asian cook

Terry Tan

photography by

Michael Paul, Sian Irvine, Peter Cassidy,
Gus Filgate and Richard Jung

asian cook

This revised and expanded edition published in 2010 by Jacqui Small, an imprint of Aurum Press Ltd, 7 Greenland Street, London NW1 0ND
First published by Jacqui Small in 2003

Publisher Jacqui Small
Art Directors Valerie Fong, Maggie Town, Ashley Western
Tools Photography Nat Rea
Food Styling Sunil Vijayakar, Terry Tan, Kit Chan, Emi Kazuko, Jayne Cross
Props Styling (this edition) Jenny Iggleden
Project and Copy Editor Siobhán O'Connor
Production Peter Colley

British Library Cataloguing-in-Publication Data
A catalogue record for this book is available from the British Library.

ISBN 978 1 906417 35 2

2014   2013   2012   2011   2010
10 9 8 7 6 5 4 3 2 1

Printed and bound in Singapore

RECIPE NOTES

Oils Unless otherwise specified, all recipes require the use of a light oil with a neutral taste and preferably a high smoke point, such as groundnut (peanut), rapeseed (canola), corn, sunflower, grapeseed or safflower oil. If you do use olive oil, unless otherwise specified, choose a mild or light olive oil – not extra virgin. **Eggs** are large in UK sizes (USA: large to extra large; Australia: extra large). **Sugar** is granulated white or caster (superfine) sugar unless otherwise specified. **Spoon measurements** Recipes use standard measuring spoons. Spoon measurements are level unless otherwise specified. **Preparation time** includes cooking time; soaking or marinating time is given separately.

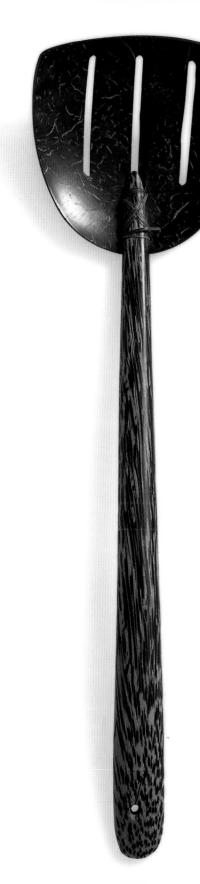

contents

introduction

Most people in the West believe that Asian kitchens are exotic, full of strange and rustic implements, of granite mortars that need forklifts to move them and cast-iron woks that rust before you can say 'stir-fry'. True, some tools used in Asian cooking can seem esoteric, even mystifying at times, but most are very simple to use. Take the granite mortar and pestle: it has been around for centuries and is small and light enough for even a child to use. I inherited mine from my grandmother, which makes it older than I am! It has now worn to a silky smoothness and grinds spices and aromatics beautifully into emulsion-like pastes.

It is fascinating and therapeutic to grind, grate, slice and chop using age-old tools and implements. They seem to impart an extra and mysterious dimension of flavour to the dish cooked, and, despite the introduction of food processors, true quality and authenticity for many dishes are often achievable only by using the traditional tools that have stood the test of time. Most are easy to use, and few require painstaking instructions; however, frequent practice helps to produce perfect results. In the pantheon of good, authentic cooking, there is much to be said for using implements designed for specific tasks. Even better, they make wonderful heirlooms to hand down to the next committed or aspiring cook in the family.

For generations, Asians have used a wide range of the tools chronicled in this book. Some implements have been threatened with extinction, but more than a few have been saved from the back burner of history, modernized and even adapted into exciting new electrical appliances. Much of what can be found in Asian kitchens is available in speciality stores and ethnic supermarkets, many of which now have their own websites. Some tools may be harder to track down, but most avid cooks agree this is all part of the fun of exploring the cuisines of other lands.

Geographically, the Asia we refer to here embraces China; India, Pakistan and Sri Lanka; Japan and Korea; the five distinct countries of Burma, Laos, Cambodia, Thailand and Vietnam; and the islands of the Indonesian archipelago and neighbouring Malaysia and Singapore, collectively known as Southeast Asia. Although Laotian and Cambodian cooking are relatively unknown to many people in the Western world, they do share some characteristics with their neighbouring countries; the recipes in the book will help you to explore both connections and differences.

What's more, even though contemporary lifestyles dictate the need for high-tech appliances, Asian kitchens still contain tools that are evocative of the agrarian way of life. There is a special relationship between their aesthetic and their functionality. For instance, banana leaf serves as a mat for steamed coconut rice, while also imparting a distinctive fragrance to the dish. When Thai sticky rice is served in a woven banana-leaf basket, the flavour of the dish is subtly enhanced.

High-tech appliances may well make short work of food processing, but speed is not the be-all and end-all of kitchen craft. The true enjoyment of food often dictates that some effort must be made. The split-second timing of stir-frying, the consistency and delicacy of dumpling dough, and the smoothness of spice pastes are all dependent on using the correct tool. Even the simplest items can be used ingeniously. Two-foot-long chopsticks are a good example. When you deep-fry food, if you pick up the cooked morsels using a conventional ladle or pair of tongs, you run the risk of hot oil splattering on you. With very long chopsticks, the distance between cook and wok provided by these lengthy utensils ensures that there is no danger.

Several of the tools and foods featured in this book have traditional symbolic, religious or mystical significance, and it can only enhance your enjoyment to dwell a little on the hidden symbolism. Every Japanese dish reflects a mood dictated by a season, whereas the Chinese people love roundness (as in shape) because it symbolizes eternity. Whatever your reason for exploring the East, be it buying a wok, re-creating food sampled on holidays, or looking for an exciting wrap for dumplings, I hope that you enjoy using this book and the tools featured in it.

choice of materials

This list explains the pros and cons of the principal materials from which the eclectic range of Asian cooking equipment is made or naturally derived, and gives guidance on care, preparation, cleaning and storing.

ALUMINIUM

Uses Pots, steamers, tiffin carriers, storage tins, cake moulds, ladles and woks.

Pros Cheap, lightweight and conducts heat well and evenly as long as the gauge is heavy enough.

Cons Reacts with acidic elements in food juices and therefore discolours certain foods or imparts a metallic taste. The metal itself also tends to discolour and pit. Thin-gauge aluminium warps easily and heats unevenly.

Care Wash with hot soapy water, using a scouring pad if necessary. Remove stains by boiling in a weak solution of vinegar, bicarbonate of soda or cream of tartar.

ANODIZED ALUMINIUM

Uses As for aluminium.

Pros An electrochemical process, anodizing gives aluminium a hard, dense oxide coating that resists corrosion. It also changes the molecular structure of the aluminium, making it harder than steel while maintaining excellent heat distribution and conduction.

Cons Dishwasher detergents cause coloured anodized aluminium pans to fade and discolour.

Care Wash anodized aluminium with hot soapy water. Do not use scouring pads, as they will damage the coating.

BAMBOO

Uses Utensils, steamers and lids, barbecue skewers.

Pros Cheap, portable and nonreactive to foods, its porous nature is an advantage when used for steaming.

Cons Can become brittle with frequent use, relatively short life, will warp and burn if not handled carefully.

Care Wash with hot water only, never with detergents or other cleaning products, as this natural material is porous and absorbs cleaning fluids.

BRASS

Uses Cake moulds, mortars and pestles, karahis.

Pros An alloy of copper and zinc, with other metals such as aluminium and tin added for strength and anti-corrosion properties. It is tough, corrosion- and rust-free, and both beautiful and functional.

Cons Can be extremely heavy.

Care Wash with hot soapy water and detergent.

CAST IRON

Uses Pots, pans, griddles, grill pans, casseroles, teppanyaki hotplates, and teapots.

Pros Durable, strong, does not warp, conducts heat evenly and retains it well. Marvellous for long, slow cooking using minimal fat.

Cons Very heavy, so best for a pan that remains fairly static during cooking, such as a casserole or frying pan. Its density makes it slow to heat. If dropped on a hard floor, it may break. If uncoated (for example, if it does not have an enamel or nonstick surface), a cast-iron implement must be seasoned with oil to prevent sticking and rusting.

Care Avoid uncoated cast iron. Wipe with kitchen paper. Remove stuck-on food by lightly scouring under hot running water. Dry well, and coat with oil before storing. Brush the cooking surface with oil before each use, then wipe off before adding oil for cooking. Wash coated cast iron with hot soapy water, but do not scour. To remove stubborn residue, leave the pan to soak for an hour or so.

CLAY AND TERRA COTTA

Uses Cooking pots, yogurt pots, mortars and pestles, dishes.

Pros Attractive, rustic, nonreactive. Chinese clay pots have supportive wire mesh to help prevent breakage.

Cons Cracks easily if roughly handled. Clay pots do not take well to cooking over a direct flame, and are best used over charcoal embers or in the oven.

Care Wash and dry, but never use detergents because the material is absorbent. Dishwasher-safe. Never store clay or terra-cotta implements stacked one in another, as this will cause cracking.

COCONUT SHELL

Uses The outer hard casing of the coconut is shaped into all sorts of practical and attractive implements, including bowls, ladles, serving utensils, spoons and spatulas.

Pros Nonreactive, inexpensive, rustic, versatile.

Cons Can be hard to come by, cracks easily, few matching sets. Some discoloration can occur when coconut shell is used for spices.

Care Wash with hot soapy water. If you need to remove stubborn stuck-on food, you can scrub or scour coconut shell, but not with detergents because the material is absorbent.

COPPER

Uses Karahis, moulds, wire mesh ladles.

Pros The traditional choice of Western chefs, but used much less in Asia because of its high cost. Some utensils have a light copper plating, but it is mainly used for mesh. Never rusts or turns brittle.

Cons Pricey and needs cosseting.

Care Wash with hot soapy water. Never use scouring pads. Soak with a little vinegar, and dry with a soft cloth to bring up the shine.

EARTHENWARE

Uses Casseroles, herbal pots, mortars and pestles.

Pros Nonreactive, cheap, porous, retains heat and moisture well. Excellent for slow, moist cooking in the oven, for use in a microwave and on the stovetop for gently simmered soups and stews if protected.

Cons Dislikes sudden or extreme temperature changes. It is not flameproof, but good-quality earthenware can be used over a low flame when a heat diffuser is in place to disperse the direct heat.

Care Wash glazed or partially glazed pots with hot soapy water without scouring. Completely unglazed pots should be scrubbed clean with salt water. Do not use detergent because this will taint the flavour of any food that is subsequently prepared or cooked using the implement.

GRANITE AND STONEWARE

Uses An ancient material used mainly in heavy grinding tools, and for serving dishes such as the traditional Korean bibimbap bowl.
Pros Virtually indestructible, but will break if dropped from a height. Does not stain and is nontoxic and nonreactive.
Cons Heavy, clumsy and difficult to clean.
Care Wash with hot water and a light detergent. Scrub out with a steel-wool scouring pad after grinding spices, and soak in hot water for an hour to remove strong smells.

LACQUERWARE

Uses Plates, bowls, bento boxes, trays and other serving dishes. The sap from the lacquer tree is applied in multiple layers, then heated and allowed to dry.
Pros Beautiful, lightweight, portable, delicate, but still tough enough for dishwasher cleaning. Retains heat well, does not stain and is nontoxic and nonreactive.
Cons Cannot be used for cooking and may chip if knocked or dropped.
Care Wash with hot soapy water, and dry with a clean soft cloth to prevent staining.

LEAVES, DRIED

Uses Mainly from bamboo and lotus plants, dried leaves are used for wrapping savoury and sweet dishes that are then steamed or boiled.
Pros Impart distinctive fragrance, have a long shelf life if stored properly. Cheap and disposable.
Cons Crack and tear easily if not handled gently.
Care Must be kept in a cool, dry place.

LEAVES, DRIED BASKETWARE

Uses Many types of dried leaves are employed in the endless range of baskets used throughout Asia. Dried leaves of the pandanus (screwpine) family (usually found in mangrove swamps), coconut tree, rattan plant, bamboo and other broad types are woven into baskets of varying shapes and sizes, fans and food containers.
Pros This type of basketware is relatively cheap (except when crafted and sold as exotic ornaments in gift shops). Excellent for steaming dryish dishes and for serving. Unless waxed or otherwise treated with a coating, they do not react to cooking agents such as oil and vinegar, except for taking on a dark tan colour after use.
Cons They are not everlasting, being of a handicraft nature, and strips may come away after a while. They can become misshapen too.
Care Easy to wash and dry, but not dishwasher-safe because of the delicate weave.

LEAVES, FRESH

Uses Leaves such as banana, pandanus (screwpine), bamboo and yam are used for wrapping, encasing and perfuming foods, especially when steaming. Banana leaves are also cut into large pieces and employed as serving plates in tropical parts of Asia. Although scented, some fresh leaves are not edible because of their fibrous nature.
Pros They are inexpensive and disposable, and give a natural, authentic presentation.
Cons Fresh leaves are delicate, tear easily and have a short shelf life. Some are available fresh only in the country in which they are grown.
Care Keep wrapped in a cool, dry place for 3–4 days.

PORCELAIN

Uses Plates, bowls, spoons, rice scoops and tureens.
Pros Can be delicate or tough, depending on manufacture. Chinese and Japanese porcelain have been famous for centuries for their beauty and function. Very aesthetic, elegant, retains heat well, but cool to the touch. Nonporous and nonreactive. Microwave-friendly, except for those glazed or decorated with metallic paints.
Cons Should not be used over direct heat, fragile, and needs careful cleaning, particularly with some types of glaze or finish.
Care Wash in hot soapy water, and soak to remove stubborn stuck-on food, dishwasher-safe unless otherwise specified.

STAINLESS STEEL

Uses Pots, pans, woks, ladles, scoops, serving dishes, storage containers, knives and cleavers.
Pros One of the toughest and most enduring materials, used in a wide range of tools and utensils. Contains chrome, which is what makes it stainless. Pristine-looking, long-lasting and hygienic, rustproof and nonreactive. Immune to corrosion and pitting. Stainless-steel utensils also contain nickel, described as 18/10, which means the ratio of chrome to nickel is 18 per cent and 10 per cent, respectively. The stainless steel used in knives contains a lower level of chrome (at least 12 per cent) and 0.15–0.8 per cent carbon, which gives the steel strength, as in professional Japanese carbon-steel knives. The reduced amount of chrome means that such items are more prone to staining.
Cons Stainless steel is a poor and uneven conductor of heat, but some woks and pots are made with a sandwich base of aluminium or copper to alleviate this problem. Good stainless-steel utensils have a base containing at least 5mm (¼in) of aluminium or 3mm (⅛in) of copper. Stainless steel is not entirely stainless and will discolour if left in contact with hard water, salt water, acidic juices or even some detergents if not rinsed out thoroughly after washing. Small pits may form.
Care Clean with hot soapy water, using a nylon scourer if necessary. Avoid bleach and harsh abrasives. Soak stuck-on foods, and remove stubborn stains with a proprietary stainless-steel cleaner.

WOOD

Uses Asian woods come in a range of types and varying degrees of hardness. They are used for cake moulds, trays, bowls, pot covers, steamer trivets, chopsticks, pot rests, tongs and rolling pins.
Pros Durable, inexpensive, nonreactive.
Cons Can be heavy, prone to discoloration if used with highly coloured ingredients such as certain spices.
Care Wash with hot soapy water, and scrub gently with a soft-bristled brush, especially when cleaning cake moulds that feature deeply etched, intricate designs.

china

'If there be only one note, there can be no music. If there be one flavour, there would be no satisfaction. If sugar is added to vinegar, there would be the universal harmony of sweet and sour.' So said Yen Tzu, a disciple of Confucius, circa 600 BC. This is the philosophy that underscores Chinese cuisine.

china and its regions

China is a vast country with enormous climatic and geographical variations. The cuisine has evolved over more than 3000 years and developed in an environment of constant flux, with occasional periods of relative permanence. Today, ancient traditions and culinary innovations exist in delicious synergy.

Some 80 per cent of the nation's 1.6 billion people still live a rural life, engaged in agriculture. Despite a shortage of fertile arable land, Chinese farmers have learned to nourish their terrain to produce bountiful harvests. Centuries-old terraced paddy fields maximize use of water, even though there are frequent droughts. Despite the advent of refrigeration, Chinese people still insist on the freshest foods available and often shop several times a day to ensure this.

There are distinct regional schools in Chinese cuisine, which run in line with the geographical boundaries of the northern, eastern, southern and western regions, and are better known as Beijing, Shanghainese, Cantonese and Sichuan cuisine, respectively. Each is steeped in indigenous traditions. There are also lesser-known types such as the Muslim school of northeast China, Hunanese, Hainanese (of Hainan Island) and several subschools within the southern Chinese province of Guangdong. Hong Kong, although a part of South China, has also evolved its own distinctive style.

The name of China's northern capital city has undergone no fewer than eight changes since it was first named Chi in 481 BC. At various stages throughout the next 2500 years of rising and falling dynasties, political upheaval and other changes, it has been called Yenking, Chungtu, Tatu and Khanbalyk (both under the thirteenth-century ruler of the Mongol empire and founder of the Yuan Dynasty, Kublai Khan), Peking, Peiping and finally now Beijing.

Severe winters, short growing seasons and an arid climate have created a hearty cuisine designed to nourish and nurture the body. The staples grown throughout the region are wheat, millet and soya beans. Rice does not grow happily here and therefore rarely features in northern Chinese meals; the preference is for steamed wheat-flour buns and noodles.

Northern Chinese cuisine is regarded as the most sophisticated of all, although it is robust and features simple ingredients. Its chief characteristic is the frequent and lavish use of soya bean paste, which is the basis of many well-known sauces, including hoisin and yellow bean. More influenced by the vast hinterland of Mongolia and beyond than the sea on its eastern shores, northern China has menus that are rich in lamb and duck, as well as roasted, braised and barbecued dishes. The world-famous Peking duck is widely regarded as a national treasure.

The Yangtze River, or Chang Jiang, is China's longest waterway and the third-longest in the world after the Amazon and the Nile. It leaves its mountain source in Qinghai province, high in the Tibetan Plateau, and flows through Sichuan, before eventually ending in the East China Sea just north of Shanghai. There is a vast network of lakes and tributaries in eastern China, which is a leading

OPPOSITE 1 baby bok choy (pak choi) **2** mustard greens **3** mangetout (snow peas) **4** spring onions **5** mung beansprouts
BELOW 1 bean thread noodles **2** rice noodles **3** egg noodles **4** rice **5** egg dumpling skins, or wrappers (egg roll skins) **6** rice dumpling skins, or wrappers (spring roll wrappers or rice paper wrappers)

agricultural region boasting some of the most fertile land in the country. Barley, wheat, rice, corn, sweet potatoes, peanuts and soya beans grow there in abundance. The region offers diverse cooking styles, but all emphasize freshness and pure, natural flavours. Eastern China's stir-fried dishes are often plain, seasoned only with soy sauce and pepper. Lotus plants grow profusely in the ponds, lakes and streams throughout the region, and as a result many dishes are wrapped in lotus leaves, then steamed.

The mountains of the warmer southern reaches of eastern China feature many tea plantations. Fujian is perhaps the best-known of China's tea-growing provinces. Trade of the precious leaf with Europe in the early nineteenth century brought prosperity to the local residents, whose leisured classes were subsequently able to cultivate a fine taste for exquisite cooking. Fujian chefs are extremely fond of pork, using all the offal in highly imaginative ways, including dishes of steamed pig's blood. The long coastline, riverine areas and freshwater lakes are fecund with the seafood that also typifies this cuisine.

In the west, the province of Sichuan has a tongue-tingling reputation as a fiery cauldron of chilli peppers. Chillies are not the be-all and end-all of the region's cooking, however, and several festive and banquet dishes are completely devoid of fire. The purpose of chillies is not, as can sometimes seem the case, to paralyse the tongue, but rather to stimulate the palate, making it more sensitive and receptive to the multiple flavours. Many of the sauces are a hotchpotch of hot, sweet, sour, aromatic and fragrant flavours, and Sichuanese dishes often break traditional culinary rules to brilliant effect. The range of dishes is delectable, from exquisite jade shrimp and fire-exploded kidney flowers (*huo bao yao hua*) to popular sweet and sour pork (*suan tien zhou rou*), aromatic crispy duck, and hot and sour soup (*suan la rou si tang*). A spread of cold dishes is typically served at the start of a Sichuanese feast to tempt the palate.

The name Sichuan literally means 'Four Rivers', although there are actually more than twice this number in the province, all tributaries of the mighty Yangtze River. A region of fertile soil, abundant rain, searingly hot summers and mild winters, Sichuan supports an astonishing range of plant foods and a wealth of subtropical fruits, including oranges, limes, apples, plums and lychees. Sichuan teas are also justly famous, especially those from the West Lake area. The supreme variety is dragon well, or longjing, tea, a green tea that is renowned for its superior quality and is still produced mostly by hand.

Historically, the southern province of Guangdong was allied to the former Guangxi province, now an autonomous region. Lying in the shadow of the Guangdong-Guangxi mountains, the region is crisscrossed by three tributaries of the Yangtze, the best-known of these being the Pearl River, which has given its name to soy sauce and other products such as yellow rock sugar. Rice is the dominant grain here. Peanuts, coconuts, pineapple, sugar cane, tea and coffee, as well as tobacco and rubber plants, all thrive in this part of China and are grown in profusion. There was much contact with Indian, Persian and Arab traders before the fifteenth century, and, later, Portuguese, British, Dutch and French entrepreneurs and merchants called regularly.

The magic of this region's cooking, usually termed Cantonese, is concentrated on texture. Natural flavours are not altered, and preparation is kept to a minimum. Absolute freshness is vital. The aim is to control crispness and subtlety, but perhaps the most distinctive aspect of Cantonese cuisine is savouriness. Seafood flavours are often incorporated into meat cookery, such as in the use of oyster and shrimp sauces. Salted and fermented black beans also impart their distinctive highly savoury taste, while ginger counteracts fishiness and garlic provides perfume.

The former British colony of Hong Kong, which was in many ways separated from the fold of mainland China until once again coming under Chinese rule, is a magnet for world travellers and business people, and its cuisine has evolved accordingly. Demand for superb food has forced local chefs to be constantly inventive and to maintain high professional standards, and they have developed an international reputation for cutting-edge cooking. Today, many Chinese restaurants around the world take pride in promoting 'Hong Kong–style' dishes, which essentially means Cantonese food with an innovative twist. It may not be a separate school of cooking as such, but Hong Kong chefs relish the universal regard for their style as a supreme version of Cantonese cooking. This has made the chef brigade that much more pushy in culinary competitions. The island's restaurateurs are deadly serious about promoting themselves as not merely offering a re-creation of the best of Cantonese cuisine, but rather resolutely fine-tuning that cuisine in resplendent, individualistic Hong Kong culinary mode.

OPPOSITE 1 dark soy sauce **2** oyster sauce **3** bamboo shoots **4** salted and fermented black beans **5** light soy sauce **6** hoisin sauce **7** sesame oil **8** five-spice powder **9** Sichuan pepper **10** water chestnuts **11** white sesame seeds **12** fresh root ginger **13** dried Chinese mushrooms

cleaver and chopping board

China's characteristic knife, the cleaver, may well seem like a lethal guillotine to the uninitiated, but it is surprisingly easy to use. Its versatility as chopper, slicer, crusher, tenderizer and scooper effectively eliminates the need for a battery of knives in the kitchen. With care, a cleaver lasts more than a lifetime, and in China (as well as countries such as Singapore, Indonesia and Malaysia, where it is also used) the family knife is often passed on to the next generation, to continue its service as a culinary stalwart.

1

2

3

4

1 CHOPPING BOARD

Chinese people traditionally use a block of natural hardwood that is a complete round cut from a whole tree trunk, rather than several pieces of wood fused together, as is the case with many chopping boards today. The furious chopping action of the heavy Chinese cleaver will inevitably chip a synthetic board, but natural wood can absorb the blows without splintering. Cleaning such boards can be a problem. Chinese chefs use their cleavers to scrape off any bits of embedded food to prevent contamination. As a result, the boards become slightly concave over time.

2 3 4 CLEAVERS

Heavier than most other knives, the cleaver is honed to razor sharpness and balanced to give the leverage needed to cut through joints of meat and even bone. There are several sizes and weights of cleaver, made from a variety of materials. They may have wooden or plastic handles, or be cast from a single piece of metal. While modern stainless-steel models produced by Western manufacturers can look impressive, they do tend to require frequent sharpening, as do the old-fashioned iron knives sold in Chinese supermarkets and Asian grocers. A far better choice is carbonized steel, which should always be wiped rather than washed after use, to prevent discoloration, then given a light coating of vegetable oil to prevent rusting.

using a cleaver

Peeling With the fingertips of one hand, hold down the piece of root vegetable firmly. Hold the cleaver in your other hand, with its sharp edge positioned between the skin and the vegetable flesh. Press down firmly all the way to peel off one strip at a time. Turn the vegetable, and repeat until all the skin has been peeled.

Tenderizing meat Turn the cleaver over so that the blunt end is facing down. Make heavy blows all over the sliced meat, turning it over once to do the other side. When properly tenderized, the meat should have slight ruts in it and be roughly 20 per cent larger and flatter than when you started.

Scooping Tilt the cleaver at an angle, with the sharp edge pointing away from you. Run the flat side of the blade underneath the prepared food in one movement, and scoop up the pieces ready to place on a serving dish, or in a bowl or wok. If necessary, lightly rest your hand on top of the food to help it onto the cleaver.

Chopping To prepare bok choy for cooking, hold the leaf of one stem lightly with one hand. Place the cleaver at a slight angle, resting the flat of the blade gently against the hand holding the bok choy. Measure the required distance from the thick edge of the stalk and press down, making clean cuts to separate leaf and stalk.

Shredding To cut fine julienne of firm ingredients such as fresh ginger, place the food on the cutting board and slice off the skin, removing the broadest sides first. Slice finely, keeping the food together in one piece as much as possible. Next, layer several slices one on top of the other. Cut through the layers to make fine shreds.

Crushing Bash the cloves of garlic with the broad, flat side of the blade; the skin will slide off smoothly. Apply pressure with one hand on the blade's flat side, near its blunt edge, and crush the garlic to the desired size. Rapid chopping will give you fine slivers, but less garlic juice will be produced than when crushing.

woks and their accessories

The wok has a mystical history dating back some 3000 years, yet in all that time has never changed its ingenious shape. Riding on the popularity of stir-frying as a healthy cooking method, it is now endorsed by chefs of many nationalities, and can be a best friend in the home kitchen, too, serving as a deep-fryer, steamer, braiser and boiling pot, all in one pan. The wok's shape ensures that heat is concentrated at the base and less intense at the sides, making it ideal for stir-frying. A flat-bottomed frying pan simply does not do the job as well. Avoid trendy reinterpretations of the timeless design. To get the most out of your wok, familiarize yourself with its accompanying tools, which help to transform it from simple pan into multitasking wonder cooker.

1 3 WOKS

Today, woks come in a wide range of materials and sizes. The best are made of heavy cast iron and usually need only to be seasoned before use. New ones, however, must be filled with oil and heated through before being drained and dried. For other metals given to rusting, use a metal scouring pad to remove any traces of rust before you start cooking. Nonstick woks are not suited to rapid stir-frying because the action of the ladle may chip the pan's synthetic coating. A wok made from stainless steel will conduct heat very rapidly, so is liable to burn food too easily. Electric models are not ideal for stir-frying, as they conduct heat at a rapid and uneven rate; however, they are good for braising and steaming. Choosing either a single- or double-handled wok is largely a matter of preference. One-handled versions are favoured by restaurants because they allow the chef to easily toss large quantities of ingredients during stir-frying, which aids the action of the wok ladle.

2 WOK LID

Wok lids are necessary for braising, steaming and smoking; they are also used to facilitate the stir-frying process. When placed on the wok during cooking, they create a flash of dense moist heat, thereby speeding up cooking.

4 WOK STAND

The wok's round base does not sit well on the stove top. Circular wok stands, typically made of iron, have four teeth that are strategically placed to grip the crossbars of the stove, allowing the wok to sit firmly without tipping.

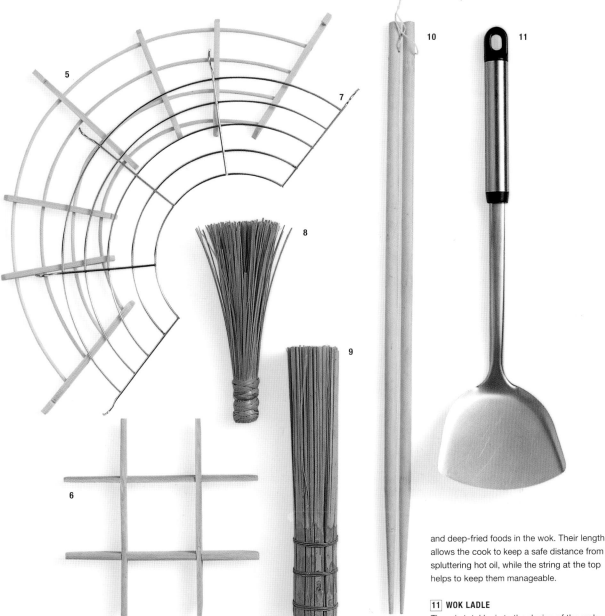

5 **7** **DRAINING RACKS**

These come in bamboo or metal, and are placed at the side of the wok to drain deep-fried food such as spring rolls. Hooks at the end of each crossbar keep them steady.

6 **STEAMING TRIVET**

Originally made of bamboo or wood, these are now often metal. Simple grids made up of two crossbars, they rest at the bottom of the wok, and cradle plates and bowls during steaming, keeping them above the boiling water.

8 **9** **BAMBOO WOK-CLEANING BRUSHES**

A precursor of the ubiquitous plastic washing brush, this is no more than a bunch of bamboo or fine wooden slivers bundled together to form a thick brush that is comfortable and easy to use. Excellent for removing stubborn stains and charred grit, wok-cleaning brushes come in various sizes.

10 **LONG CHOPSTICKS**

These large extended chopsticks (up to 45cm/ 18in long) are used for manipulating noodles and deep-fried foods in the wok. Their length allows the cook to keep a safe distance from spluttering hot oil, while the string at the top helps to keep them manageable.

11 **WOK LADLE**

There is total logic to the design of the wok ladle, which is a little like a shovel. The size and shape correspond exactly to the base of the wok so that, in one scooping action, almost all the food is tossed and turned for effective stir-frying. The slightly raised sides prevent spillage, and the angle of the head corresponds to the gradient of the wok for ergonomic comfort. Wok ladles are traditionally made of metal with a wooden handle, or shaped from one piece of rust-resistant metal alloy; today, they are available in stylish stainless steel or wood, and are sometimes slotted to aid draining.

how to stir-fry

This classic vegetable dish of bok choy with ginger and oyster sauce is a good opportunity to practise your stir-frying technique. For best results, prepare all the ingredients before starting to cook, get the oil really hot, and keep the food constantly moving in the wok.

Step 1 Trim off the hard stalk ends of 200g (7oz) bok choy; cut the rest into 5cm (2in) pieces (about 3 cups). Peel a small knob of fresh root ginger, and slice into 1 tbsp fine shreds. Heat 2 tbsp groundnut (peanut) or similar oil in a wok until very hot. Add the ginger, and stir with a wok ladle until light brown.

Step 2 Add the firm white stem sections of the bok choy, and continue stir-frying over a high heat for 2 minutes, constantly flipping the ingredients away from the hot base of the wok using the ladle. Moving the food rapidly and constantly in the wok ensures that it does not overcook and also that it cooks evenly.

Step 3 Stir in the green leafy parts of the bok choy, then add 1 tbsp oyster sauce and 100ml (scant ½ cup) water. Continue stir-frying until the liquid comes to a rapid boil. Quickly transfer the contents of the wok to a serving dish – the wok's sloping sides help to make this easy – and serve immediately.

easy vegetable stir-fries

mushrooms with bamboo shoots

Soak 6 dried Chinese mushrooms in enough hot water to cover until soft. Squeeze out the water, discard the stalks and cut the caps into quarters. Halve 6 straw mushrooms. Cut 100g (⅔ cup) bamboo shoots into 1cm (½in) strips. Heat 2 tbsp vegetable oil such as groundnut (peanut) in a wok over a high heat. Stir-fry 1 tbsp crushed garlic for 1 minute. Add the bamboo shoots and stir-fry for 2 minutes, then add the mushrooms and stir-fry for a further 1 minute. Now add 2 tbsp sesame oil, 1 tbsp light soy sauce, 1 tsp freshly ground black pepper, 100ml (scant ½ cup) water mixed with 1 tsp cornflour (cornstarch), and 2 tbsp Chinese rice wine such as Shaoxing. Bring to the boil, and serve at once.

sichuan four harmonies

Slice 1 large carrot diagonally, and blanch in boiling water for 2 minutes. Halve and deseed 1 yellow (bell) pepper, and cut into pieces the same size as the carrot. Quarter 1 large red onion. In a wok over a high heat, stir-fry 1 tbsp crushed garlic and 1 tsp crushed fresh root ginger in 2 tbsp vegetable oil such as groundnut (peanut) for 1 minute. Add 1 tbsp sesame oil and the quartered onion, and stir-fry for 2 minutes. Add the carrot, yellow pepper and 16 mangetout (snow peas), plus 1 tbsp light soy sauce; stir-fry for 2 minutes. Mix 100ml (scant ½ cup) water with 2 tsp cornflour (cornstarch), and add to the wok with 2 tbsp Chinese rice wine such as Shaoxing. Bring to a boil, and serve as soon as the sauce thickens.

celery with straw mushrooms

Cut off the root end from a whole head of celery, and trim off the leaves. Cut the stalks into 5cm (2in) lengths, then into julienne. Wash and drain 150g (5½oz/ about 1 cup) canned straw mushrooms. Heat 2 tbsp groundnut (peanut) or similar vegetable oil in a wok over a high heat. Stir-fry the celery for 1 minute, then add the straw mushrooms. Continue stir-frying for 2 minutes. Add 1 tsp salt and 2 tbsp water, and stir constantly until the liquid comes to a quick boil. Serve immediately.

beansprouts with spring onions

Wash 350g (12oz/3½ cups) beansprouts in a colander, and drain thoroughly. Deseed 2 large fresh green chillies, and cut into julienne. Cut 4 spring onions (scallions) into 5cm (2in) lengths. Heat 2 tbsp vegetable oil such as groundnut (peanut) in a wok over a high heat, and toss the spring onions in it for 30 seconds. Add the drained beansprouts and chillies, and stir-fry for 1 minute. Sprinkle over 1 tsp salt, and continue stir-frying for a further 30 seconds. Serve immediately.

yangzhou fried rice

Fried rice must be the best-travelled Chinese dish of all. It turns up in myriad guises – from simple to elaborate – all around the world, even though it was born from the pragmatic and somewhat mundane need to recycle leftovers. This classic version is believed to have originated in the southern province of Jiangsu and is positively ambrosial, with lots of premium ingredients, including roast pork, crabmeat and juicy prawns (shrimp).

SERVES 4   PREPARATION TIME: 20 MINUTES

TOOLS
Cleaver
Chopping board
Wok and ladle

INGREDIENTS
800g (1¾lb) cold cooked rice
100g (3½oz) raw prawns (shrimp)
2 tbsp groundnut (peanut) oil
2 spring onions (scallions),
    chopped, plus extra, to garnish
3 eggs
150g (5½oz) roast pork or
    cooked ham, diced
100g (3½oz) cooked
    white crabmeat
2 tbsp frozen green peas
2 tbsp light soy sauce
1 tsp freshly ground
    black pepper
1 chicken stock
    (bouillon) cube

1 Give the cold cooked rice a thorough raking with a fork to separate the grains. (It is best to use rice that has been cooked the day before, cooled quickly and refrigerated until needed.) Peel and devein the prawns (shrimp), making a deep slit down the back of each one.

2 Heat the oil in the wok, and fry the spring onions (scallions) for 1 minute. Push them to one side of the wok. Crack in the eggs, and cook until set. Remove from the wok, cut up roughly and set aside.

3 Add the rice, prawns, pork or ham, and crabmeat. Stir-fry vigorously for 3 minutes until the prawns are turning pink and opaque. Tip in the frozen peas, cooked egg, soy sauce and pepper, and crumble in the stock cube. Stir-fry for 3 minutes more, then serve hot, garnished with the extra spring onion.

wok cooking techniques

The wok's versatility obviates the need for a battery of utensils for different methods of cookery, but it is helpful to have two woks, of 25cm (10in) and 35cm (14in) diameter. The larger one is better for holding bamboo steamers and for smoking, while the smaller wok can be used for deep-frying and braising. When storing, they can be stacked one in the other, thus taking up less kitchen space.

1

1 Deep-frying The wok's curvature means that it demands much less oil to deep-fry than does a conventional deep-fryer. Always choose an oil with a high smoke point for deep-frying and stir-frying. Groundnut (peanut) oil (the preferred choice of Chinese cooks), rapeseed (canola) oil and light olive oil (not extra virgin) are all good choices. Place a draining rack on the side of the wok. Add oil to a depth of one-third, and heat. Fry only a few pieces of food at a time. When done, remove each item, holding it at an angle so that the excess oil drains away. Sit on the draining rack to drain completely.

2 Steaming To steam foods in a wok, simply place the food on a dish resting on the steaming trivet. Choose a dish large enough to sit steadily on the trivet, but allow room at the sides for easy removal. Fill the wok with water, making sure that it does not touch the base of the dish. Bring to the boil, cover with the wok lid and let the steam circulate. Alternatively, use a bamboo steamer of a slightly smaller diameter than the wok. Ensure that it sits at least 4cm (1¾in) above the water level, and cover with the steamer's lid.

3 Tea-smoking Smoking is a slow, gentle heat process for cooking and flavouring foods that are not too thick or chunky, such as fish or thin slices of meat and poultry. Fill the wok to a depth of one-third with uncooked rice mixed with a few handfuls of barley grains. Sprinkle over 1 tbsp black or green tea leaves. Sit the food on a double layer of foil, wrap firmly and lay it directly on the grains. Cover with the wok lid, and smoke over a low heat for about 1 hour, opening the foil parcel for the last 30 minutes of cooking. Avoid using highly flavoured teas such as lapsang souchong for smoking.

4 Braising This technique involves cooking food gently in a flavoursome liquid in a closed container. The liquid should just cover the main ingredients; the long, gentle simmering process will reduce it by about half. Open the lid occasionally during cooking, and top up with a little liquid if it is too dry. Remove the food when it is cooked, and reduce the sauce further by boiling vigorously until thickened, which intensifies its flavour.

FUCHSIA DUNLOP fish braised in chilli bean sauce

British-born writer and radio and television journalist Fuchsia Dunlop speaks fluent Mandarin and trained to be a chef in Chengdu. This dish, *dou ban xian yu*, from her highly acclaimed book *Sichuan Cookery,* is typical of Sichuanese home cooking and one of her favourites. It beautifully demonstrates the region's famous love of chilli.

SERVES 4   PREPARATION TIME: 30 MINUTES

TOOLS
Cleaver
Chopping board
Wok and ladle
Wok lid

INGREDIENTS
1 whole carp, trout or grey
   mullet, weighing about 750g
   (1lb 10oz), with head and tail
   still attached
160ml (about ⅔ cup) groundnut
   (peanut) oil

For the marinade
¾ tsp salt
1–2 tbsp Shaoxing wine

For the sauce
4 tbsp Sichuanese chilli
   bean paste
1 tbsp finely chopped fresh
   root ginger
1 tbsp finely chopped garlic
300ml (1¼ cups) chicken stock
1 tsp white granulated sugar
1–2 tsp light soy sauce
¾ tsp potato flour
½ tsp Chinkiang or black
   Chinese vinegar
3 spring onions (scallions), green
   parts only, finely sliced

1 Use a cleaver to make 4 or 5 shallow diagonal cuts into each side of the fish, and to pierce its head (this releases more flavoursome juices). Place in a large dish, and rub the fish inside and out with the salt and Shaoxing wine. Leave to marinate while you assemble the other ingredients.

2 In a wok, heat 100ml (scant ½ cup) of the oil over a high heat until smoking. Dry the fish with kitchen paper, and fry it briefly on each side, just long enough to crisp up the skin. Remove and set aside. Rinse and dry the wok.

3 Return the wok to a medium heat with the remaining 4 tbsp fresh oil. When it is hot, add the chilli bean paste, and stir-fry for 20–30 seconds until the oil is red and smells delicious. Add the ginger and garlic, and stir-fry for another 20 seconds or so until you can smell their fragrance. Next, pour in the stock, increase the heat and bring the liquid to the boil. Season to taste with the sugar and soy sauce.

4 Gently place the fish in the wok, and use the wok ladle to spoon some sauce over it. Reduce the heat, cover with the wok lid and simmer for 8–10 minutes until the fish is cooked and has absorbed some of the flavours of the sauce. Turn the fish once during cooking, spooning over some more sauce.

5 Carefully remove the cooked fish to a serving dish. In a small bowl, dissolve the potato flour in 1 tbsp cold water, and add to the sauce, stirring briefly until it thickens. Throw in the vinegar and green spring onions (scallions), stir a few times, then pour the sauce over the waiting fish and serve.

braised five-spice belly pork

Originally from northern China, this popular dish has transcended the provincial borders and is now cooked in almost every Chinese kitchen. In the north it is traditionally served with a steamed bread known as *man dou,* while in the south it is most commonly served with rice.

SERVES 4   PREPARATION TIME: 45 MINUTES

TOOLS
Cleaver
Chopping board
Wok and ladle
Wok lid

INGREDIENTS
2 tbsp groundnut (peanut) oil
1 tbsp sugar
500g (1lb 2oz) belly pork, sliced
5 tbsp dark soy sauce, plus a little extra, to taste
2 tsp five-spice powder
1 tsp salt

1 Heat the oil in the wok over a medium-high heat, and add the sugar. Cook, stirring, until the sugar dissolves and caramelizes, turning a light brown. Add the pork slices, and turn them in the caramelized mixture until they are well coated.

2 Add the 5 tbsp soy sauce, five-spice powder, salt and 1 litre (4 cups) water. Cover and cook gently over a low heat for 40 minutes, turning once or twice during braising. Top up with more water if necessary.

3 Adjust the seasoning by adding extra soy sauce to taste, then serve with fluffy rice.

sizzling lamb with ginger wine

When the winter chill of northern China bites, home cooks and restaurant chefs alike turn out sizzling dishes such as this. Lamb has great affinity with ginger and Chinese wine – better yet when served on a preheated cast-iron hotplate. Most Chinese stores sell these cast-iron plates fitted on a wooden base. Simply heat the cast-iron plate over a gas flame or similar, and carefully replace it on the wooden base for safe serving at the table.

SERVES 4   PREPARATION TIME: 1 HOUR 20 MINUTES

TOOLS
Cleaver
Chopping board
Wok and ladle
Cast-iron hotplate on
    wooden base
Pair of chopsticks

INGREDIENTS
450g (1lb) boneless lean lamb
    or best end of neck, trimmed
    of any fat or sinew
2 tbsp Chinese rice wine
    such as Shaoxing
½ tsp salt
1 tbsp crushed or puréed
    fresh root ginger
1 tsp crushed or puréed garlic
1 tbsp sesame oil
2 tbsp groundnut (peanut) oil
3 spring onions (scallions),
    sliced on the diagonal into
    5cm (2in) lengths
1 tsp cornflour (cornstarch)

1 Using a cleaver, cut the lamb into thin julienne, each about 5cm (2in) long and the thickness of your little finger. Put the lamb in a large glass or ceramic bowl. Blend the Chinese rice wine with the salt, ginger, garlic and sesame oil. Pour over the lamb, cover with cling film (plastic wrap) and marinate in the refrigerator for at least 1 hour. Turn with chopsticks once or twice while it is marinating.

2 Heat the groundnut (peanut) oil in a wok over a high heat. Stir-fry the spring onions (scallions) rapidly for 10 seconds, then add the drained lamb (reserve the marinade). Stir-fry rapidly for 1 minute.

3 Meanwhile, mix the reserved marinade with 100ml (scant ½ cup) water and the cornflour (cornstarch); stir to blend well. Tip into the wok, and stir-fry for about 30 seconds until the sauce thickens.

4 Turn off the heat, and leave the lamb sitting in the wok while you heat the cast-iron hotplate over a direct flame for about 5 minutes until very hot. Carefully transfer the lamb to the hotplate, which will sizzle furiously for a few seconds, and serve immediately.

sichuan chilli beef

China's western provinces of Sichuan, Hunan and Hupei are mavericks when it comes to regional cooking. This is the unique western school of cooking, often generically called Sichuanese. It is the only regional style of cooking that uses chillies with great abandon – and the famous Sichuan peppercorns with their distinctive liquorice flavour.

SERVES 4   PREPARATION TIME: 30 MINUTES

TOOLS
Cleaver
Chopping board
Wok and ladle

INGREDIENTS
450g (1lb) sirloin or rump steak
1 tbsp light soy sauce
2 garlic cloves, coarsely ground
1 tsp Sichuan peppercorns,
   crushed
1 tbsp cornflour (cornstarch)
2 dried red chillies, cut into
   thin rounds
100ml (scant ½ cup) groundnut
   (peanut) oil
½ tsp sugar

1 Using a cleaver, cut the beef into thin slices across the grain. In a bowl, combine the beef with the soy sauce, garlic, Sichuan peppercorns, cornflour (cornstarch) and 100ml (scant ½ cup) water. Leave to marinate for at least 10 minutes.

2 Heat half of the oil in a wok over a medium-low heat. Add the sliced dried chillies, and stir-fry very quickly for 5 seconds or a little longer, making sure that they do not scorch. Transfer the chillies and the chilli-infused oil to a small bowl to cool. Carefully wipe out the wok with kitchen paper.

3 Drain the beef, and reserve the marinade. Heat the remaining oil in the clean wok over a medium-high heat, and stir-fry the beef for 1 minute. Add the reserved marinade, and dribble about half of the chilli oil into the beef. Increase the heat to high, and stir-fry very quickly for 30 seconds.

4 Continue to stir-fry for about 1 minute until the beef slices are almost dry. Transfer to a serving plate, and serve hot with the remaining chilli oil on the side for those who like a baptism of fire.

peking-style caramel walnuts

Although these delicious 'lacquered' nuts are best started the day before serving, don't let this put you off. They are well worth the effort. They can be served hot or cold, and make a great talking point at drinks parties. Cashews can be used instead of, or as well as, walnuts if preferred.

SERVES 8   PREPARATION TIME: 25 MINUTES, PLUS 2–12 HOURS' DRYING

TOOLS
Pot
Colander
Baking tray
Wok
Wire strainer
Wire rack

INGREDIENTS
450g (1lb/about 4 cups)
    shelled walnuts
200g (1 cup) granulated sugar
450ml (scant 2 cups) groundnut
    (peanut) oil
6 tbsp sesame seeds

1 Bring a large pan of water to the boil, add the walnuts, and simmer, uncovered, for 5–10 minutes until the water becomes dark and the nuts begin to turn pale. Drain and rinse the walnuts under cold running water until the water runs clear.

2 Dry the nuts thoroughly with kitchen paper, and spread them out over a baking tray or sheet. Pour the sugar evenly over them, then roll the nuts in the sugar so that they are completely coated. Sit the tray in a cool place, under a mesh food cover and preferably in a light breeze, and leave to dry overnight or for a minimum of 2 hours.

3 When ready to proceed, heat the oil in the wok to a medium heat. Divide the nuts into small batches so that you do not crowd the wok. Add the first batch to the oil, and cook for 2 minutes or until the sugar dissolves and the nuts are golden.

4 Using a wire-mesh strainer, lift out the nuts from the oil, and lay them on a wire rack, keeping them well separated. Sprinkle with some of the sesame seeds.

5 Repeat with the remaining walnuts, and serve warm or cold. Alternatively, the caramelized nuts will keep in a screw-top jar for up to 2 weeks.

cooking pots

While the wok reigns supreme in every Chinese kitchen, stir-frying is by no means the only cooking method; one-pot dishes are common among rural Chinese families in colder regions. Various types of pot play important roles in preparing stocks, stews and braised dishes. A good stock is vital to Chinese soups, and the wok's open shape and rapid evaporation rate make it unsuitable for stock making.

3 DOUBLE-BOILER

This ancient Chinese utensil is much like a French bain-marie, and used for slow simmering and stewing; this model is enamel. A single-handled lower container (for water) is fitted with a slightly smaller upper container (for the food to be cooked), which has with its own handle and a tight-fitting lid. In ancient times in China, it was used strictly for herbal stews that required long, slow and gentle cooking from an indirect heat source. Today, such pots are widely used in Southeast Asia for sweet coconut custards.

1 STOCKPOT

Soups and stocks play important roles in Chinese cuisine, so large conventional cooking pots, much the same as those used in Western kitchens, are necessary. The most basic pot used would be a plain aluminium one; however, today they are largely of modern design and made of stainless steel.

4 HUNAN POT

Originating from the province of Hunan, these finely crafted delicate clay or terra-cotta pots with a funnel in the centre are typically used for festive rituals. They were originally used for serving medicinal brews and herbal soups that only well-to-do families could afford. Hunan pots are not robust enough to be placed over direct heat, and so herbal soups are poured into them after being cooked in other pots.

2 CLAY OR SAND POTS

These glazed or unglazed lidded pots need gentle handling, as they crack easily under intense heat. They can be used directly on an electric ring or ceramic hotplate, but not over a gas fire (a heat-diffusion mat can help to prevent cracking). Clay pots serve as an oven-to-table utensil when food must be presented piping hot or still sizzling. The best way to do this is to cook the dish in a wok, then transfer it to a clay pot that has been preheated in a very hot oven for 30 minutes. Always use a wooden spoon with clay pots.

soup and congee

Most Chinese people have a penchant for soups, derived from the yin–yang philosophy that they are sustaining because their ratio of substance to liquid is purported to right any bodily imbalance. The variety of soups is wide. Some are practically stews, with lots of meat, seafood or noodles, and meant as complete meals in themselves. Lighter soups have a different role to play as refreshing dishes, or to help dry dishes go down well. Congee is a rice porridge, the staple of most rural communities in South China and typical breakfast fare. Traditionally, it is made with broken rice grains. For variety, the basic mixture can be flavoured with a wide range of tasty extras such as white fish, shredded chicken, mushrooms, dough sticks, fresh coriander (cilantro) and sliced chillies.

chicken and mushroom soup

Cut 1 skinless chicken breast fillet into 1cm (½in) cubes. Wipe clean 250g (9oz) fresh mushrooms such as enoki, shiitake, oyster and chestnut (cremini) mushrooms (or use a mixture) with a piece of damp kitchen paper. Cut into bite-sized pieces. Put the mushrooms and chicken in a pot with 800ml (3¼ cups) water, 1 chicken stock (bouillon) cube, crumbled, and 1 tbsp light soy sauce. Bring to the boil, reduce the heat slightly and simmer for 25 minutes. Stir through 1 tbsp chopped flat-leaf parsley and ½ tsp freshly ground black pepper. Serve hot.

congee with shrimp and spring onions

Wash thoroughly 200g (1⅓ cups) jasmine rice, and put in a pot with 1.5 litres (6 cups) water. Bring to the boil, cover, reduce the heat slightly and simmer for 40 minutes until the rice grains are slightly pulpy and the surrounding liquid is opaque white. Peel and devein 150g (5½oz) small raw prawns (shrimp). Tip them into the congee, and simmer for 5 minutes until pink and opaque. In the last minute of cooking time, stir through 1 tbsp sesame oil and ½ tsp freshly ground black pepper. Garnish the congee with 2 tbsp finely chopped spring onions (scallions) just before serving hot.

clay pot rice with saltfish and chicken

This traditional Cantonese dish successfully combines seafood with meat, and is redolent with ginger, garlic and sesame oil. Saltfish is much loved in China, not only as a savoury ingredient, but also as a fragrant salting agent, eliminating the need for additional salt. Generally, only a small amount is used and cut up into tiny pieces so that the salty flavour is well distributed throughout the dish.

SERVES 4   PREPARATION TIME: 45 MINUTES

TOOLS
Clay pot
Rice cooker
Cleaver
Chopping board
Wok and ladle

INGREDIENTS
200g (1⅛ cups) jasmine rice, rinsed
1 skinless chicken breast fillet
2 Chinese sausages
150g (5½oz) saltfish fillet
3 tbsp groundnut (peanut) or rapeseed (canola) oil
2 tbsp grated fresh root ginger
3 garlic cloves, sliced
2 tbsp sesame oil
2 tbsp oyster sauce
2 tbsp dark soy sauce
1 tsp freshly ground black pepper
2 tbsp chopped spring onions (scallions)

1 Preheat the oven to 240°C/475°F/Gas 9, and place the clay pot in it to heat through while you cook.

2 Using a rice cooker, cook the rice in 750ml (3 cups) water for 12 minutes. Meanwhile, cut the chicken into 2cm (¾in) cubes, slice the sausages diagonally into pieces 5mm (¼in) thick, and finely dice the saltfish.

3 Heat the oil in a wok over a medium-high heat, and stir-fry the ginger and garlic until lightly golden. Add the chicken, sausage, saltfish, sesame oil, oyster sauce, dark soy sauce and pepper, and toss through well for 4 minutes.

4 Combine the contents of the wok with the cooked rice, and transfer to the heated clay pot. Garnish with the chopped spring onions (scallions), and serve immediately.

DEH-TA HSIUNG tung-po mutton

Su Tung-Po (1036–1101) was a poet, painter, calligrapher and epicure. A native of Sichuan, he spent most of his life travelling around China and is credited with the invention of this famous dish. This version comes from cookery author and teacher Deh-ta Hsiung, who has written dozens of authoritative books on Chinese cuisine.

SERVES 4   PREPARATION TIME: 1 HOUR

TOOLS
Cleaver
Chopping board
Wok and ladle
Deep pot

INGREDIENTS
4 tbsp groundnut (peanut) or
    other vegetable oil
400g (14oz) stewing mutton
    or lamb, cubed
2 large potatoes, peeled
    and cubed
1 large carrot, cubed
100ml (scant ½ cup) Chinese rice
    wine such as Shaoxing
2 tbsp dark soy sauce
1 tbsp crushed or puréed
    fresh root ginger
1 tsp five-spice
    powder
1 tsp sugar
1 tsp salt

1 Heat the oil in a wok over a medium-high heat. Stir-fry the meat until well sealed and browned. Remove from the wok, and set aside to drain on kitchen paper.

2 Using the same oil, stir-fry the potatoes for a couple of minutes until light brown. Add the carrot, and stir-fry for 2 minutes. Remove the vegetables, and set aside.

3 Transfer the meat to a deep pot. Add the rice wine, soy sauce, ginger, five-spice powder, sugar and salt. Pour over 1 litre (4 cups) water, and simmer, covered, for 40 minutes until the gravy is thick.

4 Add the reserved potatoes and carrot, and continue to simmer for a further 15 minutes, before serving hot.

steamers and related tools

The culinary technique of steaming food is steeped in yin–yang philosophy. In China, the belief is that fried foods must be counteracted by those that contain less or no oil, and are therefore healthier. Steaming uses minimal amounts of flavourings, allowing the natural flavours of food to come through. It is an excellent way of cooking the seafood that is so prolific in China's coastal and inland riverine areas. Lean meats and lean poultry joints become more succulent and flavoursome when steamed, and no nutrients are lost, as they are with boiling. Last but certainly not least, steaming requires very little skill from the cook. Clearly, there are many good reasons to incorporate more steamed dishes in your culinary repertoire.

1 BAMBOO STEAMERS

These steamers are traditionally made of woven bamboo and come in various sizes between 15cm (6in) and 35cm (14in) in diameter. The larger the steamer, the larger the wok or saucepan that needs to be used with it. Generally, steamers of about 24cm (10in) diameter will suffice for most domestic cooking needs. The wonderful thing about steamers is that you can stack them one on top of the other, and cook various foods using the same steam power. Steamers need only be rinsed in cold water and dried after use. Never use detergents to wash bamboo steamers, as they readily absorb cleaning agents.

2 LOTUS LEAVES

The large dried leaf of the lotus plant looks like a grey-green fan measuring some 40cm (16in) in diameter. After soaking, it is extremely tough and pliable, and suitable for wrapping all kinds of foods, to which it imparts a faint floral perfume during steaming. The lotus plant is held in reverence by Buddhists and Taoists, and is symbolically related to Guanyin, the goddess of mercy, who is regarded as the patron saint of seafarers in some parts of China.

3 ALUMINIUM STEAMER

This modern version of the bamboo steamer comes in multiple layers and has a high domed lid; there is also a bottom section to hold water, so it can be used without a wok. Although it is useful for similar steaming jobs, the solid lid tends to create too much condensation, so that water drops back onto the food, resulting in an unwanted 'soup'. You can prevent this by using the aluminium steamer in conjunction with the lid of a bamboo steamer, or by puncturing several small holes in the metal lid to create a vent.

4 ONE-PORTION ALUMINIUM STEAMER

A handy small steamer for cooking dim sum and reheating, this is just large enough to hold two small dumplings. Several of these little steamers can fit inside a large bamboo steamer to keep individual dim sum servings hot without letting them overcook.

5 LITTLE METAL CUPS

These small cups are used for steaming individual portions of savoury or sticky rice flour cakes, a popular Chinese street food. The cakes are unmoulded onto plates or dried palm leaves, or eaten with a spoon straight from the cup.

steamed seared scallops with ginger, garlic and chilli

Steamed scallops prepared in this way are a Cantonese speciality – although the roe is usually removed and used for another recipe, and the scallops are steamed without searing first. As with all Cantonese cooking, the secret is to use the freshest of prime ingredients and treat them simply. When you are searing the scallops, by the time you put the last scallop in the pan, the first one will be ready to take out.

SERVES 4   PREPARATION TIME: 20 MINUTES

TOOLS
Sharp knife
Chopping board
Frying pan or skillet
Wok
Bamboo steamer
Baking parchment or
   heatproof steaming plate

INGREDIENTS
12 fresh large or queen scallops
   on the shell (use the rounded
   side of the shell, rather than
   the flat side)
2 tbsp groundnut (peanut) or
   light olive oil
2 tbsp light soy sauce
2 tbsp Shaoxing wine
8cm (3in) piece of fresh root
   ginger, finely shredded
2 spring onions (scallions) or
   baby leeks, finely sliced
2 garlic cloves, finely chopped or
   cut into slivers
2 small fresh red or green
   chillies, deseeded and finely
   chopped
freshly ground black pepper

1 Remove the small muscle from the side of the scallop, to detach the scallop from the shell. You can remove the orange-coloured roe if you wish (and reserve it for another use), or simply leave it on. Pat the scallops dry with kitchen paper. Clean the rounded havles of shells, and set aside for serving. Lightly season the scallops with black pepper.

2 Fill a wok or saucepan about one-third full with water, and bring to a simmer, so that it is ready for steaming the scallops as soon as they have been seared.

3 Heat the oil in a heavy frying pan or skillet over a high heat. When it is very hot, add the scallops, dotting them in a circle around the pan. Sear for 30 seconds. Remove from the pan, and sit each scallop seared-side up in a reserved shell.

4 Mix together the soy sauce and wine, and sprinkle over the scallops. Scatter a little ginger and spring onion (scallion) or leek over each one, and sprinkle with a little of the garlic and chilli. Sit half of the scallops, shell and all, in a bamboo steamer lined with baking parchment, or sit them on a flat plate resting inside the steamer. Cover, and steam over the wok of simmering water for 5–6 minutes until cooked – do not to overcook or the scallops will be rubbery. Carefully remove from the steamer, and keep warm while you steam the rest of the scallops. Serve immediately, and don't neglect to enjoy the delicious juices as well as the meat!

glutinous rice in lotus leaf

Chinese chefs are adept at cooking glutinous rice, usually wrapped around savoury mixes and often cloaked in lotus leaves. This is known as *lor mai fun* in Cantonese. The dried leaves are fragile and, before using, need to be soaked in hot water until soft, so that they are pliable enough for wrapping.

SERVES 4   PREPARATION TIME: 45 MINUTES, PLUS 1 HOUR'S SOAKING

TOOLS
Colander
Bamboo steamer
Heatproof steaming plate
Cleaver
Chopping board
Wok and ladle
1 dried lotus leaf for wrapping
Flat square presser

INGREDIENTS
400g (2½ cups) glutinous rice, soaked for
    1 hour in cold water, rinsed and drained
For the stuffing
4 dried Chinese mushrooms
2 tbsp groundnut (peanut) or light olive oil
2 garlic cloves, crushed
200g (7oz) skinless chicken fillet, diced
1 Chinese sausage, finely sliced

8 canned Chinese chestnuts
2 tbsp light soy sauce
2 tbsp oyster sauce
2 tbsp sesame oil
2 tsp salt
1 tsp freshly ground black pepper
1 tbsp dark soy sauce
2 tbsp chopped spring onions (scallions)
chilli sauce, to serve (optional)

1 Steam the soaked rice for 20 minutes, and set aside. Put the mushrooms in a bowl, just cover with hot water and leave to soak for 10 minutes; drain, chop and set aside.

2 Heat the oil in a wok over a medium-high heat, and fry the garlic for 2 minutes; take care not to burn. Add the chicken and Chinese sausage, and stir-fry for 5 minutes. Add the remaining stuffing ingredients, including the chopped mushrooms, and stir-fry for a further 5 minutes. Sprinkle a little water on top. Remove from the heat.

3 Soak the lotus leaf in hot water for a few minutes, then remove, wipe dry with kitchen paper and trim off the hard stalk. Spread out the cooked rice over the lotus leaf to a thickness of about 1cm (½in), and use the presser to firm it up.

4 Pile the stuffing ingredients in the centre of the rice (above left). Lift up two opposite sides of the lotus leaf, line them up together, and fold them over and over to seal like a parcel (above centre).

5 Gather the remaining two sides, and fold them so that the edges of the leaf tuck in and under (above right).

6 Pat the parcel firmly so that it holds its shape, then turn over, so that the seam-side is underneath. Sit seam-side down on a plate in a bamboo steamer set over a wok of simmering water. Cover and steam for 10 minutes.

7 Unwrap, and serve straight from the leaf with chilli sauce to accompany, if liked.

steamed winter melon soup

Winter melons are about the size of footballs, and are often used as a cooking pot, as well as a type of serving bowl to be brought to the table. The ingredients of this nourishing soup are all contained within the scooped-out melon, and the soft melon flesh should be eaten as well as the soup.

SERVES 6   PREPARATION TIME: 1 HOUR

1 Bring 1 litre (4 cups) water to a boil in a large pot, and simmer the barley for 15 minutes. Meanwhile, cut off the top third of the melon, and reserve to use as a lid for steaming the soup. Discard the pith and seeds from the centre of the melon, and scoop out and discard the melon flesh, leaving a rim of about 2.5cm (1in) thickness all the way around the inside of the shell.

2 Add the chicken, ham and lotus seeds to the simmering barley, and continue cooking for a further 15 minutes.

3 Transfer the contents of the pot to the melon shell, sprinkle in the salt and sugar, and gently stir through. Carefully sit the melon on a plate in a bamboo steamer. Replace the melon's top, and cover the steamer tightly. Cook for 30 minutes.

4 To serve, bring the whole melon to the table, with a few finely sliced spring onions (scallions) sprinkled over the soup as a garnish.

TOOLS
Large pot
Cleaver
Chopping board
1 whole winter melon
Bamboo steamer with
   high-domed lid
Heatproof steaming plate

INGREDIENTS
100g (scant ⅔ cup) pearl barley
200g (7oz) skinless chicken
   breast fillet, cubed
100g (3½oz) Chinese or cooked
   ham, diced (about ¾ cup)
150g (5½oz) canned lotus
   seeds, drained
2 tsp salt
1 tsp sugar
finely sliced spring onion
   (scallion), to garnish

steamed chicken with chinese wine and mushrooms

This is probably the most oft-cooked dish throughout all of China, although it is believed to have originated from South China's Hainan Island. It takes a liberal leaf from the iconic Hainan chicken rice that is served up in just about every Southeast Asian restaurant. Serve with plain steamed rice or noodles, and bok choy, with side dips of chilli and vinegar.

SERVES 4   PREPARATION TIME: 1½ HOURS

TOOLS

Cleaver
Chopping board
Large pot
Steamer
Deep heatproof steaming plate
    or bowl

INGREDIENTS

1 whole chicken, about 1.5kg
    (3lb 3oz)
8 dried Chinese mushrooms,
    soaked in hot water until soft
1 tbsp crushed or minced garlic
2 tbsp Chinese rice wine such
    as Shaoxing
1 tbsp thinly sliced fresh
    root ginger
1 tsp salt
2 tbsp sesame oil
handful of fresh coriander
    (cilantro) leaves, to garnish
    (optional)

Chilli and vinegar dipping sauce
1 tbsp finely ground fresh chilli
3 tbsp rice vinegar
pinch of salt

1 Trim off any excess fat from the chicken, and discard. Put the chicken in a large pot. Rub the garlic all over the chicken, including the insides. Do the same with the wine, then put the slices of ginger and whole mushrooms inside the chicken cavity. Sprinkle the salt all over the chicken.

2 Sit a deep plate or large bowl in a steamer – traditional Chinese bamboo, modern aluminium and stainless-steel steamers all produce much the same results – and carefully sit the chicken on top. Steam, covered, for at least 1½ hours. To check whether the chicken is done, pierce the deepest part of a thigh with a metal skewer. If the juices run clear, the chicken is cooked. With the steaming method, there is less fear of overcooking; an extra 15 or 20 minutes make the chicken even more tender and succulent.

3 To make the chilli dip, simply blend the ground chilli with the vinegar and salt in a small bowl. To serve, discard the skin from the chicken, and carve the chicken into slices and portions. Arrange on a large plate with the mushrooms and a little of the ginger, with some fresh coriander (cilantro) sprinkled over the top (if using) and the chilli dip in a small bowl on the side for dipping.

dim sum utensils

The phrase *dim sum* means 'food to touch the heart', and the range of dim sum foods is endless, especially when you consider that every regional Chinese cuisine has its favoured recipes. There are, however, specific types of dim sum dish, including fried, steamed, savoury and sweet, plus a small range of rice-based dishes such as congee with century egg, salt fish or chicken.

1 CUP CAKE MOULD

Popular Chinese street food items, such as *chui kueh* (water cakes) or Little Buddhas (steamed rice cakes with a savoury radish mixture) are made in these small aluminium cups.

2 JELLY AND TART MOULDS

These come in aluminium or plastic, with simple scalloped patterns or pineapple, fish, turtle and rabbit motifs. Each motif is symbolic: pineapple for nobility (in Chinese, the word sounds the same as that for 'emperor'); fish for rebirth; rabbit for wisdom; and turtle for longevity.

3 REEDED PASTRY BRUSH

Thin pieces of bamboo are fused together to make an easy-to-grasp handle for this broad fine-haired brush, which is as functional as it is beautiful. It can be used for egg-washing or basting tarts and other festive cakes, as well as lightly dusting foods with flour before cooking.

4 WON TON SPREADER

A thin, short piece of finely honed wood is used to scoop up and spread small amounts of minced pork or seafood when making won ton or similar dumplings. The flat shape ensures that just enough of the filling mixture is placed on the won ton skins.

5 DUMPLING DOUGH ROLLER

This tool is much smaller and thinner than a conventional rolling pin, and fits nicely into the palm of one hand, leaving the other free to manipulate the dumpling dough when rolling it out. The roller is made of light wood and is about 25cm (10in) long.

small cooking utensils

While Chinese kitchens are not cluttered with equipment, there are a number of small tools that can be very handy for specific jobs. On occasions when you feel the urge to make special dishes and snacks such as sweet tofu, home-made noodles, and steamed or fried vegetable cakes, these tools help to make the job a cinch.

1 2 TOFU SCOOPS
A plain round piece of metal, with or without a handle, serves as a scoop for tofu when portions need to be cut from a large slab. Commonly used in factories, they are also employed by Chinese street food vendors, who scoop out individual portions of sweet tofu for customers.

3 STOCK SCOOP
A good stock base (especially chicken stock) is essential to China's large variety of soups. This small aluminium bucket on a long handle is used to ladle the prepared stock from large, deep pots.

4 FLAT SQUARE PRESSER
This aluminium square with a handle is used to press down steamed cakes made from mashed radish or yam, to prevent air bubbles forming during cooking.

5 THREAD NOODLE SLICER
Noodles are fundamental to Chinese cuisine, and are most commonly made with wheat or rice flour, although bean thread vermicelli or cellophane noodles, made from mung bean starch, are also popular. Making fresh noodles at home in small quantities is relatively easy (in fact, it is very similar to pastry or pasta making), and the results taste much better than store-bought noodles. Chinese noodle makers make their noodles from rolled-out sheets of dough and cut them to varying widths with this tool – wider ribbons for soups; thinner for stir-fries. The noodle slicer, a broad stainless-steel blade measuring about 12.5cm x 7.5cm (5in x 3in), is attached to a wooden handle and is used to cut and scoop up the strands of uncooked noodle dough.

1

2

3

5

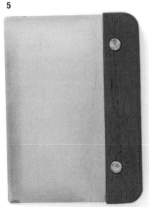

4

MING TSAI mushroom and leek spring rolls

A long sojourn in France inspired esteemed American chef Ming Tsai of the Blue Ginger restaurant in Boston to devise this recipe, which uses leeks to give a French twist to traditional Chinese spring rolls. They make excellent party canapés.

SERVES 4–6   PREPARATION TIME: 1 HOUR

TOOLS
Cleaver
Chopping board
Vegetable shredder
Strainer or large sieve
Wok and ladle
Large spoon
Wire mesh ladle

INGREDIENTS
75g (2½oz) cellophane noodles
2 tbsp groundnut (peanut) oil,
   plus extra for deep-frying
1 tbsp finely chopped garlic
1 tbsp finely chopped fresh
   root ginger
2 fresh serrano or similar chillies,
   finely chopped
125ml (½ cup) hoisin sauce
125g (4½oz) shiitake mushroom
   caps, thinly sliced
2 large leeks, white parts only,
   cut into julienne
8 tbsp (½ cup) chopped
   coriander (cilantro) leaves
100g (3½oz) spring onions
   (scallions), chopped (about
   1 cup chopped)
16 spring roll wrappers, about
   20cm (8in) square
1 egg, beaten with 4 tbsp water
salt and freshly ground
   black pepper

1 Soak the cellophane noodles in a bowl of hot water for 10–15 minutes until soft. Drain thoroughly, then chop into pieces 5cm (2in) long.

2 Heat a wok over a high heat. Add the 2 tbsp oil, and swirl to coat the pan. When the oil is hot, add the garlic, ginger and chillies, and stir-fry for about 2 minutes until soft. Do not allow the aromatics to burn.

3 Reduce the heat to medium, add the hoisin sauce, and cook for about 3 minutes until it loses its raw taste. Add the shiitake mushrooms and leeks, and stir-fry for about 6 minutes until soft. Season with salt and black pepper.

4 Transfer the filling mixture to a strainer or sieve, and, using a large spoon, press the mixture well to drain it thoroughly. Leave to cool.

5 Transfer the filling mixture to a medium bowl, and add the coriander (cilantro), spring onions (scallions) and softened cellophane noodles. Stir to blend.

6 Dampen a clean tea towel or kitchen cloth. Arrange 4 wrappers side by side on a work surface, with one point of each one near you, and cover the remainder with the damp towel or cloth to prevent them drying out.

7 Place about 4 tbsp of the filling on each of the wrappers just above the near corners. Bring the corner nearest you up and over the filling, and roll halfway. Fold in the side corners, brush the edges with the egg wash, then continue rolling to enclose the filling completely, rolling as tightly as possible. Cover with the damp towel or cloth, and allow the rolls to rest, with seam-side facing down, while you fill and roll the remaining wrappers. Cover, and leave to rest for at least 2 minutes.

8 Carefully wipe out the wok with kitchen paper. Fill about one-third full with enough oil for deep-frying, and heat to 180°C (350°C) over a high heat (a small cube of bread dropped into the oil should brown in about 40 seconds). Working in batches, fry the spring rolls until golden, turning as needed, for about 5 minutes until crisp and golden. Remove with a wire mesh ladle, and drain on kitchen paper. Slice the rolls on the diagonal or in half, and serve hot with a dipping sauce (you can look for inspiration among the dipping sauces on the following pages).

making potstickers and dumplings

These delightful dumplings, known as potstickers in China, are a relative of the Japanese *gyoza*. The pastry for the dumpling skins is rolled out as thinly as possible, but not so thinly that the potstickers break when fried, because the crimped and pleated edges look nicer when the pastry remains delicate.

Step 1 Working as quickly as possible, take a dumpling skin, and sit flat in the palm of one hand. Using a won ton spreader, mound a good dollop of the filling in the centre of the skin.

Step 2 Carefully dab around the edge of the skin with a little water with your fingertip, being careful not to make the dough soggy.

Step 3 Fold the skin over to make a half-moon shape, and seal the edges together firmly using your thumb and forefinger.

Step 4 Holding the sealed edge with both hands, make a folded pleat in the dough on one side of the dumpling, along the seam edge.

Step 5 Repeat the preceding step two or three times, so that you end up with a row of folds much like the pleats on a curtain.

Step 6 Press down gently on the pleats so that they remain in shape, and lightly flatten the bottom of the dumpling, so that the pleated seam sits upright and runs along the centre.

shanghai pork dumplings

The traditional method of cooking potstickers is to fry them until their bases are brown, literally 'sticking' to the pan, hence the name. A little water is then added to flash-steam the dumplings until they are fully cooked, but be careful because it will spatter upon hitting the oil.

SERVES 6   PREPARATION TIME: 45 MINUTES

TOOLS
Cleaver
Chopping board
Won ton spreader
Lidded frying pan or skillet
Wok ladle

INGREDIENTS
100g (3½oz) spring
   onions (scallions), finely
   chopped (about 1 cup)
300g (10oz) pork mince
   (ground pork)

1 tsp salt
1 tsp freshly ground
   black pepper
2 tbsp sesame oil
1 tbsp cornflour (cornstarch)
24 round dumpling skins
   (you can use shao mai skins
   or thicker potsticker wrappers)
a little groundnut (peanut)
   oil for frying
To serve
Chinkiang or Chinese black vinegar
finely shredded fresh root ginger

1 In a bowl, mix together the spring onions (scallions) and pork. Add the salt, black pepper, sesame oil and cornflour (cornstarch), and blend thoroughly so that the seasoning is well incorporated and evenly mixed.

2 Take a dumpling skin and, using a won ton spreader, place a good dollop of mixture in the centre. Dab around the edge of the skin with a little water, and fold the skin over to make a half-moon shape. Using your thumb and forefinger, firmly seal the edges together.

3 Holding the sealed edge with both hands, make 3 or 4 pleats along the seam edge of the dumpling (see steps 4 and 5, opposite). Press down gently on the pleats so that they hold their shape. Cover the finished dumpling with a clean damp cloth. Repeat with the remaining dumpling skins and pork mixture.

4 Heat a little oil in a frying pan over a medium-high heat. Place about 6 of the dumplings in the pan, bottom-side down, pressing a little so that they sit firmly with the seam pointing up. Fry the dumplings until the bottoms are golden brown.

5 Add about 2 tbsp water to the pan, quickly cover with a lid and steam-cook the dumplings for 15–20 minutes until the pan is dry and the dough is translucent. Serve hot with a dipping sauce of Chinkiang vinegar and shredded ginger.

chinese chive dumplings

Chinese chives have a more pungent flavour than ordinary chives, and give their distinctive aroma and garlicky taste to these moreish dumplings with characteristically translucent pastry. You can serve these dumplings as potstickers, or simply steam them in the more delicate *shao mai* skins if you prefer.

SERVES 6   PREPARATION TIME: 45 MINUTES

TOOLS
Large pot
Cleaver
Chopping board
Won ton spreader
Lidded frying pan or skillet
Wok ladle
Small pot

INGREDIENTS
250g (9oz) Chinese chives, trimmed and cut into 1cm (½in) lengths
125g (4½oz) raw prawns (shrimp), peeled, deveined and finely diced
60g (2oz) fresh water chestnuts, peeled and diced, or 60g (2oz) canned water chestnuts, rinsed and drained (about ¼ cup diced)
2 tsp light soy sauce
1 tsp Shaoxing wine
1 tsp salt
1 tsp freshly ground black or Sichuan pepper
1 tsp toasted sesame oil
1 tsp cornflour (cornstarch)
18–20 round dumpling skins (*shao mai* skins) or potsticker wrappers
about 1 tbsp groundnut (peanut) oil for frying
Soy and vinegar dipping sauce
60ml (¼ cup) light soy sauce
3 tbsp Chinkiang or Chinese black vinegar
2cm (¾in) piece of fresh root ginger, grated
1–2 tsp sugar
1 spring onion (scallion), finely chopped

1 Bring a large pot of lightly salted water to the boil over a high heat. Add the chives, and blanch for 1 minute. Drain in a colander, and rinse under cold running water to stop the cooking and keep the chives' bright green colour. Shake the colander to get rid of any excess water, then gently squeeze the chives dry.

2 Transfer the chives to a bowl, and add the prawns (shrimp), water chestnuts, soy sauce, Shaoxing wine and sesame oil. Season with the salt and pepper, and sprinkle over the cornflour (cornstarch). Mix thoroughly.

3 Working with about 6 dumpling skins at a time, put a little filling (about 2 tsp) in the centre of the round of dough, leaving enough room around the edges for folding and pinching together to seal. Bring up the dough from four sides to meet in the middle to form a cross shape. Pinch together firmly at the centre point and along the seams, being careful not to tear the dough. Sit on a floured work surface, and cover with a clean damp tea towel or kitchen cloth. Repeat with the remaining dough and filling until all the mixture has been used.

4 Heat the groundnut (peanut) oil in a large frying pan or skillet over a medium-high heat. When the oil is hot, carefully arrange the dumplings, seam-side up, in the pan. Cook in batches, leaving enough space between the dumplings that they do not touch each other. Fry for 2 minutes until turning golden brown on the bottom and starting to crisp. Pour in about 125ml (½ cup) water, being careful to avoid any spatter, cover the pan tightly and reduce the heat to low. Cook for 4–5 minutes until the dough is starting to become translucent. Remove the lid, increase the heat to medium, and cook for about 3 minutes more until the water has evaporated.

5 To make the dipping sauce, mix together the soy sauce, vinegar, ginger, sugar and 2 tbsp water in a small pan. Gently heat for a couple of minutes until the sugar has dissolved. Remove from the heat, and transfer to small bowls for dipping. Garnish with the spring onion (scallion) just before serving.

6 To serve, transfer the dumplings to a serving plate, and serve hot with the soy and vinegar sauce for dipping.

Variation To steam the dumplings, arrange the dumplings on a lightly oiled heatproof steaming plate inside a bamboo steamer, making sure that they do not touch other. Steam in batches over simmering water for 12 minutes until the dough is translucent, topping up the water level with fresh boiling water if needed. Or vary the filling if you like. Try substituting the prawns with some minced pork (ground pork) fried with a little hoisin sauce or some finely diced cooked chicken breast fillet.

steamed prawn shao mai

Shao mai, or *siu mai*, is just one of hundreds of items within the dim sum range. These delicate pea-topped dumplings are filled with a savoury prawn (shrimp) mince flavoured simply with ginger, garlic, spring onions (scallions) and sesame oil. *Shao mai* wrappers, or dumpling skins, are available ready-made from Chinese grocers.

SERVES 4   PREPARATION TIME: 30 MINUTES

TOOLS
Cleaver
Chopping board
Heatproof steaming
    plate
Won ton spreader
Bamboo steamer
Wok

INGREDIENTS
500g (1lb 2oz) raw tiger prawns
    (shrimp), peeled and deveined
1 tbsp minced or puréed garlic
1 tbsp minced or puréed fresh
    root ginger
2 tbsp sesame oil
1 tbsp cornflour (cornstarch)

1 tsp freshly ground black pepper
1 egg, lightly beaten
1 tsp salt
1 tbsp light soy sauce
2 spring onions (scallions),
    finely chopped
20–30 round dumpling skins
30 large frozen green peas

1 Mince the prawns (shrimp) with a cleaver until their texture resembles chopped nuts. Put in a bowl with the garlic, ginger, sesame oil, cornflour (cornstarch) and black pepper, and stir well. Add the beaten egg, salt, soy sauce and spring onions (scallions), and mix thoroughly.

2 Using a won ton spreader, place a good dollop of filling onto the centre of a dumpling skin (above left). Draw up the sides of the wrapper, and shape into a little straight-sided dumpling (above right). Trim off the ends of the dumpling skin, so that the edge of the skin is flush with the filling. Sit a single green pea on top and in the centre of the filling, pushing it down just slightly so that it stay in place. Repeat with the remaining prawn mixture and dumpling skins.

3 Arrange the *shao mai* on a lightly oiled steaming plate, making sure that they do not touch each other. Fill a wok about one-third full with water, and bring to the boil. Sit the plate in a bamboo steamer over the simmering water, cover and leave to steam for 20 minutes, topping up the water level with extra boiling water if needed. Transfer the *shao mai* to a serving plate, and serve immediately.

scallop dumplings

Using fresh scallops may make these *shao mai* a little more expensive, but they are perfect for a special occasion. Their scallop and prawn (shrimp) filling is overlaid with strips of fresh scallop meat and topped with red caviar in a final flourish.

SERVES 6–8   PREPARATION TIME: 45 MINUTES

TOOLS
Cleaver
Chopping board
Wok
Won ton spreader
Heatproof steaming plate
Bamboo steamer

INGREDIENTS
1 tbsp groundnut (peanut) or
    other vegetable oil
1 small carrot, finely diced
90g (3oz) oyster mushrooms,
    torn into small pieces
6–8 canned water chestnuts,
    drained, rinsed and finely
    diced (if using fresh water
    chestnuts, peel before dicing)
3–4 garlic cloves, very finely
    chopped
5cm (2in) piece of fresh root
    ginger, finely chopped
250g (9oz) scallops, finely
    diced, plus a few extra, cut
    into horizontal slices, to top
    the *shao mai*
150g (5½oz) peeled and
    deveined cooked prawns
    (shrimp), finely diced
1 tbsp light soy sauce
2 tsp Chinese rice wine such
    as Shaoxing
1 tsp toasted sesame oil
1 tsp salt
½ tsp freshly ground
    black pepper
1 tsp cornflour (cornstarch)
24–30 round dumpling skins
    (*shao mai* skins)
a little red caviar, to garnish
Chinese or other fresh chives,
    to garnish
To serve
Soy and Vinegar Dipping Sauce
    (see page 50)
chilli oil (optional)

1 Heat the groundnut (peanut) oil in a wok over a medium-high heat. When the oil is hot, add the carrot, mushrooms, water chestnuts, garlic and ginger, and stir-fry for 2 minutes. Transfer to a bowl, and allow to cool. Carefully wipe out the wok with kitchen paper.

2 One the mixture has cooled completely, add the 250g (9oz) scallops, prawns (shrimp), soy sauce, rice wine, sesame oil, salt, pepper and cornflour (cornstarch). Stir until well combined and evenly mixed. Cover with cling film (plastic wrap), and chill until needed.

3 Using a won ton spreader, place a good dollop of filling onto the centre of a dumpling skin. Draw up the sides of the wrapper, and shape into a little straight-sided dumpling (see page 53, above right). Trim off the ends of the dumpling skin, so that the edge of the skin is flush with the filling. Sit a couple of slices of extra scallop on top so that the filling is covered. Repeat with the remaining scallop mixture and dumpling skins until all the mixture has been used.

4 Arrange the *shao mai* on a lightly oiled steaming plate, making sure that they do not touch each other. Fill the wok about one-third full with water, and bring to the boil. Sit the plate in a bamboo steamer over the simmering water, cover and leave to steam for about 15 minutes, carefully topping up the water level with extra boiling water if needed.

5 Transfer the *shao mai* to a serving plate, and garnish each one with a little caviar and a trimmed length of chives. Serve at once with the dipping sauce and some chilli oil, if liked.

festive crab and pork dumplings

Dumplings are staple festive fare throughout China and come in a wide range of types, but with basically the same pastry covering. They can be open types such as *shao mai* or closed like the northern Chinese potstickers that are *de rigueur* during Chinese New Year celebrations. This crab and pork version derives more from the latter. It uses store-bought potsticker skins, which are more translucent than won ton skins, but still thick enough to stand up to frying.

MAKES 16 DUMPLINGS   PREPARATION TIME: 30 MINUTES

TOOLS
Cleaver
Chopping board
Wok
Won ton spreader
Heatproof steaming plate
Bamboo steamer

INGREDIENTS
120g (4½oz) pork mince
   (ground pork)
60g (2oz) picked crabmeat
1 tsp cornflour (cornstarch)
½ tsp salt
½ tsp cracked black pepper
1 tbsp sesame oil
1 spring onion (scallion),
   finely chopped
2 garlic cloves, finely ground
16 round dumpling skins
   (potsticker wrappers)
For the dipping sauce
2 tbsp Chinkiang or malt vinegar
1 tsp finely shredded fresh
   root ginger

1 To make the filling, in a bowl, mix together the pork, crabmeat, cornflour (cornstarch), salt, black pepper, sesame oil, spring onion (scallion) and garlic cloves. Stir to blend thoroughly.

2 Using a won ton spreader, put a teaspoon of the filling on the centre of each dumpling skin. Fold the skin over to form a half-moon, and pinch together the edges to seal. Make 3 pleats along the seam edge of each dumpling, folding inwards, and press to seal firmly (see page 48). Pat the bottom of each dumpling so that it will sit on the steaming plate without toppling.

3 Arrange the dumplings on a lightly oiled steaming plate. Fill the wok about one-third full with water, and bring to the boil. Sit the plate in a bamboo steamer over the simmering water, cover and leave to steam for about 20 minutes, carefully topping with extra boiling water if needed. If you like, you can make these dumplings as potstickers, following the instructions on page 49.

4 To make the dipping sauce, in a small bowl, mix together the vinegar and ginger. Serve the dumplings with the dipping sauce at the table, so that people can help themselves.

barbecued pork buns

This star item, *char siu bao*, is a dim sum classic, a fluffy, light dough encasing savoury-sweet roast pork, or sometimes chicken. The same dough can be used for sweet buns, made by simply placing a spoonful of mashed red beans, sold canned in all Chinese food stores and Asian supermarkets, in the centre of the dough.

SERVES 4   PREPARATION TIME: 45 MINUTES, PLUS 2 HOURS' RISING TIME

TOOLS
Cleaver
Chopping board
Fine sieve
Roasting pan with rack
Steamer and lid
Pastry brush

INGREDIENTS
For the dough
1 tsp sugar
250ml (1 cup) warm water
2 tsp active dry yeast
450g (4 cups) plain (all-purpose) flour
pinch of salt

For the barbecued pork filling
250g (9oz) rib-cut pork
2 tbsp hoi sin sauce
2 tbsp Chinese wine such as Shaoxing
1 garlic clove, crushed
½ tsp five-spice powder
1 tsp sugar

1 To make the dough, dissolve the sugar in the warm water, and sprinkle the yeast over the top. Stir. Leave to stand for 15 minutes in a warm place until a froth begins to form.

2 Sift the flour and salt into a large bowl. Add the yeast mixture, and mix to a dough. Knead on a floured work surface for 15 minutes or until the dough is elastic and smooth. Put the dough in a warm, dry bowl, and leave to rise in a warm place for about 2 hours.

3 Meanwhile, to make the filling, cut the pork into thick strips, and marinate in the hoi sin sauce, Chinese wine, garlic, five-spice powder and sugar for 15 minutes, or longer if possible. Preheat the oven to 200°C/400°F/Gas 6.

4 Arrange the pork strips on a rack in a roasting pan, and roast in the oven for 35 minutes. Leave to cool, then cut into 1cm (½in) dice.

5 Shape the dough into a cylinder about 5cm (2in) in diameter. Cut into rounds 1cm (½in) thick, then roll each into a thin circle about 8cm (3in) in diameter. Put 1 tbsp of the roast pork in the centre of a circle, then bring up the sides of the dough and pinch to seal firmly. Repeat with the remaining circles of dough.

6 To finish, prepare a steamer by filling the base with water and bringing to the boil. Cut several squares of greaseproof paper or baking parchment the size of the bottom of the dumplings. Lightly oil the paper or parchment, and place a dumpling on each square. Sit the dumplings in the steamer, cover and steam for 20 minutes. Serve hot or at room temperature.

crisp-fried stuffed aubergine

At their best piping hot and fresh from the pan, these morsels are a pleasing contrast of textures and flavours, with their crisp coating and herby prawn (shrimp) filling. Try serving with some pea shoots tossed in stir-fried garlic and a little sesame oil and soy sauce.

SERVES 6–8   PREPARATION TIME: 40 MINUTES

TOOLS
Cleaver
Chopping board
Wok
Wire mesh strainer
Frying pan or skillet

INGREDIENTS
For the filling
175g (6oz) raw prawns (shrimp), peeled, deveined and coarsely ground or chopped
2 spring onions (scallions), green part only, finely chopped, plus extra, julienned, to garnish
2 tbsp finely chopped Chinese chives
2 tbsp finely chopped coriander (cilantro) leaves
1 tsp salt
1 tsp Shaoxing rice wine
1 tsp light soy sauce
1 tsp cornflour (cornstarch)
For the aubergine (eggplant)
1 large egg
45g (⅓ cup) plain (all-purpose) flour
3 tbsp cornflour (cornstarch)
pinch of salt
½ tsp Sichuan pepper
100 g (3½ oz) fine breadcrumbs such as panko
500 g (1 lb 2 oz) aubergines (use Chinese or Japanese aubergines if you can)
groundnut or olive oil for deep-frying
chilli oil, to serve
For the dipping sauce
2 tsp groundnut (peanut) oil
1 spring onion (scallion), thinly sliced
125ml (½ cup) chicken stock
1 tsp fermented black beans, rinsed and lightly mashed (optional)
1–2 tsp light soy sauce
pinch of salt
½ tsp sugar
1 tsp cornflour (cornstarch)

1 To make the filling, mix together the prawns (shrimp), spring onions (scallions), salt, rice wine and cornflour (cornstarch) in a bowl until well combined. Use your hands if necessary to make sure that all the ingredients are blended. Cover with cling film (plastic wrap), and chill until needed.

2 Trim off the ends of the aubergines (eggplants) diagonally, and discard. Cut the aubergines into slices about 2.5cm (1in) thick, again on the diagonal. Using a sharp knife, cut out a deep wedge about 5mm (¼in) wide at the top from the skin side of each slice, about two-thirds of the way down into the slice. Put the slices in a colander, and sprinkle with salt. Leave to stand for 20 minutes, then rinse thoroughly, drain and pat dry with kitchen paper.

3 Stuff about a teaspoon of the filling into each wedge in the aubergine slices, and smooth the top. In a small bowl, whisk the egg with 1 tbsp water, and set aside. Sift together the flour, cornflour and pinch of salt in a separate wide bowl. Put the breadcrumbs in another shallow bowl.

4 In a wok, heat enough oil for deep-frying to 180°C/350°F. When the oil is hot (a small cube of bread dropped into the oil should brown in about 40 seconds), dip each piece of aubergine into the egg mixture, then in the flour to coat, shaking off any excess. Lastly, coat in the breadcrumbs. Using a slotted spoon, carefully lower the aubergine slices into the hot oil, cooking 4 or 5 pieces at a time. Deep-fry for 4–5 minutes until golden brown all over, turning several times during cooking. Remove with a slotted spoon or wire strainer, and drain in a single layer on kitchen paper. Continue until all the slices have been cooked. Transfer to a warm serving plate, and keep warm until needed.

5 To make the sauce, heat the oil in a frying pan or skillet over a medium heat. When it is hot, add the spring onion and stir-fry for 30 seconds. Pour in the chicken stock, fermented black beans (if using), soy sauce, pinch of salt and sugar. Bring to the boil. Make a paste of the cornflour and 1 tbsp water. Stir into the boiling stock, and cook for a minute or so until the sauce has thickened.

6 To serve, arrange the aubergine slices on a serving platter, and drizzle a little sauce over the top. Put the rest of the sauce in a small bowl for dipping, with some chilli oil in another small bowl, if liked, and a bowl of pepper and salt dip (see below). Garnish the aubergine with a little spring onion (scallion), and serve at once.

Sichuan pepper and salt dip Toast about 2 tbsp whole Sichuan peppercorns in a dry wok over a low heat for about 5 minutes until fragrant, being careful not to scorch them. Using a mortar and pestle, grind the peppercorns to a powder, then sift out any husks or lumps. Mix with about 3 times the quantity of sea or ground rock salt, and use as a condiment with deep-fried foods.

serving utensils

Unlike in a formal Western meal, where the types of crockery and cutlery depend on the kind of food on the menu, a Chinese table is relatively simple and constant whatever food is being served. Chinese meals are generally communal in nature, with a selection of different dishes served all at once, with or without a central bowl of soup. Diners have their individual set of rice bowl, chopsticks and porcelain spoon, and simply help themselves from the dishes available.

1 TEAPOT

Tea is the favourite accompaniment to food in Chinese restaurants, although, contrary to popular belief, it is rarely served with food in Chinese homes. The tea leaves are placed in the pot, and hot water added again and again as needed. The traditional shape of Chinese teapots is round and squat, although they are taking on other shapes as fashions change.

2 TEA CUPS

Tea is served in small cups and replenished often. When offered in the home as refreshment to guests, the tea is presented with both hands and drunk likewise, hence the absence of saucers and handles.

3 PORCELAIN RICE BOWL

The shape and size of traditional Chinese rice bowls have remained unchanged for centuries. To hold the bowl, place your thumb on the upper rim and four fingers on the lower rim. The bowl is supposed to be held near the mouth and rice delicately pushed in with chopsticks. Rice is not meant to be picked up a few grains at a time – in China, the grains dropping between the chopsticks denotes bad luck.

4 SOUP NOODLE BOWL

Noodles are meant to be one-dish meals in themselves, and large bowls such as this are used for serving soup-based noodle dishes.

5 SMALL SAUCE DISHES

These come in various sizes and shapes, some compartmentalized so that they can contain a few items such as soy sauce, grated fresh root ginger, chilli sauce, sliced chillies, mustard or vinegar.

6 DINNER PLATE

The Chinese do not serve rice on a dinner plate, except as a token gesture to Westerners who are not used to eating rice from a bowl. Plates such as this one are used only when a one-dish meal is served – for example, fried noodles. Such plates are, however, commonly used in Southeast Asia and Indochina.

7 SOUP BOWL

The traditional family mode of eating soup is for all diners to dip into a large, central bowl for repeated mouthfuls. Today, individual soup bowls such as this are a common sight, owing to modern hygiene standards. Individual portions of congee are also served in this type of bowl.

8 9 PORCELAIN SPOON AND REST

As porcelain conducts heat badly, these are sensible implements for drinking hot soup without scalding the lips and tongue because the spoon remains cool. Such spoons are also used for mixing and stirring sauces and marinades that contain vinegar; a metal spoon can react with acidic ingredients. The spoon rest prevents stains on the tablecloth.

10 CHOPSTICKS REST

The porcelain chopstick rest helps to keep the food-stained tips of the chopsticks off the tablecloth, and decorated versions of these rests are one of the formal touches to be expected at banquets.

11 CHOPSTICKS

Chopsticks for eating are usually about 24cm (10in) long and are traditionally made from bamboo or wood. In ancient China, the imperial classes used ivory or even solid gold. Plastic chopsticks are not ideal for eating noodles, as they are slippery. Lacquer chopsticks are intended for ornamental use, rather than eating, but can be used for cold dishes.

12 SOUP TUREEN

A soup tureen is generally used for serving soup at the centre of the table. It also makes an ideal serving container for stews. The lid keeps heat in effectively. There are no handles, and it is important to wear padded oven gloves when moving the hot tureen.

13

12

14

13 SOUP LADLE

A large porcelain ladle such as this is used to serve soups from tureens. It usually features a slightly curved handle and flat-bottomed bowl section.

14 SOY SAUCE BOTTLE

The Chinese equivalent of the Western salt and pepper cruet, the soy sauce bottle is typical of restaurant rather than home use. It is placed on the dining table for individual seasoning of meals. In a Chinese home, however, any extra sauce is meant as a dip, and as such is presented in small dishes or bowls for shared use.

how to use chopsticks

Whether made of wood, bamboo or classy silver, chopsticks can be exasperating for those not familiar with their use. But don't despair: they can be mastered. With a little practice at holding and clicking them together, it will soon be easy to pick up even the tiniest and slipperiest of morsels.

1

2

3

4

Beginners will find bamboo or wooden chopsticks easier to use than plastic, and square-cut Chinese chopsticks are easier to handle than pointed Japanese models. Practise clicking the chopsticks together before moving on to pick up food with them. The most important thing to remember is that only the top chopstick should move.

Step 1 Grasp one of your chopsticks about a third of the way along from the thick end, between the base of the thumb and the tip of the third finger. This chopstick must be kept steady throughout use. Some people (especially children) find it easier to hold their chopsticks about halfway along, but, if you hold them too far back or forward, they will not provide enough leverage and will be unwieldy to use.

Step 2 Hold the second chopstick between the tips of the thumb, first and second fingers, holding it above the other chopstick, again about a third of the way along. When the chopsticks are held parallel to each other, there should be a space of about 2cm (¾in) between them.

Step 3 Keeping your thumb as the anchor, use the tip of your second finger to raise the front of the top chopstick, thus opening the set.

Step 4 Maintain control by keeping the bottom chopstick steady, and use your second finger to lower the top chopstick, bringing the tips together with a light pressure so that you can grasp a piece of food.

cold sesame noodles

Cold noodles are eaten with relish and relief during the muggy hot summers in China, and are a popular snack and picnic food. Every region has its own take on cold noodles, which make a refreshing change from hot ones, and you will find many street food vendors selling their particular versions of this simple but delicious dish.

SERVES 4–6   PREPARATION TIME: 30 MINUTES

TOOLS
Large cooking pot
Cleaver
Chopping board
Colander

INGREDIENTS
500g (1lb 2oz) fresh wheat
    or egg noodles
2 tbsp sesame oil
1 tbsp dark soy sauce
2 eggs
pinch of salt
1 tbsp groundnut (peanut) oil
250g (9oz) roast pork tenderloin,
    cut into 5cm (2in) strips
75g (¾ cup) beansprouts,
    blanched for a few seconds,
    then refreshed in cold water
roughly chopped roasted
    skinless peanuts or toasted
    sesame seeds, to garnish
3 spring onions (scallions), finely
    sliced, to garnish

For the sesame sauce
2 tbsp sesame seed paste,
    diluted with 3 tbsp warm
    water
2 tbsp dark soy sauce
2 garlic cloves, finely
    chopped
2 spring onions (scallions),
    finely sliced
1 tbsp rice wine vinegar
2 tsp sugar
2 tsp chilli oil
1 tsp salt
1 tsp ground Sichuan
    pepper

1 Cook the noodles in a large pot of slightly salted boiling water for 4–5 minutes. Drain in a colander, and rinse under cold running water. Drain again thoroughly. Transfer to a bowl, add the sesame oil and soy sauce, and toss well. Cover, and chill until needed.

2 In a small bowl, whisk together the eggs and a pinch of salt. Set aside for 10 minutes. Heat a scant 1 tsp oil in a wok over a medium-high heat. Add a quarter of the beaten egg, and swirl around the pan to make a small omelette. Carefully lift the edges using a spatula, and turn and cook briefly on the other side. Repeat with the remaining egg mixture, adding a little oil to the pan as needed, so that you end up with 4 small omelettes. Allow to cool, and slice into strips about 5cm (2cm) long. Set aside.

3 To make the sesame sauce, mix together all the sauce ingredients in a small bowl.

4 When you are ready to serve, add the sauce to the noodles, and toss well. Transfer the noodles to a serving plate, and top with the egg strips and pork. Toss through, then garnish with the chopped peanuts or toasted sesame seeds, and the spring onions (scallions).

NINA SIMONDS hot and sour prawn lo mein

'When I was growing up, "ordering Chinese" invariably meant *lo mein* noodles,' says US culinary expert Nina Simonds. 'The Cantonese *lo mein* I loved as a child, however, bears little resemblance to this bright, fresh-tasting and virtually greaseless version. Whenever I'm feeling nostalgic, I toss noodles in this spicy sauce laced with garlic, vinegar and hot chillies.'

SERVES 6   PREPARATION TIME: 30 MINUTES

TOOLS
Cleaver
Chopping board
Small pot
Large pot
Colander
Wok and ladle
Wire mesh strainer

INGREDIENTS
175g (6oz) canned water
　chestnuts, rinsed, drained
　and sliced (about ¾ cup)
225g (8oz) wide flat noodles
700g (1½lb) medium raw
　prawns (shrimp), peeled,
　deveined and rinsed
3½ tbsp groundnut (peanut) oil
1 red onion, thinly sliced
2½ tbsp finely chopped garlic
1 tsp hot chilli paste
225g (8oz) mangetout (snow
　peas), ends snapped and
　strings removed

For the ginger marinade
3 tbsp Chinese rice wine
　or sake
1½ tbsp finely chopped fresh
　root ginger
1 tsp sesame oil

For the hot and sour sauce
340ml (1⅓ cups) Chinese
　chicken stock or water
85ml (scant ⅓ cup) light
　soy sauce
2 tbsp Chinese rice wine
　or sake
2 tbsp sugar
2 tbsp Chingkiang or
　Chinese black vinegar or
　Worcestershire sauce
1 tsp toasted sesame oil
1 tbsp cornflour (cornstarch)

1 Bring a small pan of water to the boil, and blanch the water chestnuts for 10 seconds, then refresh under cold water, drain and pat dry with kitchen paper. Set aside.

2 Bring a large pot of water to the boil, add the noodles and cook according to the packet instructions until they are just tender. Put the noodles in a colander, and rinse under cold water. Set aside to drain thoroughly.

3 To make the ginger marinade, mix together the Chinese rice wine or sake, ginger and sesame oil in a bowl. Add the rinsed prawns (shrimp), toss lightly to coat in the marinade, and set aside. To make the hot and sour sauce, in a separate bowl, mix together the stock, soy sauce, Chinese rice wine or sake, sugar, vinegar, sesame oil and cornflour (cornstarch), then set aside.

4 Heat a wok over a high heat. Add 2 tbsp of the oil, and heat until very hot but not smoking. Lift the prawns from the marinade, and add to the wok. Toss lightly for about 1½ minutes until they turn pink. Remove with a wire mesh strainer, and drain in a colander. Set aside. Wipe out the wok with kitchen paper.

5 Reheat the wok over a medium-high heat. Add the remaining 1½ tbsp oil, and heat for about 20 seconds until hot. Add the onion, garlic and chilli paste, and stir-fry for 1½–2 minutes until the onion is slightly softened.

6 Add the water chestnuts and mangetout (snow peas), increase the heat to high, and toss until heated through. Pour in the hot and sour sauce. Cook for 2–3 minutes, stirring constantly to prevent lumps, until the sauce is thickened.

7 Add the reserved prawns and noodles, and mix gently. Transfer to a serving plate, and serve immediately.

japan
and korea

Japanese culture may be difficult for non-Japanese to fathom because of its near-mystical symbolism. The true genius of Japanese cooking, however, lies in its simplicity – the marrying of a few flavourings with the natural goodness of fresh ingredients, and each dish a manifestation of the Japanese love of nature.

japan and korea

The objective of Japanese cooking is to let each ingredient, and each dish, reveal its particular beauty and flavour. This may be seen in the use of an autumn leaf to garnish, an artfully arranged vegetable pickle, or the rustic colours of carefully selected porcelain and lacquer serving dishes.

Indeed, it is this very simplicity that makes Japanese cuisine so wonderfully enchanting. It imparts an almost Zen-like karma, with the focus not on quantity, but on reverence for the essence of each morsel. It is said that the Japanese eat not only with their mouths, but also with their souls, as witnessed when you see people contemplating every mouthful as though it were poetry.

The key flavourings used in Japanese cuisine are essentially simple ones. They include bonito flakes (dried smoked fish), dashi (a base stock made with various flavourings such as bonito flakes, seaweed and dried shiitake mushrooms), and sake, as well as fermented soya bean products such as soy sauces and hundreds of different types of yeasty miso paste. Other common Japanese ingredients are bamboo shoots, daikon (a large white radish; also known as *mooli*), ginger, shiitake mushrooms, nori (seaweed sheets), kombu (dried kelp; also called *konbu*), shirataki noodles and soba (buckwheat) noodles. Perhaps the most memorable thing for first-timers is wasabi paste, an extremely pungent condiment of green horseradish that literally 'gets up your nose'.

There are seven main types of cooking methods used in Japan. A typical meal will consist of a selection of small dishes, often three dishes each made by a different cooking method, plus miso soup, rice and pickles. Grilled dishes are known as *yakimono*, and these are familiar to many Westerners as *yakitori* and *teriyaki*. *Agemono* are deep-fried foods such as tempura, while *nimono* are simmered or poached foods – essentially the stews of Japanese cooking. *Mushimono* are steamed items, *itamemono* are sautéed or pan-fried, *sunomono* are vinegared, and *aemono* are dressed dishes often featuring a substantial sauce.

The Japanese insist on serving foods in tandem with the seasons – the ultimate seasonal food. The best Japanese restaurants maintain separate sets of dishes and serving utensils for each season. The pattern of waitresses' kimonos and sashes reflects the season – red for autumn (fall), white for winter, green for spring and orange for summer. The ambience will harmonize with the dishes served, and food will be arranged to reflect the shapes, colours and textures of the seasons.

It is sushi that perhaps most captures Western imagination. Frequently confused with sashimi, which is simply raw fish, sushi is cooled sticky rice that has been flavoured with vinegar, often topped with pieces of raw fish or shellfish, and either eaten as a starter or as the main focus of a meal. The Japanese consider raw fish to be the high point of a meal, and all dishes that follow are merely co-stars. Sushi is an art form in itself, but does not have to be purist. Nor does it have to feature raw fish.

Up until the end of the sixteenth century, the island nation of Japan was almost completely isolated from the rest of the world. The first Europeans to reach her shores were Portuguese seamen,

OPPOSITE 1 daikon **2** shimeji mushrooms **3** shiso leaves **4** spinach **5** enoki mushrooms **6** shiitake mushrooms **7** edamame **8** burdock root
BELOW 1 sushi rice **2** kombu seaweed **3** bonito powder **4** hijiki seaweed **5** shichimi togarashi, or Japanese seven-spice **6** dried red chilli flakes **7** wakame seaweed **8** nori seaweed **9** udon noodles **10** white sesame seeds **11** soba noodles **12** black sesame seeds

and in their wake trade between the two countries began in earnest. Jesuit missionaries began arriving, hoping to convert the Japanese to Christianity. They also noticed that the Japanese consumed practically no meat and ate large quantities of rice and seafood. The Portuguese incomer, however, began to interfere with the Japanese feudal system. This, coupled with fear of an invasion by Spaniards based in the Philippines, led to the Portuguese being forcibly expelled from Japan in 1638. All foreigners were banned, and all Japanese were forbidden to leave the country on pain of death. Once more, Japan's doors were locked against the world, until the arrival of US Navy Commodore Perry in the nineteenth century, who compelled the opening up of Japan to foreigners once again with the Kanagawa Treaty of 1854, which allowed trade between the United States and the once-closed nation.

What the Portuguese did leave behind, however, were their recipes for deep-fried seafood and vegetables that came to be known as *tempura*, a corruption of the Latin word *tempora*. Use of this term came about as a result of the Portuguese Catholics' observance of Ember Days, which they called by the Latin name of *quattuor anni tempora* (the four 'times', or 'seasons', of the year). The eating of meat was strictly forbidden at these times, as well as at others in the liturgical calendar such as during Lent and on Fridays. The Portuguese would ask instead for seafood, usually prawns (shrimp). Eventually, the name *tempura* became attached to the fried prawns, and so it remains to this day, although other foods such as salmon, tofu, bamboo shoots and vegetables are also cooked in the tempura style and have come to be seen as quintessentially Japanese.

The Korean peninsula, immediately to Japan's west, is blessed with a largely friendly subtemperate climate that yields abundant produce. For centuries, Koreans have eaten the produce of the sea, the land and the mountains. Korean cuisine is fragrantly spicy and hearty, with basic seasonings coming from garlic, ginger, black pepper, spring onions (scallions), soy sauce and sesame seeds. Chillies are used liberally; fermented soya bean paste, mustard, vinegar and rice wine also feature. The permutations of these ingredients in marinades and seasonings are seemingly endless.

No Korean person could be without *kimchi*, the region's spicy pickled cabbage, for more than a few days, and there are many versions of it. Often two or three varieties of *kimchi* are served as part of a meal. The pickling liquid is a blend of salt, chilli powder, fresh red chillies, ginger, soy sauce and sugar. Layer upon layer of sliced cabbage is placed in a stone jar, covered with several pieces of muslin (cheesecloth) to allow the pickle to 'breathe' and, after about a week, the jar is opened to reveal an intoxicating dish.

Beef is the favourite meat on the Korean peninsula and most frequently turns up as *bulgogi* (marinated barbecued beefsteak) or *bulgabi* (barbecued short ribs). It is the sauce that distinguishes these two national favourites. *Yang yeum kanjang* is a pungent mix of soy sauce, sesame oil, bean paste, wine, spring onions, chilli paste, garlic and sugar. Both the steak and ribs are marinated in this paste for several hours, then grilled over hot coals or cooked on a cast-iron griddle at the table.

The Koreans often use a fermented soya bean paste similar to the Sichuan chilli bean paste. Known as *gochujang*, it has a surprisingly mellow flavour given the amount of ground chilli in it. Seaweed is used in many different ways, the Korean *kim* being similar to Japanese *nori* and used in much the same way, as a wrapper, or shredded and added to soups.

Korea has some unique noodles in the form of *naengmyun*, a rubbery buckwheat noodle made so long that the dried strands are folded in half, and when cooked are cut with scissors at the table. The name means 'cold noodle' and, while they can be served hot, they are most frequently featured floating in a tangy cold broth, accompanied by raw julienne vegetables, slices of Asian pear and perhaps a hard-boiled egg or sometimes cold beef.

Historically, poor farming families ate a diet of boiled rice and vegetables, often eking out their supply of rice with the addition of other grains and pulses. The vegetables would be stir-fried with a sharp seasoning such as chilli and bean paste during winter, and served raw and cold in summer. The Korean diet has changed much over the past few decades, and with more Koreans travelling abroad, as well as foreigners in turn visiting South Korea and its more reclusive neighbour to the north, taste buds are being shaped by the introduction of international foods. Korean chefs, especially those working in restaurants outside their own country, are not averse to tweaking their traditional dishes. While some chefs may use ingredients not indigenous to Korea, accompanying seasonings remain firmly within Korean kitchen practices. As the basis for many dishes, these time-honoured seasonings are revered and practically sacrosanct.

OPPOSITE 1 kimchi yang yeum **2** umeboshi plums **3** gochujang (Korean chilli bean paste) **4** miso **5** fried tofu, or bean curd **6** shoyu (Japanese soy sauce) **7** mirin **8** fresh tofu **9** pickled daikon **10** brown vinegar

knives and chopping board

Top-quality Japanese kitchen knives are truly the razor-sharp progeny of the samurai fighting sword and are among the most prized possessions in Japanese homes. Forgers of these blades are regarded as living national treasures. Japanese knives are forged so that only one side of the blade holds the cutting edge, usually on the right, so that the knifes cut much faster and more cleanly than the double-edged knives typical of Western manufacturers. Two materials are favoured: carbon steel and stainless steel. Carbon steel is superior, and honed so sharply that it can literally split a hair. Always hold a Japanese knife lightly – not with a stranglehold. With the correct movement and rhythm, a knife is an extension of your hand, and there should be no awkward tension while cutting.

1 KITCHEN CARVER

Known as a *deba*, this functions like a Chinese cleaver, but is narrower and lighter, usually measuring 18cm (7in) long and 4cm (1¾in) wide. It is basically a fish knife, used for removing the head, tailing and boning, but can also be used for poultry and meat. Indeed, there is no reason why this versatile implement cannot be used for other jobs, including heavy chopping.

2 FISH SLICER

Traditionally used for sashimi, this long, slender knife with blunt end is known as a *tacobiki*, or octopus knife. It is ideal for slicing fish fillets, as well as cutting neat sushi rolls. Another type of sashimi knife, the *yanagi-ba*, or willow-leaf blade, is also long and slender, but looks more like a Western knife because the blade ends in a fine point. Serrated knives will never do for fish slicing because they tear instead of making clean cuts. Always have a folded clean damp cloth close by, and wipe the blade frequently to keep it clean while you are working.

3 VEGETABLE KNIFE

Shaped and weighted like a Chinese cleaver, albeit narrower, this is used mainly for vegetable cutting, but its weight and leverage make it suitable for delicate cutting, chopping and fine slicing, even bashing garlic. Choose brands made of carbon steel.

4 ALL-PURPOSE KNIFE

With its 24cm (9½in) single-sided blade, this knife is a Japanese version of an all-purpose chef's knife and known as an *oroshi*. It can be used for preparing fish, beef, poultry and vegetables. Like the others shown here, it has a non-slip wooden handle and should be sharpened on a whetstone.

5 CHOPPING BOARD

The Japanese use conventional chopping boards, but chefs have a preference for square or rectangular shapes made of pine. Japanese cuisine relies heavily on cutting, so these tend to be noticeably larger than the chopping boards usually seen in the West.

how to prepare fish

Presentation is key in Japanese cuisine. Using the right tool in the right way will help you to achieve the best results, especially when it comes to preparing raw fish for sashimi or sushi.

1 Cutting fish Holding the fish slicer or similar sharp knife at a slight angle, cut the fillet on a slight diagonal in one firm, smooth action by drawing the knife towards you.

2 Skinning fish Carefully separate the skin and the flesh at one end of the fish; holding the skin down on the board, insert the blade of a fish slicer or similar sharp knife at a slight angle between the skin and flesh. Draw the knife blade along the skin.

3 Peeling the filament from skin Using your fingers, carefully separate the filament from the skin at the head end of the fish, and pull back towards the tail.

sashimi

It is imperative that fish for sashimi be impeccably fresh, as is the case whenever you are serving raw fish. Lay your fillet on a wooden chopping board, and hold the sashimi knife so that the blade is inclined slightly to the left. With a sweeping motion, draw the knife towards you from its base to the tip, applying gentle pressure, but letting the weight of the knife do the work. Use the knife to move the slice of fish a little to one side on the board, then lay the slice on its side. Continue until all the fish is sliced. Serve with shredded daikon, shiso leaves and wasabi.

simple japanese pickles

Traditionally, Japanese pickles are much more than condiments. The art known as *tsukemono* is actually a very extensive domain, with each accompaniment regarded with the same reverence as the main course. For centuries, every home in Japan has had its own pickling crock or barrel. Pickles are relished for their piquant, salty flavours, which juxtapose artfully with raw fish and unseasoned meats. They also have a sharp, cleansing effect on the palate and aid digestion. As with any pickle, the ones here will keep for weeks if stored properly in a jar with a tight-fitting lid, but they are best eaten within a week.

daikon pickle

Finely grate 1 large daikon into a mixing bowl. Sprinkle 2 tsp salt all over the radish strands, and stir well. Leave to stand for 20 minutes to pickle in the salt, then squeeze out as much moisture from the daikon as possible. Add 2 tbsp rice wine, 1 tbsp sugar and 1 tsp white sesame seeds, and toss through well.

aubergine pickle

Wash and dry 4 baby aubergines (eggplants), and cut into quarters lengthways. Rub with 1 tbsp salt, and set aside on a piece of kitchen paper for at least 1 hour. Combine 150g (5½oz) miso paste, 2 tbsp mirin and 1 tbsp finely grated fresh root ginger in a small bowl. Gently squeeze out the moisture from the aubergines, and put in a shallow bowl. Pour the pickling liquid over the top, cover and leave to steep overnight or for several days. Serve with grilled fish or chicken.

turnip pickle

Peel 500g (1lb 2oz) large turnips, then rinse and cut into thin julienne. Put in a bowl, and sprinkle liberally with 2 tbsp salt. Set aside for 10 minutes, then squeeze out the moisture from the turnips using your hands. Add 1 tbsp kombu strips and 1 tbsp finely grated lemon zest. Leave to stand at room temperature for 30 minutes. To serve, drain off any excess liquid, and arrange in a mound next to fish or meat dishes.

EMI KAZUKO
seared swordfish sashimi salad with miso vinegar dressing

Sashimi salad is one of the most popular fusion dishes at Japanese restaurants outside Japan because it makes an easy starting point for newcomers to the art of eating fish raw. At home, if you cannot get sashimi-quality fresh fish to eat completely raw, Emi suggests you either sear or blanch raw fish as in this recipe.

SERVES 4   PREPARATION TIME: 15 MINUTES

TOOLS
Fish slicer or sashimi knife
Vegetable knife
Chopping board

INGREDIENTS
500g (1lb 2oz) fresh
   swordfish fillet, skinned
½ onion
120g (4½oz/about 6 cups) mixed
   salad leaves
For the dressing
2½ tbsp white miso (soya paste)
1½ tbsp rice vinegar or
   white wine vinegar
2 tbsp sake or white wine
1–2 tsp mustard such as
   neri-garashi (Japanese
   mustard paste)
To garnish
white sesame seeds,
   lightly toasted

1 In a very hot pan lightly brushed with oil (add the oil only once the pan is hot), quickly sear the swordfish on both sides until just the surface is cooked and the centre is still pink. Slice thinly crossways, inserting the knife blade slightly diagonally.

2 Slice the onion into very thin half-moons, and put in ice water to freshen and to reduce some of the sharpness. Drain and pat dry with kitchen paper. Mix with the salad leaves.

3 Whisk together the dressing, and put some in the centre of each of 4 individual plates. Arrange a quarter of the salad on top of each pool of dressing, and a quarter of the swordfish slices around the salad. Drizzle the remaining dressing over the fish, sprinkle with sesame seeds and serve.

sushi equipment

While many people associate sushi with raw fish, the term actually means 'vinegared rice', and consequently the rice preparation is the most important element. Having the proper tools makes all the difference to the results. The rice has to be cooled to the right temperature, and it must have the correct texture and sheen. Natural materials, such as bamboo and wood, have a special quality that ensures that the rice comes out perfectly because, unlike metal, they do not react chemically with foods. Furthermore, it is virtually impossible to get the precise shape required for rolled sushi without using a genuine sushi mat.

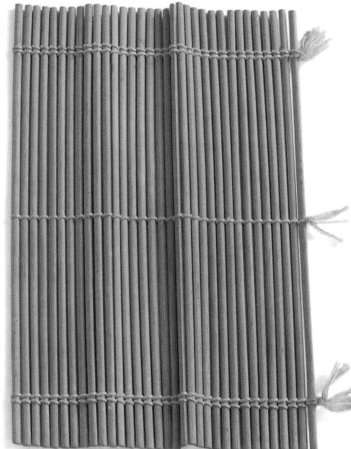

1

2

1 BAMBOO MAT

This 25cm (10in) square-shaped mat of fine bamboo is for forming and pressing rice and other soft foods into cylindrical shapes. For *norimaki*, for instance, nori sheets are toasted and placed directly on the mat, and warm rice is heaped on top and flattened. The mat is then rolled up and over to make perfect nori rolls. To avoid musty smells, wash the mat in tepid water after use, then wipe and allow to dry completely before storing.

2 RICE COOLING TUB

Known as a *hangiri*, this tub is made from the wood of a special cypress tree and bound with copper hoops. Perfect for rapid cooling of sushi rice (which always has to be freshly made), the wood also helps to give the rice its proper gloss and malleable texture. This cooling process is hastened by the use of the fan to drive off moisture and create the right flavour.

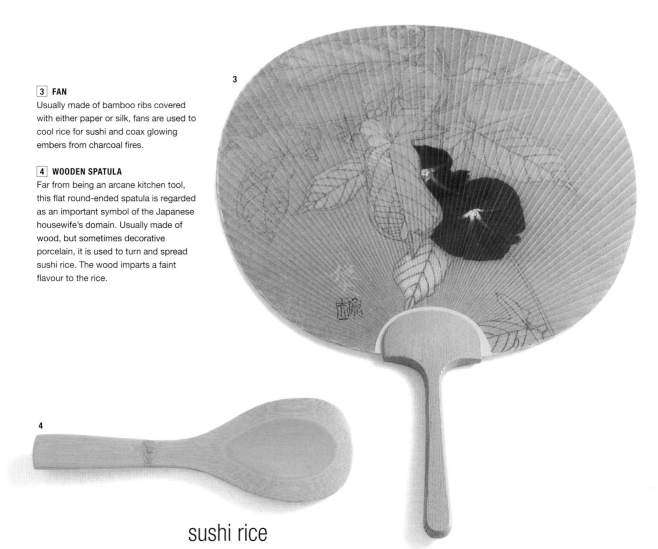

3 FAN

Usually made of bamboo ribs covered with either paper or silk, fans are used to cool rice for sushi and coax glowing embers from charcoal fires.

4 WOODEN SPATULA

Far from being an arcane kitchen tool, this flat round-ended spatula is regarded as an important symbol of the Japanese housewife's domain. Usually made of wood, but sometimes decorative porcelain, it is used to turn and spread sushi rice. The wood imparts a faint flavour to the rice.

sushi rice

Following the instructions below will help to ensure that your sushi rice has the silky glossiness so prized by Japanese chefs and that is fundamental to top-quality sushi.

MAKES ENOUGH FOR 8–10 ROLLS   PREPARATION TIME: 30 MINUTES, PLUS 1 HOUR'S DRAINING

TOOLS
Colander
Electric rice cooker
Wooden cooling tub
Fan
Small saucepan
Wooden spatula

INGREDIENTS
300g (1¾ cups) Japanese
   sushi rice
50ml (¼ cup) rice vinegar
1 tbsp sugar
1 tsp salt

1 Wash the rice in several changes of fresh water until the water runs clear, and leave to drain in a strainer or colander for at least 30 minutes (and preferably 1 hour). Put the drained rice in the rice cooker with enough cold water to rise 3cm (1¼in) above the level of the rice, then switch on the cooker. When done, leave to stand for 10 minutes, then transfer the cooked rice to the cooling tub.

2 Meanwhile, mix together the vinegar, sugar and salt in a small pan. Place over a medium heat until the sugar has dissolved, stirring occasionally. Cool using the fan.

3 Sprinkle the vinegar mixture over the rice. Using the wooden spatula, gently fold through the rice for 2 minutes. Using a fan, cool quickly as you fold until the rice is cool enough to handle.

sushi techniques

Sticky rice is, as the name says, sticky. This can make it difficult to work with, as the grains stick to your fingers. The Japanese solution is to keep a bowl of acidulated water nearby, and to dip the hands in it before picking up the rice. To make this 'hand vinegar', use 2 tbsp rice vinegar per 125ml (½ cup) water.

rolling norimaki

Toasting the nori seaweed used for *norimaki* over a gas flame darkens it and makes it more pliable for rolling. Toast very briefly over a medium heat to make it more crispy and to bring out the flavour, holding the sheet of nori about 10cm (4in) away from the heat source.

1 Place the bamboo sushi mat on a dry chopping board, and lay the toasted nori on top, with the shiny side facing down. Add 2–3 tbsp vinegared sushi rice and, using hands wet with hand vinegar, gently spread out the rice over the nori in a thin, even layer. Leave a gap of 1.5cm (⅝in) around the edge of the rice. Top the bed of rice with the fillings of your choice.

2 Pick up the bamboo mat at the near side, and roll it over to meet the other side, enclosing the rice in the nori in a cylinder shape and ensuring that the filling is at the centre of the roll.

3 Lift the bamboo mat a little, then press it gently down and over the cylinder. Roll the cylinder in the mat a little to help the sushi firm up – but be careful not to squash the rice. Pat both ends in firmly, and trim away the excess seaweed.

4 Lay the *norimaki*, or nori roll, on the cutting board, seam-side down. Using a sharp knife, cut the roll into 3cm (1¼in) pieces.

rolling uramaki

Also known as inside-out or reverse-roll sushi, *uramaki* are a pretty alternative to *norimaki* and have the crunch and nutty taste of sesame.

1 Cover a bamboo sushi mat with a sheet of cling film (plastic wrap). Place a sheet of nori crossways on top of it, with the shiny side facing down. Wet your hands with hand vinegar (see opposite), and mould a portion of vinegared sushi rice into a cylinder; gently spread out the rice until it covers the nori. Sprinkle toasted white sesame seeds evenly over the rice.

2 Turn over the rice bed on the cling film–covered bamboo mat, so that the rice side is facing down. Arrange the desired fillings in a row across the centre of the nori.

3 Pick up the side of bamboo mat nearest you and, keeping the filling in the centre, roll the mat over, overlapping about 1cm (½in) so that the rice sticks onto the nori. Roll the *uramaki* over a little inside the mat so that the join will remain sealed. Remove the *uramaki*, and cut into 3cm (1¼in) pieces.

shaping nigiri-zushi

This type of hand-moulded sushi looks relatively easy to make, yet the Japanese consider it one of the most difficult types to get exactly right and usually leave it to the skills of the professional sushi chef. It takes trained hands to shape the rice gently but firmly so that it is cohesive enough to pick up in one piece, while still being deliciously light-textured in the mouth.

1 Wet your hands with hand vinegar (see opposite) to prevent the rice sticking. Take a handful of vinegared sushi rice, and mould it into a neat oblong measuring about 5cm x 2cm x 2cm (2in x ¾in x ¾in). Using the tip of your finger, smear a little wasabi paste (be careful not to use too much) along the top of the rice.

2 Cover with a piece of thinly sliced raw tuna, salmon, sea bream or skinned squid (calamari), cut so that it measures about 7cm x 3cm (3in x 1¼in). Alternatively, top the moulded rice with a cooked tiger prawn (shrimp), peeled, deveined and split open along the belly so that it sits flat on the rice. You can also make *nigiri-zushi* with rolled omelette (see page 86), cutting the omelette into pieces measuring 7cm x 3cm x 1cm (3in x 1¼in x ½in), and omitting the wasabi paste.

nori roll

Japanese chefs train for many years to perfect their craft, yet some types of sushi are relatively easy to make at home. Below are instructions for making *norimaki*, or nori roll (pictured at bottom left, opposite). As you become more proficient, try your hand at *uramaki* (see page 81 and opposite bottom right) or, the hardest to master, *nigiri-zushi* (see page 81 and opposite top).

SERVES 4   PREPARATION TIME: 40–60 MINUTES, PLUS DRAINING

TOOLS
Sharp knife
Chopping board
Bamboo mat
Wooden spatula

INGREDIENTS
1 quantity vinegared sushi rice
    (see recipe on page 79)
a few pieces of deseeded
    cucumber, pickled daikon
    or fresh tuna fillet
2 sheets toasted nori
½–1 tsp wasabi paste, plus
    extra, to serve
pickled ginger and *shoyu*
    (Japanese soy sauce),
    to serve

1 Make the sushi rice (see page 79). Meanwhile, prepare the filling ingredients. Cut the deseeded cucumber, pickled daikon or fresh tuna into batons measuring about 1cm (½in) square, and set aside.

2 Take a sheet of nori seaweed, and gently warm over a gas flame (or similar heat source) for a few seconds to toast and crisp slightly, holding it about 10cm (4in) from the flame.

3 Sit the bamboo mat on a dry chopping board, and lay the toasted nori on top, with the shiny side facing down. Using hands wet with acidulated water (see page 80), add 2–3 tbsp of the vinegared sushi rice, and gently spread it out over the nori until the layer of rice is thin and measures about 12cm x 8cm (5in x 3¼in). Leave a gap of 1.5cm (⅝in) between the edge of the rice and that of the nori.

4 Use your finger to smear a faint line of wasabi paste along the centre of the rice (remember to be sparing because of the wasabi's heat), then cover with a strip of your chosen filling.

5 Pick up the mat at the near side, and roll it over to meet the other side and form a cylinder, enclosing both the rice and the filling in the nori (see page 80). Roll the cylinder in the mat a little to help it firm up.

6 Remove the cylinder from the bamboo mat, and set aside to rest, seam-side down, while you repeat the rolling process with the remaining ingredients.

7 Using a sharp knife, cut each cylinder into 3cm (1¼in) pieces. Arrange the sushi on a sushi bench or other serving plate, and serve with pickled ginger, *shoyu* and a dab of extra wasabi paste, if desired.

Note Always work gently and with deliberation when rolling or shaping sushi. You need to press down just firmly enough that the grains of rice adhere slightly to each other, so that the finished sushi will keep its shape and not fall apart in the hand when being eaten. Take care not to press so hard that the grains are squashed or the nori wrapping (if using) tears.

EMI KAZUKO california roll

This is probably the first and the most well-known 'fusion' sushi invented outside Japan, using avocado, abundant in California, and is now a fixture at most sushi shops, even in Japan. Seafood sticks are usually used in this roll, but make a point to use the real thing – king crab leg meat – and taste the difference.

MAKES 4 ROLLS (24 PIECES)   PREPARATION TIME: 40–60 MINUTES, PLUS DRAINING

TOOLS
Mandolin or vegetable peeler
Sharp knife
Chopping board
Bamboo mat
Wooden spatula

INGREDIENTS
1 quantity sushi rice
  (see page 79)
1 or 2 large pieces of cooked
  fresh king crab leg meat or
  6 seafood sticks
1 avocado, peeled and stoned
2 sheets nori, halved
  crossways
4 tbsp *tobiko* fish roe or white
  sesame seeds, lightly toasted
1 bunch of fresh chives
2 tbsp mayonnaise, optional
To serve
vinegared ginger (see right)
shoyu (Japanese soy sauce)
wasabi paste

1 Make the sushi rice. Meanwhile, prepare the filling ingredients. Cut each piece of king crab leg meat lengthways into two or four, depending on thickness, to make 4 sticks of about 'fountain pen' size. If using seafood sticks, cut these in half lengthways. Cut the avocado into 8 slices lengthways.

2 Prepare a nori rice bed following the method for *uramaki* (see page 81). Sprinkle 1 tbsp of the *tobiko* or sesame seeds over the rice, and gently pat so that it sticks to the rice.

3 Turn over the whole rice bed onto the bamboo mat covered with cling film (plastic wrap) in the same way as you would for *uramaki*. Lay 2 slices of the avocado side by side horizontally across the centre of the rice bed with 1 piece of the crabmeat or 3 seafood stick halves. Lay 6–8 sprigs of chives alongside the avocado and crab, allowing them to stick out at the ends by 3–4 cm (1¼–1¾ in). Spoon about ½ tbsp mayonnaise, if using, over the top of the ingredients.

4 Pick up the bamboo mat from the side nearest you, and roll once according to the method on page 81. Remove the roll from the bamboo mat. Repeat to make 3 more rolls with the remaining ingredients. Cut each roll into 6 pieces, and serve garnished with some vinegared ginger, *shoyu* and a little wasabi in a small dish for people to help themselves.

Vinegared ginger Using a fine mandolin or peeler, very finely slice 100g (3½oz) peeled fresh root ginger. Cook in a pan of boiling water over a medium heat for 2 minutes. Drain, and pat dry with kitchen paper. To make the marinade, in a small bowl, mix together 100ml (scant ½ cup) rice vinegar, 50ml (¼ cup) water and 2½ tbsp sugar, stirring until the sugar has dissolved. Marinate the ginger for 5–6 days before using. It will keep for months in a sterilized screw-top jar in the refrigerator.

SHIRLEY BOOTH rolled omelette

Japan's distinctive sweetened egg roll, the *tamagoyaki*, is a common sight in sushi bars. The recipe here comes from *Food of Japan* author and film-maker Shirley Booth, who lived in the country for six years and studied Zen temple cookery. 'If you become quite deft at this and really want to show off, you can put a sheet of nori between one of the layers as you cook,' she says. 'Once rolled and then cut through, it will reveal an impressive spiral effect.'

SERVES 4   PREPARATION TIME: 30 MINUTES

1 In a mixing bowl, dissolve the sugar in the dashi, soy sauce and mirin to make a broth. Crack the eggs into a separate bowl, and lightly beat. Making sure that the broth is at room temperature, pour in the beaten egg, and lightly combine.

2 Heat the omelette pan until quite hot, then brush lightly with oil. If you are using a large pan, pour in one-third of the egg mixture. If using a smaller pan, pour one-sixth of the mixture into the pan. Tilt the pan backwards and forwards as you pour until you have a very thin layer of egg just covering the bottom (top left). The egg should immediately sizzle around the edges. Cook over a medium heat until the egg is cooked around the edge, but soft and runny on top.

3 Using chopsticks or a spatula, carefully roll up the cooked omelette (top right), and gently push it to the back of the pan.

4 Brush the empty bottom of the pan with oil, then push the roll away and brush underneath it too. Push the roll back, all the time keeping the pan on the heat.

5 Pour another third (or sixth) of the mixture onto the empty base (centre left), tilting the pan and lifting the cooked roll so that the liquid egg flows underneath (centre right). Cook until almost done as before.

6 Using the first roll of omelette as the core, roll up the second section around it (bottom left).

7 If using a large pan, repeat the process with the final third of the mixture. If using a small pan, repeat the process with batches of the remaining mixture, rolling each new omelette around the previously cooked one. Tip the completed egg roll from the pan (bottom right), and set aside to cool.

8 Cut the omelette into 5cm (2in) pieces, and serve either alone or, if preferred, sitting on a wad of sushi rice, with a thin strip of toasted nori wrapped around the middle.

TOOLS

Omelette pan

Small pastry brush

Chopsticks or wooden spatula

Sharp knife

INGREDIENTS

For the broth

1 tsp sugar

4 tbsp dashi

2 tsp light soy sauce

1 tbsp mirin

For the omelette

6 eggs

½ tsp salt

vegetable oil for frying

prepared sushi rice (optional;
  see page 79)

½ sheet toasted nori, cut
  into strips about 1.5cm
  (⅝in) wide and 8cm (3¼in)
  long (optional)

pressed sushi with crabmeat and prawns

Oshi-zushi, or pressed sushi, is very simple to make because it does not involve rolling. Crabmeat, prawns (shrimp) and shredded thin omelette are used here, but use your imagination and experiment with other toppings such as smoked salmon, a thin layer of cream cheese, and cucumber, with sesame seeds gently folded into the sushi rice.

MAKES 16 PIECES   PREPARATION TIME: 40–60 MINUTES, PLUS DRAINING AND PRESSING

TOOLS

Sharp knife
Chopping board
Wooden sushi mould or 20cm (8in)
    square shallow container
Wooden spatula

INGREDIENTS

½ quantity sushi rice (see page 79)
250g (9oz) cooked fresh white crabmeat, flaked,
    or 250g (9oz) canned, drained
1 tbsp freshly squeezed lemon juice
115g (4oz) peeled and deveined cooked
    prawns (shrimp), sliced in half horizontally, or
    90g (3oz) smoked salmon
2 sheets of thin omelette (see right),
    finely shredded
a few sprigs of lemon thyme, to garnish
salt and freshly ground black pepper

To serve

vinegared ginger (see page 84) or pickled daikon
shoyu (Japanese soy sauce)

1 Make the vinegared cooked sushi rice following the instructions on page 79.

2 If using canned crabmeat, first heat in a small pan over a medium heat for a couple of minutes, stirring vigorously and constantly, until it is flaky. Put the canned or fresh crabmeat in a bowl, add the lemon juice and season with salt and pepper.

3 Line a wooden sushi mould or a 20cm (8in) square shallow container with cling film (plastic wrap). Spread the sushi rice evenly over the bottom so that it comes about halfway up the sides of the mould, pressing down firmly. Add a layer of prawns (shrimp) or smoked salmon to cover the rice, overlapping the salmon as needed. Spread the crabmeat evenly over the top, and press down firmly.

4 Sprinkle the omelette shreds over the top, and cover with a wooden lid. If using a shallow container, cover the sushi with cling film first, then a sheet of cardboard or similar. Weight down evenly with a heavy plate, and press until ready to serve.

5 Remove from the container, and cut into bite-sized pieces. Garnish with lemon thyme, and serve with vinegared ginger or pickled daikon, and soy sauce.

Thin omelette Whisk together 2 eggs with a pinch of salt. Heat a little vegetable oil in a 20cm (8in) omelette pan. Pour in half of the egg mixture, and swirl around the pan until evenly coated. Gently cook for about 30 seconds on each side until just set; slide from the pan, and leave to cool. Cook the second omelette as before.

EMI KAZUKO cucumber log sushi

Inro, an old word for a pillbox, is one of the most sought-after items for collectors of Japanese antiques. This *inro*-shaped sushi is made with white gourd in Japan, but here it is made with English cucumber and works beautifully.

MAKES 4 HALF CUCUMBER LOGS (ABOUT 26 PIECES)   PREPARATION TIME: 40–60 MINUTES, PLUS DRAINING AND SOAKING

TOOLS

Sharp knife
Chopping board
Citrus zester
Fruit and vegetable corer
Wooden spatula

INGREDIENTS

½ quantity sushi rice (see page 79)
2 English cucumbers, halved
2 tbsp salt, plus an extra pinch
1 piece of kombu (dried kelp), about
    10cm x 5cm (4in x 2in) (optional)
2 tbsp sake
1 tbsp sugar
2 tsp mirin
6 raw tiger prawns (shrimp), deveined, or
    100g (3½oz) peeled and deveined
    cooked prawns (shrimp)
To serve
shoyu (Japanese soy sauce)
wasabi paste

1 Make the vinegared cooked sushi rice following the instructions on page 79.

2 Meanwhile, prepare the other ingredients. Trim the cucumber halves and, using a citrus zester, cut away fine strips of peel lengthways down the cucumber skin, to make a striped pattern. Chop the strips of peel very finely, and set aside.

3 Using a corer, cut a neat round hole down the centre of each cucumber half. Soak the hollow cucumber halves in a mixture of the 2 tbsp salt, the kombu (if using) and 1 litre (4 cups) water for 30 minutes. Drain and leave to dry. Discard the kombu, or reserve for use in other recipes.

4 Mix together the sake, sugar, mirin and extra pinch of salt in a small saucepan. Bring to the boil, add the unpeeled tiger prawns (shrimp) and cook over a medium heat for 5–6 minutes until almost all the cooking juice has been absorbed. When cool, peel and finely dice the flesh. If using cooked prawns, heat the seasoning mixture, and use it to marinate the prawns for 10 minutes. Drain and finely dice.

5 Gently fold the reserved cucumber peel and the prawns into the sushi rice, and use it to firmly stuff the central hole of each cucumber half. Cut crossways into rounds 1–2cm (½–¾in) wide. Arrange on a serving platter, and serve with sauce and a little wasabi in individual dishes.

EMI KAZUKO rainbow roll

Tazuna, meaning 'rein' in Japanese, is a twisted rope. *Tazuna-maki*, or rainbow roll, has a pattern on top resembling this, and uses ingredients of various colours and tastes. It is quite complicated to make, but makes a stunningly beautiful party dish.

MAKES 3 ROLLS (18 PIECES)   PREPARATION TIME: 40–60 MINUTES, PLUS DRAINING AND SOAKING

TOOLS
Vegetable peeler
Sharp knife
Chopping board
2 bamboo mats
Wooden spatula

INGREDIENTS
½ quantity sushi rice
   (see page 79)
2 pickled or Bismarck herring
   fillets, skin on
1 cucumber, about 10cm
   (4in) long
2 tbsp salt
120g (4½oz) smoked trout or
   smoked salmon
For the hand vinegar
2 tbsp rice vinegar
To serve
shiso leaves
lemon wedges
vinegared ginger (see page 84)
wasabi paste
shoyu (Japanese soy sauce)

1 Make the sushi rice. Meanwhile, prepare the other ingredients. Pat dry the herring fillets with kitchen paper, and cut each one lengthways into 2 fillets. Cut the smoked trout or salmon into strips about 10cm (4in) long and 3cm (1¼in) wide. Mix together the vinegar and 250ml (1 cup) water in a bowl for the hand vinegar.

2 Using a wide peeler, carefully cut about 4 very thin strips lengthways from one side of the cucumber; repeat on a further 3 sides, leaving the core; discard the outer strip of peel. In a shallow bowl, mix together the salt and 250 ml (1 cup) water. Add the cucumber strips, and leave to soak for 10 minutes; drain and pat dry with kitchen paper.

3 Wet your hands in the hand vinegar, then take a third of the sushi rice (about 90g/3oz), and shape into a firm cylinder about 20cm (8in) long. Sit on a bamboo sushi mat covered with cling film (plastic wrap). Lay a strip each of cucumber, smoked trout and herring (with the silver pattern facing up) at a slight diagonal, like a forward slash, on top of the rice, all slightly overlapping. Repeat until the rice is completely covered. Cover with a cling film-covered bamboo mat, and press to shape. Remove from the bamboo mat, and keep wrapped in the cling film until ready to serve.

4 Repeat this process to make 2 more rolls using the remaining ingredients. Cut each roll into 6, and arrange on shiso leaves on a serving plate. Serve garnished with lemon wedges, vinegared ginger, and wasabi and *shoyu* in individual dishes.

rice cookers, pots and pans

The Japanese are extremely fond of simmered dishes that are not unlike the casseroles of Europe. Indeed, a full and well-balanced Japanese meal would always contain a simmered dish, along with something grilled, something steamed, a few deep-fried morsels, a sautéed dish and a plate of vinegar-marinated foods or dressed salad. These pots and pans help to produce a real feast.

1 JAPANESE RICE COOKER

Although this utensil is used throughout Asia, it is a Japanese invention, first produced in rudimentary form in the 1920s. Over the decades, the basic pot has been modernized and altered to serve the purpose better, with all sorts of innovations, including thermostatic control and warming capability. The rice cooker consists of an inner aluminium pot within an outer one that has a spring base at the bottom. Heat is generated around the sides between the two pots. The machine works on the principle of weight; when all the water has been absorbed, the inner pot, now lighter, springs up and the electric power is cut off automatically. No more burnt or scorched rice! Electric rice cookers can be used for making soups, but in this case have to be switched off manually. They can even be used for Korean firepots and fondues. They range in size from small models for two people, to huge machines for catering and restaurant use that can prepare rice for up to 50 people.

2 OMELETTE PAN

Known as a *makiyaki-nabe*, the Japanese omelette pan is oblong or square with a wooden handle, and essential for the preparation of rolled egg dishes (*dashimaki*), for which the Japanese are renowned. Omelette pans can be made of heavy copper with tin coating (which is the most expensive), cast iron, or heavyweight aluminium with a nonstick surface. They should be used for nothing else but eggs, and seasoned with a little oil before each use.

3 EARTHENWARE CASSEROLE

Warming simmered dishes are traditional to Japanese cuisine, and the favoured utensil is an earthenware casserole called a *do-nabe*. It is often intricately patterned because it is taken directly from the oven to the table.

4 TEMPURA POT

Some people think that the Chinese wok can be used for tempura, but this is not true. A Japanese tempura pot has straighter sides, and is designed to keep the oil at an even temperature, which is imperative for perfect tempura. A wok, on the other hand, maintains different temperatures at different points and is too erratic for delicate deep-frying. Tempura pots come with their own racks, so that the fried food can be placed on the side to drain.

5 DROP LID

Known as an *otoshibuta* in Japan, this wooden lid, usually made of cedar, is placed inside saucepans during cooking. This helps to concentrate the heat on the food being cooked, and to prevent the food from bouncing around and breaking up during boiling.

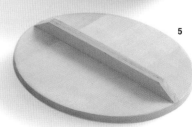

three simple soups

Whether it is breakfast, lunch or dinner, a nourishing soup is served at every Japanese meal. Slightly cloudy miso soups, made with one of the many varieties of soya bean paste, are perhaps the best known, but clear soups are also popular. All are based on dashi, Japan's ubiquitous stock, made from kombu seaweed and bonito flakes. It is available as a convenient concentrated powder.

prawn soup

Soften a small piece of wakame seaweed in a little cold water for 10 minutes. Trim away any hard bits, then cut the remaining wakame into 2cm (¾in) pieces. Meanwhile, peel and devein 8 medium-sized raw prawns (shrimp). Bring a small pot of water to the boil, and blanch the prawns for 2 minutes, then drain and set aside. Bring some more water to the boil, blanch the wakame for 1 minute, then rinse under cold running water and drain. Mix 800ml (3¼ cups) water and 1 tbsp dashi concentrate in a saucepan, and bring to simmering point. Add salt to taste. To serve, place 2 prawns and a small amount of wakame in the bottom of each of 4 bowls, and top up with the dashi. Garnish each bowl with ½ tbsp fresh coriander (cilantro) leaves, and serve.

miso shiru

Drain 200g (7oz) firm tofu, and cut into 2cm (¾in) cubes. In a saucepan, blend 3 tbsp miso and 2 tbsp dashi concentrate with 800ml (3¼ cups) water, and heat until the liquid just reaches scalding point. Add the cubed tofu and 4 tbsp chopped spring onions (scallions). When they are piping hot, serve immediately.

clam soup

Gently scrub 16 fresh clams under cold running water to remove all grit. Soak in a bowl of cold water for 30 minutes, then drain in a colander. (Make sure that you discard any that have cracked or broken shells, or that remain open after soaking.) Put the clams in a pot with 800ml (3¼ cups) water and a 10cm (4in) piece of kombu, and bring to a quick boil. Remove the kombu after 5 minutes, and continue cooking the clams until their shells have opened (discard any that remain closed), which should take no more than 4–5 minutes. Scoop out the clams with a slotted ladle, and set aside. If preferred, you can cut out the clam meat and serve it without the shells. Reduce the kombu stock to a simmer. Thinly slice 2 celery sticks, and add to the simmering stock with 2 tsp salt and 2 tbsp finely grated lemon zest. Simmer for 2 minutes, then return the clams to the pot. Simmer for another minute or so until the clams have just heated through, and serve immediately.

udon noodle soup with bamboo shoots and enoki mushrooms

Miso broth makes the perfect base for adding a variety of ingredients to make a tasty soup. Here, bamboo shoots and udon noodles are used, but you can vary the type of noodles you add and experiment with different vegetables. You could even poach a little chicken, salmon or tuna in the broth, and serve that way.

SERVES 4   PREPARATION TIME: 25 MINUTES

TOOLS
Soup pot and ladle
Earthenware casserole
Chopping board
Vegetable knife

INGREDIENTS
2 tbsp miso paste or about 30g
    (2 cups) bonito or tuna flakes
    (if you prefer a clearer soup)
200g (2 cups) canned bamboo
    shoots, rinsed, drained and
    cut into fine julienne
300g (10oz) cooked udon
    noodles, rinsed and drained
8 spring onions (scallions),
    finely sliced
200g (7oz) enoki mushrooms
pinch of salt
shichimi togarashi, to
    serve (optional)

1 Bring 800ml (3¼ cups) water to the boil in a small pot, and add the miso or seasoning flakes. Simmer for 10 minutes, then reduce the heat to low and keep the soup on a gentle simmer.

2 Add the bamboo shoots, noodles and mushrooms, together with a pinch of salt. Bring the soup to a brisk boil once again, reduce the heat slightly and simmer for 5 minutes.

3 Transfer the soup to an earthenware casserole, and serve piping hot in individual soup bowls as a starter. Have a small bowl of shichimi togarashi ready at the table for sprinkling over the top, if liked – for those people who like a little added heat and spice.

chilled soba noodles

High summer in Japan can be oppressive, with unforgiving 40°C (104°F) heat and high humidity. Small wonder, then, that chilled noodles are a great comfort, innocent of all but the lightest mirin dressing. Traditionally, this is served in a smart bamboo box with a separate beaker of dipping sauce, held close to the chest while eating to minimize splashing.

SERVES 4   PREPARATION TIME: 15 MINUTES

TOOLS
Large pot
Small pot
Wire mesh drainer

INGREDIENTS
140g (5oz) soba or
    somen noodles
300ml (1¼ cups)
    dashi stock
150ml (⅔ cup) mirin
60ml (¼ cup) soy sauce
1 tbsp sesame oil
To serve (optional)
ice cubes
strips of toasted
    nori seaweed

1 Bring a large pot of water to a rolling boil. Add the noodles gradually, so as not to stop the boiling action. Stir through gently to prevent sticking, and cook according to the packet instructions until just softer than al dente.

2 Meanwhile, make the dipping sauce. Combine the dashi, mirin and soy sauce in a small saucepan, bring to the boil and simmer for 5 minutes. Cool the sauce quickly by placing the pan in a sink filled with cold water.

3 When the noodles are done, rinse them in a wire mesh drainer under a cold tap, and set aside to drain thoroughly.

4 To serve, drizzle the noodles with the sesame oil and a little of the cold dipping sauce, and toss well. Divide the noodles among the serving boxes, and put the remaining dipping sauce in a beaker. If desired, add a couple of ice cubes to each serving, or garnish with thin strips of nori seaweed.

tempura prawns

Japanese chefs have turned deep-frying into an art form. Only the best oil is used, and the results are remarkably grease-free, crisp on the outside and perfectly cooked inside. The secret lies in the featherlight batter made at the very last moment before frying. This recipe can be easily adapted to cook other ingredients. Virtually any vegetable can be cooked this way – aubergine (eggplant), okra, courgette (zucchini) and sweet potato are all good choices.

SERVES 4   PREPARATION TIME: 40 MINUTES

TOOLS
Sharp knife
Chopping board
Tempura pot
Fine sieve
Bamboo draining basket
Cooking chopsticks
Grater

INGREDIENTS
8 large raw tiger prawns
    (shrimp), peeled and
    deveined, but with tails left on
vegetable oil for deep-frying
For the tempura batter
3 tbsp plain (all-purpose) flour,
    plus extra for dusting
1 tbsp cornflour (cornstarch)
½ tsp baking powder
600ml (2¼ cups) ice-cold water
1 large egg white
To serve
grated daikon
shoyu (Japanese soy sauce)
wasabi paste

1 Devein the prawns (shrimp), and make a deep slit down the back. Spread out each prawn like a butterfly, and press down gently.

2 In the tempura pot, heat enough oil for deep-frying to 180°C/350°F. To check whether the oil is at the right temperature, fry a small cube of bread; if it sizzles and turns golden brown in about 40 seconds, the oil is ready to cook with.

3 Meanwhile, make the batter. Sift the 3 tbsp plain (all-purpose) flour, cornflour (cornstarch) and baking powder into a bowl. Add the ice-cold water a little at a time, whisking to combine until smooth.

4 In a separate clean, dry bowl, whisk the egg white until stiff peaks form, then gently fold into the batter.

5 To cook, dip each prawn into a little plain (all-purpose) flour, shaking off any excess, then dip into the batter and deep-fry for 2–3 minutes until golden and crisp.

6 Drain on kitchen paper, and serve with grated daikon, soy sauce and a little wasabi.

Variation To make aubergine and okra tempura, slice 1 aubergine (eggplant) lengthways, then into half-circles about 1cm (½in) thick. Or try to find Japanese or finger aubergines, and slice these lengthways into strips of about the same thickness. Remove the stem ends from a handful of fresh okra. Dredge the vegetables in a little flour, then dip into the batter. Transfer to the hot oil, and deep-fry for 2–3 minutes until the batter is crisp and golden.

pork tonkatsu

Like that other Japanese favourite, tempura, *tonkatsu* is derived from European culinary elements – or, more precisely, that of the Portuguese. Breaded pork cutlets, likely as not, came with Portuguese traders and missionaries when they were making their presence felt in Japan a few centuries ago. Today, both *tonkatsu* and tempura are firmly entrenched as part of the line-up of Japanese food styles.

SERVES 4   PREPARATION TIME: 30 MINUTES

TOOLS
Cleaver
Chopping board
Frying pan or wok and ladle
Cooking chopsticks

INGREDIENTS
4 boneless pork chops or
   pork tenderloin, each about
   2cm (¾in) thick
plain (all-purpose) flour seasoned
   with sea salt and ground
   sansho, for dredging
1 egg, lightly beaten
125g (1 cup) fine or coarse
   panko breadcrumbs
vegetable oil for deep-frying
For the tonkatsu sauce
90ml (⅓ cup) tomato ketchup
1 tbsp crushed fresh root ginger
1 tbsp crushed or minced garlic
1 tbsp sugar
2 tbsp mirin
2 tbsp *shoyu* (Japanese
   soy sauce)
2 tbsp Worcestershire sauce
2 tbsp rice wine vinegar
2 tbsp yellow mustard such as
   neri-garashi
½ tsp ground allspice
pinch of ground cloves
To garnish
pickled ginger, cut into julienne
daikon pickle (see page 75),
   cut into julienne
spring onion, green part only,
   cut into julienne
napa cabbage, finely shredded
strips of toasted nori (optional)

1 To make the *tonkatsu* sauce, put all the ingredients in a small saucepan, and whisk together until thoroughly blended. Simmer gently for about 15 minutes, skimming off any scum that rises to the surface. Strain and set aside until needed.

2 Using the blunt edge of a cleaver or a meat mallet, tenderize the pork until it is slightly thinner and evenly flattened. Cut into strips, or leave whole if you prefer. Dredge the pork first in the seasoned flour, then in the beaten egg. Lastly, roll in the panko breadcrumbs until evenly coated. Firmly pat in the crumbs, and set aside to rest for a few minutes.

3 Heat enough vegetable oil for deep-frying in a frying pan or wok over a high heat until smoking. Cooking in batches so that you do not crowd the pan or wok, carefully lower the pork into the oil. Reduce the heat to medium, and deep-fry for about 8 minutes until golden brown and just cooked through. Drain on kitchen paper, and keep warm until you have finished cooking all the batches.

4 To serve, slice the pork into bite-sized strips if left whole. Arrange on a warm serving plate, and serve hot with the *tonkatsu* sauce for dipping and the garnishes arranged on the side.

Variation If you want to add some zing to the meat, sprinkle with a little shichimi togarashi before dredging in the flour. Also, ready-made *tonkatsu* sauce is available at good Asian food stores and Japanese supermarkets, if you don't have the time or the inclination to make your own. *Tonkatsu* always works very well with prawns (shrimp). Simply follow the same method, using raw large or tiger prawns (shrimp), peeled and deveined, but with the tails left on. Deep-fry for 2–3 minutes until the prawns are just cooked through and the coating is crisp and golden.

grilling and tabletop cooking

Given the diminutive nature of most Japanese homes, large kitchens and dining rooms are rare luxuries. From this restriction has evolved a tradition of cooking at the table, thus minimizing the use of small, often cramped kitchens. Grilled foods have always been a speciality in Japan, whether enjoyed as a simple domestic sizzling affair or as high drama in a teppanyaki restaurant.

1 RIDGED GRIDDLE

A small portable barbecue grill, this useful item has a corrugated cooking surface so that fat from the food being grilled (typically meat, poultry or fish) easily drips away. The griddle can be placed over a gas or charcoal heat source. Electric models are also available.

2 TABLETOP BURNER

Indispensable to Korean and Japanese homes is the tabletop burner, which allows dishes to be cooked at the table. The one shown here is a gas-fired model that works on disposable cartridges that are inserted in the base. These machines are useful for outdoor cooking, too. Also available are small tabletop burners that are capable of gently cooking delicate foods, but are more practical for keeping dishes that have already been cooked warm at the table.

3 TEPPANYAKI GRIDDLE

The Japanese name derives from the Chinese word for 'iron pan'. This is a domestic version of the massive restaurant *teppanyaki*. Although modern in concept, it harks back to post–Iron Age Japan, when nomadic warriors cooked on makeshift iron sheets over charcoal fires. Electric or otherwise, the *teppanyaki* is no more than a flat iron pan for cooking dishes for which minimal oil is required at the table.

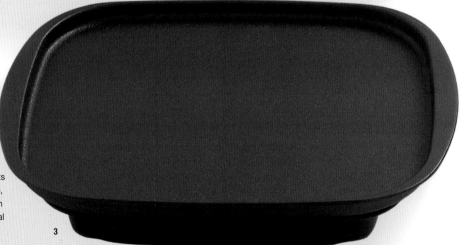

4 5 SUKIYAKI PANS

Sukiyaki is a sautéed dish of chicken or beef with assorted vegetables. As most Japanese homes are small, the cooking range is often no more than a tiny stove, so cooking at a charcoal or gas ring at the dining table is expedient. There is no need for an additional utensil to serve the cooked dish because diners help themselves straight from the pan. The traditional round cast-iron *sukiyaki* pot would be used over a charcoal or gas fire, but electric versions are available.

6 KOREAN FIREPOT

Related to the steamboat (see pages 251–2), firepots are also known as *sin sul lo* and come in aluminium or brass. When using the charcoal-burning type of firepot shown here, it is wise to place it on a heavy piece of wood to prevent your tabletop being scorched. Also watch out for any stray sparks from the burning charcoal, and ensure that the dining room has adequate ventilation. Electric firepots are cleaner and safer to use and have thermostat control to prevent overboiling, but they do lack the rustic appeal of the traditional models.

HIBACHI BARBECUE OR GRILL (not shown)

These Japanese portable barbecues or grills are made of cast iron and fired by charcoal. They have short legs so that they can be set on the ground – or on a tabletop if the table is fireproof. The height that the grill rack sits above the charcoal can be adjusted to suit the type of food being cooked.

EMI KAZUKO chicken yakitori

Yakitori, bite-sized pieces of chicken threaded on skewers and grilled over charcoal, is Japan's most popular street food and a favourite bar snack. According to distinguished food writer and journalist Emi Kazuko, who has provided this recipe, the bird's leg meat is most commonly used, but other parts of the chicken, especially the liver, are also excellent when cooked in this way.

SERVES 4–6   PREPARATION TIME: 25 MINUTES, PLUS 30 MINUTES' SOAKING

TOOLS
12–16 bamboo skewers
Sharp knife
Small saucepan
Hibachi or barbecue grill
Basting brush

INGREDIENTS
6–8 skinless chicken thigh fillets,
     about 450g (1lb) in total
lemon wedges and
     ground sansho, to serve
For the tare sauce
3 tbsp sake
scant 5 tbsp *shoyu*
     (Japanese soy sauce)
1 tbsp mirin
1 tbsp sugar

1 Soak the bamboo skewers in cold water for 30 minutes.

2 Cut the chicken thighs into 2cm (¾in) square pieces, and thread 4 pieces onto each skewer.

3 Combine all the ingredients for the *tare* sauce in a small saucepan, and bring to the boil, stirring. Simmer for 5 minutes, then remove from the heat.

4 Heat the hibachi or barbecue grill (preferably charcoal) until hot. Cook the skewered chicken until lightly browned all over. Remove the skewers from the heat, one at a time, and baste with the *tare* sauce. Return to the heat to dry the sauce, then remove and baste with more sauce.

5 Repeat this process a few more times until all the chicken pieces are golden brown. Serve with lemon wedges and ground sansho.

ROY YAMAGUCHI hibachi tuna with maui onion salad

This classy dinner-party recipe comes from chef Roy Yamaguchi of Roy's Restaurants in the United States. 'If you have any leftover marinade, refrigerate it for another time,' he says. 'Just bring it to the boil and keep adding to it. My father had a batch that he kept going for 16 years!'

SERVES 4   PREPARATION TIME: 1 HOUR

TOOLS
Saucepan
Hibachi or barbecue grill
Sharp knife
Chopping board
Wok and ladle

INGREDIENTS
4 tuna fillets, about 200g
    (7oz) each
For the marinade
225ml (scant 1 cup) soy sauce
1 tbsp chopped garlic
1 tbsp minced fresh root ginger
50g (1¾ oz) spring onions, sliced
95g (scant ½ cup) sugar
For the ponzu sauce
500ml (2 cups) sake
500 ml (2 cups) mirin
½ tsp chilli flakes
10cm (4in) piece of kombu
    seaweed
275ml (scant 1¼ cups) *shoyu*
    (Japanese soy sauce)
juice of 3 lemons
juice of 1 lime
juice of 1 orange
For the maui onion salad
1 large carrot
1 small Maui onion
1½ Japanese cucumbers,
    deseeded
110g (4oz) Japanese spice
    sprouts (daikon sprouts)
8 tbsp pickled ginger
1 tbsp vegetable oil
110g (1 cup) beansprouts
½ tbsp toasted white sesame
    seeds
½ tbsp black sesame seeds
juice of 1 lemon

1 Combine the marinade ingredients in a large bowl, and use to marinate the tuna, covered, in the refrigerator for 1 hour.

2 Meanwhile, to make the *ponzu* sauce, boil the sake, mirin, chilli flakes and kombu in a saucepan over a high heat for 10 minutes. Remove the pan from the heat, and add the soy sauce and citrus juices. Leave the kombu in the sauce until serving time.

3 About 30 minutes or so before you are ready to serve, get a hibachi or barbecue grill ready.

4 To make the salad, shred the carrot, finely slice the onion and julienne the cucumber. Combine them with the spice sprouts and pickled ginger in a bowl. Heat the oil in a wok over a high heat, and stir-fry the beansprouts for 15 seconds. Transfer the sprouts to the bowl, and toss with the vegetables.

5 Remove the tuna from the marinade, and grill over a high heat for 45–60 seconds per side.

6 Divide the salad among 4 serving plates. Sprinkle with the sesame seeds and lemon juice. Arrange the tuna, cut into slices, on top of the salad, and spoon over the *ponzu* sauce.

korean firepot

When a chill is in the air, try this heart-warming mode of cooking. Electric firepots are less smoky and easier to handle than those requiring charcoal, but you can keep a charcoal-burning pot warm with tealights if you prefer. This dish differs slightly to the steamboats of Southeast Asia and China in that the ingredients are cooked all at once; diners then help themselves.

SERVES 8–10   PREPARATION TIME: 35 MINUTES

TOOLS	INGREDIENTS	
Cleaver	400g (14oz) beef fillet, thinly sliced	4 tbsp plain (all-purpose) flour
Chopping board	2 large onions, thinly sliced	400g (14oz) white fish fillet, thinly sliced
Firepot	1.5 litres (6 cups) beef or other	200ml (scant 1 cup) vegetable oil
Wok and ladle	meat stock	5 spring onions (scallions), sliced diagonally
Wire mesh spoons	5 eggs	2 carrots, cut into julienne
		400g (3 cups) pine nuts or shelled walnuts

1 If using a charcoal firepot, light the charcoal (top left) and have all the ingredients prepared (centre). Put the beef, onions and stock in the firepot, and bring to the boil.

2 Meanwhile, lightly beat 2 of the eggs in a small bowl. Put the flour on a plate or shallow dish, and dip the strips of fish in the egg, then into the flour, to coat.

3 Heat a little oil in a wok, and stir-fry the fish until cooked. Add to the firepot.

4 Beat the remaining 3 eggs in a small bowl. Cook into an omelette in the wok, then cool and slice into thin strips.

5 Add the omelette, spring onions (scallions) and carrots to the firepot. Top with the pine nuts or walnuts, and simmer for 10 minutes before letting guests help themselves, each one dipping into the stock with their own wire mesh spoon (top right) to lift out small portions of food.

bulgogi

Korean cuisine is fragrantly spicy, and the classic barbecued marinated beef known as *bulgogi* is no exception. Chicken and pork are also sometimes marinated in this way. Basic seasonings in Korean food come from a blend of aromatics and pungent seasonings such as mustard, garlic, ginger, pepper and rice wine. The permutations found in marinades and sauces are endless, and making *bulgogi* is simplicity itself once you have the correct blend of marinade ingredients.

SERVES 4   PREPARATION TIME: 20 MINUTES, PLUS AT LEAST 25 MINUTES' MARINATING

TOOLS
Cleaver
Chopping board
Charcoal barbecue or
    grill (broiler)
Tongs

INGREDIENTS
1 kg (2¼ lb) sirloin or beef fillet
1 Little Gem lettuce, leaves
    separated, to serve
For the marinade
1 tbsp crushed or minced garlic
1 tsp crushed or minced fresh
    root ginger
1 tsp sugar
½ tsp freshly ground black
    pepper
1 tsp Korean mustard powder
1 tbsp dark soy sauce
2 tbsp rice wine such as
    Shaoxing or mirin
a little freshly squeezed Asian
    pear juice (optional)

1 To make the marinade, combine all the ingredients in a large bowl.

2 Slice the beef into thin pieces about 5mm (¼in) thick and 5cm (2in) square. Using the blunt edge of a cleaver or a meat mallet, pound the beef slices on both sides to tenderize. Add to the bowl with the marinade, tossing gently to make sure that all the beef is well coated. Leave to marinate in the refrigerator for at least 25 minutes.

3 If you are using a charcoal barbecue grill, heat the barbecue until it is hot and any flames have died away. Grill the beef directly on the wire grid until cooked to your liking, basting with the marinade as you go along. If you are using an overhead electric grill (broiler), place a double sheet of foil on a baking tray or sheet, and grill the beef for 5 minutes for rare, 8 minutes for medium and 12 minutes for well done. Use tongs to turn over once or twice, and baste with the marinade.

4 To serve, arrange small piles of the beef in the lettuce leaves. Serve with plain boiled rice and dipping bowls of the sesame seed sauce opposite.

steamed greens with cho kanjang

The sesame seed sauce here, *cho kanjang*, is a Korean favourite for serving with hot steamed or raw vegetables, or a mixture of the two. It appears on the table as a side dish at many Korean meals, where traditionally a selection of dishes – invariably including pickles and condiments – is arranged for people to help themselves. Its versatility makes it ideal for serving with grilled meats or poultry, and it is very easy to make in bulk.

SERVES 4   PREPARATION TIME: 20 MINUTES

TOOLS
Vegetable or all-purpose knife
Chopping board
Steamer
Wok and ladle
Mortar and pestle

INGREDIENTS
450g (1lb) mixed greens such as
   tenderstem or purple sprouting
   broccoli, bok choy or choi sum,
   and napa or other Chinese
   cabbage

For the sesame seed sauce
200g (7oz/scant 1½ cups) white
   sesame seeds
1 tbsp sugar
4 tbsp rice wine vinegar
60ml (¼ cup) hot water
2 tbsp light soy sauce
1 tbsp sesame oil

1 Trim the stalk ends of the broccoli, and trim off the stalks on the bok choy and napa cabbage. Slice the bok choy and napa or other Chinese cabbage in half lengthways, as needed. Steam for 8–10 minutes until just tender and starting to wilt.

2 Meanwhile, heat a wok without oil over a low heat, and toast the sesame seeds for a few minutes until they are golden brown. Watch them carefully so that they do not scorch. Using a mortar and pestle, grind the sesame seeds to a coarse powder.

3 In a small bowl, mix together the sugar, vinegar and hot water, and stir until the sugar has dissolved. Add the light soy sauce, sesame oil and ground sesame seeds, and stir to blend.

4 Transfer the sauce to a glass jar with a screw-top lid, and shake well before serving as a dressing with the hot steamed vegetables. The sauce will keep in the refrigerator for up to 2 weeks.

small cooking tools

Japanese cuisine is known for its simplicity and minimalism, and although the typical Japanese kitchen is small – even minuscule – there is a particular fondness for having the right tool for each job. Quality is valued above quantity. The Japanese have a great appreciation of natural materials such as wood and bamboo, and place strong emphasis on visual appeal, so their tools also often have a synergy between colours, shapes and textures.

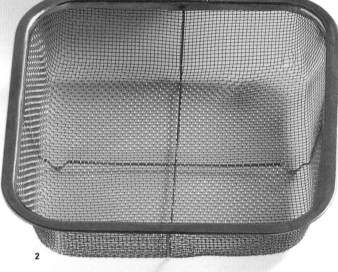

1 SURIBACHI
The sturdy Japanese grinding bowl is reminiscent of an apothecary's ceramic mortar. The high-fired pottery bowl is scored with hundreds of tiny grooves on the inside. This textured interior acts like the surface of a grater and, in tandem with the wooden pestle, processes garlic, ginger, kernels and seeds with amazing efficiency. The pestle, or *surikogi*, comes in various lengths, from 10cm (4in) to 18cm (7in). The longer and therefore heavier the pestle is, the better the leverage will be. To use a *suribachi*, rotate the pestle and press down so that the rounded end crushes the contents against the grooves of the bowl.

2 SQUARE WIRE MESH STRAINER
Known as a *zaru*, this wire mesh basket is used as a straining basket for items such as noodles. Bamboo versions are also available.

3 THREE-SECTION GRATER
This grater-cum-server is intended for small pieces of food, especially those used as condiments, such as garlic, ginger and daikon. It is designed to be taken to the table.

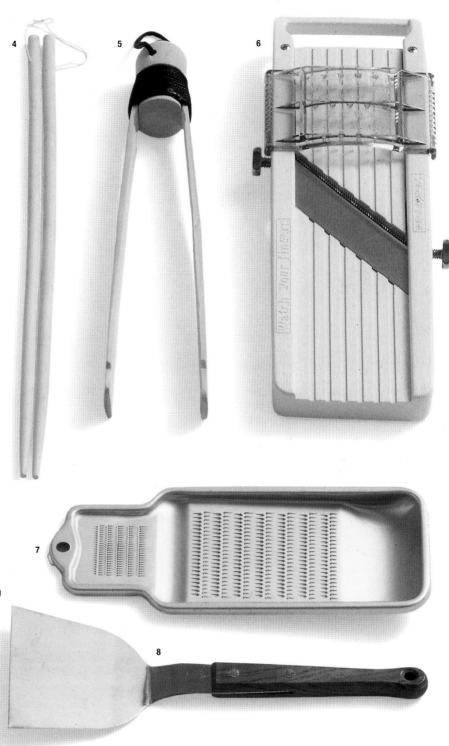

4 5 COOKING CHOPSTICKS

Some 35cm (14in) long and made of wood or bamboo, these chopsticks are indispensable in the Japanese kitchen for manipulating and turning all kinds of foods using only one hand. The length means that the cook can stay away from spluttering fat while deep-frying. Some models are held together by string; others are shaped like tongs. The tips may be flat or, more usually, pointed.

6 MANDOLIN

This curiously named and notoriously sharp implement actually looks like the musical instrument of old bearing the same name and has a case made of hard plastic or metal. It comes with several detachable blades that slot into the centre for efficient slicing, grating, crinkle-cutting, shredding and julienne. Mandolins are especially good for making paper-thin slices of hard vegetables such as carrot and daikon, and need not be restricted to Japanese vegetables – cabbage and baby artichokes are also good candidates for slicing with a mandolin. Premium models offer better protection for the hand and are the safest to use.

7 GRATER

The larger teeth of this two-sectioned grater are used to coarsely grate daikon, while ingredients such as ginger and wasabi root are finely processed using the small teeth. These graters may be ceramic, or made from metal or plastic.

8 METAL SPATULA

This wide-shaped tool is ideal for turning pieces of fish during cooking.

PETER GORDON roast pumpkin with cashew nut and gomasio dressing

At The Providores and Tapa Room restaurant in London, New Zealand-born chef, consultant and author Peter Gordon prepares his trademark fusion style of cooking, artfully blending the best of East and West cuisines. This recipe, however, is from Peter's book on home cooking. 'The most important ingredient in this relatively simple dish is the pumpkin, so make sure you hunt out the sweetest and tastiest there is,' he says.

SERVES 4–8   PREPARATION TIME: 1 HOUR 30 MINUTES

TOOLS
Vegetable or all-purpose knife
Chopping board
Suribachi

INGREDIENTS
1.5kg (3lb 3oz) pumpkin,
    peeled and deseeded
2 tbsp sesame oil
400ml (1⅔ cups) boiling water
For the dressing
50g (1¾oz/about ⅔ cup) lightly
    toasted sesame seeds
20g (¾oz) sea or kosher salt flakes
120g (4½oz) raw cashew nuts,
    toasted and finely chopped
100ml (scant ½ cup) mirin
100ml (scant ½ cup) freshly
    squeezed lemon juice
1 large bunch of rocket
    (arugula)
salt and freshly ground
    black pepper

1 Preheat the oven to 180°C/350°F/Gas 4. Cut the pumpkin into 8 even-sized chunks, and put them in an ovenproof dish. Lightly season with salt and pepper, drizzle over the sesame oil, then pour in the boiling water. Roast in the top part of the oven until tender, 40–80 minutes depending on the type of pumpkin.

2 Meanwhile, make the dressing. Using a suribachi (or other mortar and pestle), grind the lightly toasted sesame seeds and sea or kosher salt together to make a fine powder (this sesame salt is known as gomasio, or gomashio, in Japan). Transfer to a small bowl, and add the chopped cashews, mirin and lemon juice. Mix well, and leave to stand until the pumpkin is cooked.

3 Arrange the hot pumpkin on a large serving plate, and scatter some rocket (arugula) leaves over the top. Adjust the seasoning of the dressing to taste, then pour the dressing over the rocket and serve.

ELIZABETH ANDOH aubergine salad with tart sesame dressing

This recipe featuring aubergine (eggplant), from Tokyo-based cookery expert Elizabeth Andoh, makes a terrific summer salad when chilled and served on crisp leaves. She says: 'The same dressing, by the way, could transform the most mundane tomato and cucumber slices into an interesting Oriental salad.'

SERVES 2–3   PREPARATION TIME: 20 MINUTES

TOOLS
Vegetable or all-purpose knife
Chopping board
Colander
Pot
Frying pan or skillet
Suribachi

INGREDIENTS
1 aubergine (eggplant), about
    350g (12oz)
crisp salad leaves, to serve
    (optional)
For the dressing
1 tbsp white sesame seeds
½ tsp sugar
1 tbsp *shoyu* (Japanese
    soy sauce)
1 tbsp rice vinegar
pinch of salt
½ tbsp dashi or water

1 Peel the aubergine (eggplant), and cut into diagonal slices 5mm (¼in) thick. Cut these slices into strips 5mm (¼in) thick, and soak them in a bowl of cold water for 5–6 minutes to remove any bitterness and avoid discoloration.

2 Drain the aubergine, then blanch in a pot of boiling salted water for 2–3 minutes. Drain the cooked aubergine strips, and pat dry with kitchen paper to remove excess moisture. Set aside.

3 To make the dressing, in a heavy frying pan or skillet, dry-roast the sesame seeds for a couple of minutes until golden; watch them carefully, as they can quickly scorch. While the seeds are still warm, crush them in a suribachi (or other mortar and pestle). Add the remaining dressing ingredients, one at a time, stirring and grinding after each new addition.

4 Just before serving, toss the aubergine strips in the tart sesame dressing. Serve the salad at room temperature, or chilled and arranged on crisp salad leaves, if preferred.

serving dishes and lacquerware

In keeping with the insistence on serving foods in tandem with the seasons, most Japanese homes have separate sets of dishes and serving utensils for each season. Each item is carefully chosen to reflect the right synergy. Lacquer has been a part of Japanese table art for centuries, and some pieces can be very fine. In Korea, similar serving dishes are used, although there are a few unique items.

1 LARGER BOWLS

Soup noodle dishes, usually a meal in themselves, are a highly enjoyable part of Japanese cuisine and typically served in large bowls such as this.

2 SOUP SPOON

These spoons are used in Japan for dishes such as soup noodles, where the bowl is too large to be lifted to the lips.

3 CHOPSTICKS AND REST

Japanese chopsticks taper to a point. Even though disposable sets are commonplace, beautifully decorated chopsticks are considered a special gift and presented in

stunning packages. The rest is an elegant means of ensuring that the chopsticks' food-stained tips do not touch the dining table.

4 PLATE

In Japanese cuisine, flat plates are used for many dishes, not specifically for fried rice or noodles, as in Chinese service. They may be round, square or oblong.

5 LACQUER SOUP BOWL

Japanese soups are served in these lidded lacquer bowls, rather than in porcelain or pottery ones. The lids efficiently keep the heat in, and the resulting steam can make the seal very tight. You remove the lid by applying

gentle pressure around the rim of the bowl. The soup inside is then sipped directly but delicately from the bowl, as if it were a cup.

6 RICE BOWL

Whether made of lacquer or porcelain, Japanese rice bowls have a gentler curvature than the traditional round, squat dimensions found in their Chinese counterparts.

7 CONDIMENT DISHES

Shape and texture are important at the Japanese table; however, unlike in Chinese culture, where sharp corners and square shapes symbolize evil and death, there is no negative symbolism associated with angular lines. Small dishes such as these are used for serving condiments and dipping sauces.

8 KOREAN CHOPSTICKS AND SPOON

Unlike the Japanese, the Koreans commonly use spoons for eating. They also favour long pointed chopsticks made of wood or metal.

9 SOBA BASKET

Known as a *zaru*, this square bamboo rack is specially designed for serving cold soba noodles.

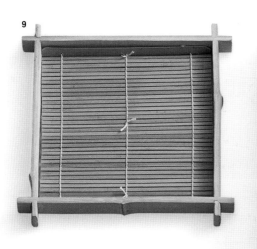

10 WOVEN BAMBOO BASKET

This small basket can serve as a napkin holder at the dining table or be used to present a single large sushi roll.

11 BIBIMBAP BOWL

A heavy stone bowl on a wooden bench, this is used for serving Korea's famous *bibimbap*.

12 BENTO BOXES

In Japan, compartmentalized lacquer boxes called *bento* are used to serve complete meals. With stunning and varied designs, individual boxes and large bento sets are considered collector's items by many, even the disposable models produced for lunch and snack sales on trains. This style of bento box is used to serve food during intermission at the theatre.

13 SUSHI BENCH

Looking like a low stool of porcelain or pale wood, a sushi bench is used only to serve sushi and sashimi portions. The idea is to create a harmony of colour and texture: jewel-like colours and rich textures of raw fish against the pale, smooth bench.

14 PORCELAIN RICE SCOOP

Japanese rice scoops are flat and often made of porcelain, with beautiful designs. As the country's rice is starchy, a flat scoop does the job easily and without spillage.

DOC CHENG'S steamed snapper with soy daikon fumet

Healthy eating East-meets-West-style is the speciality of Doc Cheng's restaurant in Singapore's legendary Raffles Hotel, whence this deliciously light recipe inspired by Japanese cooking comes. The original is made with the Japanese or tai variety of snapper, but any good-quality prime white fish such as sea bass will work, as long as it is beautifully fresh.

SERVES 4   PREPARATION TIME: 40 MINUTES, PLUS 1 HOUR STANDING

TOOLS
Medium pot
Steamer
Grater
Fine sieve
Shredder or mandolin
Cleaver
Small pot

INGREDIENTS
4 whole small snapper, gutted
    and cleaned, or 4 large fillets,
    about 130g (4½oz) each
120ml (½ cup) vegetable oil
60ml (¼ cup) sesame oil
1 tbsp finely shredded fresh
    root ginger
90g (3oz/about 8) spring onions
    (scallions), cut into julienne
salt and freshly ground
    black pepper
For the fumet
1 piece of kombu seaweed
30g (1oz) bonito flakes
125g (4½oz) daikon, shredded
60ml (¼ cup) soy sauce
4 shiso (perilla) leaves,
    finely chopped

1 To make the fumet, put 450ml (scant 2 cups) water and the kombu in a pot, and bring to the boil. Turn off the heat, and add the bonito flakes. Leave to stand for 1 hour.

2 Strain the fumet, discarding the solids. Add the daikon, soy sauce and shiso leaves.

3 Season the snapper with salt and pepper, and place in a steamer over boiling water. Cover and steam for 4–6 minutes over a medium heat until cooked.

4 Meanwhile, gently heat together the vegetable and sesame oils in a small saucepan.

5 When the fish is done, transfer to a deep serving dish. Scatter with the ginger and spring onions (scallions), then ladle the fumet over and around the fish. Spoon the hot oil mixture over the ginger and spring onions, and serve immediately.

salt-grilled trout

It is fun to serve a meal, especially lunch, in bento boxes, and this salt-grilled trout recipe is an ideal dish to feature as the main component. It can also be served as part of a Japanese meal, paired with daikon pickle. If fish does not take your fancy, chicken yakitori (see page 102) is another good recipe for bento boxes. Serve with a mound of cold cooked sticky rice sprinkled with black sesame seeds, a little green salad and some pickled ginger.

SERVES 4   PREPARATION TIME: 25 MINUTES

TOOLS
Kitchen carver or fish slicer
Chopping board
Metal or bamboo skewers
Hibachi or charcoal grill

INGREDIENTS
4 large whole fresh trout
2 tbsp fine table salt
vegetable oil for basting
2 tbsp freshly squeezed
   lemon juice
4 heaped tbsp
   daikon pickle
   (see page 75),
   to serve

1 Gut and clean the trout, but leave whole. Pat the fish dry with kitchen paper, and salt liberally both inside and out. Leave the salted fish to stand at room temperature for 25 minutes. If using bamboo skewers, soak them in cold water while the fish marinates, to prevent scorching.

2 Heat the hibachi or charcoal grill until hot. Using the metal or bamboo skewers, pierce each trout through the head just behind the eye and across 5cm (2in) of the lower body towards the tail. You should be able to lift the trout by holding the hooked end of the skewer. Grill over the charcoal for 6 minutes on each side, basting with a little oil during cooking to prevent dryness.

3 When the fish is just cooked, gently remove the skewers, and arrange the trout on a serving plate, or cut up for inclusion in a bento box. Sprinkle a little lemon juice over the fish, and serve with the daikon pickle.

bibimbap

One of the most popular dishes in Korea, *bibimbap* incorporates a variety of different vegetables (and sometimes meat), mixed with peppery sauce. It is always served over plain rice and, for panache, may be presented as it would be in Korea, in this traditional heavy granite bowl mounted on a wooden frame.

SERVES 4   PREPARATION TIME: 30 MINUTES

TOOLS
Rice cooker
Large pot
Cleaver
Chopping board
Wok and ladle
Bibimbap bowl
Colander

INGREDIENTS
8 mixed dried mushrooms
  such as shiitake and oyster
200g (1⅛ cups) jasmine rice
1 small carrot, cut into julienne
2 yard-long or snake beans,
  cut into julienne
100g (1 cup) beansprouts
3 tbsp groundnut (peanut) or
  other vegetable oil
200g (7oz) beef mince
  (ground beef)
1 tsp freshly ground or cracked
  black pepper
2 tbsp gochujang (Korean
  chilli bean paste)
6 large leaves of bok choy,
  sliced
3 tbsp sesame oil
2 eggs

1 Soak the dried mushrooms in a bowl of hot water for about 20 minutes until soft. Meanwhile, cook the rice in the rice cooker until tender.

2 In a large pot of boiling water, cook the carrot, beans and beansprouts for 5 minutes, then drain in a colander. Drain and quarter the softened mushrooms.

3 Heat 2 tbsp of the groundnut (peanut) or other vegetable oil in a wok over a medium-high heat, and stir-fry the beef for 2 minutes until well sealed and browned. Add the pepper and gochujang. Stir-fry for 1 minute. Next, add the drained blanched vegetables, and continue stir-frying for 2 minutes. Now add the bok choy and quartered mushrooms, and stir-fry for 2 minutes. Mix in the sesame oil and 100ml (scant ½ cup) water. Cook, stirring, for 2 minutes.

4 To finish, put the rice in the *bibimbap* bowl, and cover with the beef mixture. Carefully wipe out the wok with kitchen paper, then fry the eggs in the remaining 1 tbsp oil. When the yolks are just starting to set, lift the eggs out of the wok and sit on top of the *bibimbap*. Serve immediately.

simmered sweet tofu

This is one of the many simmered dishes in Japanese cuisine. It is often served cold as a starter, when it looks fabulous presented on a simple plate. The caramelized sugar gives the sauce a slightly bittersweet taste. You can use any type of tofu for this dish, including egg-flavoured, although firm tofu holds its shape better.

SERVES 1–2   PREPARATION TIME: 20 MINUTES

TOOLS
Cleaver
Chopping board
Small pot
Ladle

INGREDIENTS
1 tbsp vegetable oil
1 tbsp sugar
300g (10oz) tofu of your
    choice, cut into cubes
1 tbsp light soy sauce
1 tsp cornflour (cornstarch),
    dissolved in a little cold water
    to make a paste
½ spring onion (scallion),
    finely shredded

1 Heat the oil in a small saucepan. Tip in the sugar, and gently heat, stirring with a wooden spoon, for a few minutes until the sugar dissolves and caramelizes, turning a light brown. Remove from the heat, as this will reduce the chance of spattering when you add the other liquids to the hot syrup.

2 Very carefully add the soy sauce and 130ml (generous ½ cup) lukewarm water to the sugar syrup, then return the pan to the heat. Bring to a gentle simmer.

3 Stir the cornflour (cornstarch) paste into the sauce. Continue cooking until the sauce thickens and turns glossy, then add the tofu to the pan and simmer for 1 minute.

5 Serve hot, scattered with the spring onion (scallion). Alternatively, allow to cool, then chill for 1 hour to serve as a cold starter or appetizer.

tea and sake sets

Japan's famous tea ceremonies traditionally take place in rustic teahouses, the simplicity of the setting intended to enhance the meditative ritual of the formal ceremony. Green tea is drunk on these occasions, and is the preferred beverage for everyday meals. The Japanese rice wine sake can be drunk during meals, but more properly would be removed from the table once the rice was served.

1 SAKE SET

Possibly the smallest of all liquor containers, sake bottles (called *tokkuri*) are veritable works of art, often featuring beautiful designs reflecting Japanese life and culture. Some sake cups are so small as to be almost thimble-sized because sake is meant to be drunk in small amounts. This makes sense, given sake's potency. Deemed a drink of the Shinto gods, emperors and assorted shoguns, sake is Japan's oldest alchoholic drink, a clear essence of boiled rice with yeast added to begin the fermentation. It is a still beverage, served warm or cold.

2 TEA CUPS

Authentic Japanese tea sets come with five cups, never four or six, because the number five is considered lucky in Japan's mysterious system of numerology. Much taller than the cups traditionally used in China, Japanese tea cups are always made of fine porcelain or roughcast clay, and are usually straight-sided. They do not have handles because the cups are meant to be raised to the lips using both hands.

3 TEA WHISK

During the Japanese tea ceremony, this delicate bamboo whisk is used by the tea master to whip the bitter-tasting powdered green tea known as *matcha* to a froth in hot water. To the Japanese, bamboo is symbolic of longevity and reverence. Using a metal whisk is therefore completely inappropriate to the traditional ceremony, which is seen as a calming, spiritual experience, rather than merely a culinary one, even though food is served as well as tea.

4 TEAPOT

Japanese teapots are relatively small. Cast-iron ones such this example are expensive and are generally reserved for special guests.

ice cream desserts

A relatively modern concept, green tea ice cream probably derived from the traditional *ujigori*, a kind of sorbet first made in the river town of Uji south of Kyoto and which is famous for its green tea. Only *matcha* powdered green tea is used to make it. Below is a modified version produced quickly by infusing the tea in vanilla ice cream. In Japanese tempura bars, green tea ice cream is coated in special batter and deep-fried to make a popular sweet treat eaten at the end of a meal. Deep-fried ice cream is often thought to be a traditional Chinese dessert, too, as it is sometimes served in Western Chinese restaurants; however, the claim is that it was invented by Chinese immigrants to Australia. The easy version given here employs filo pastry, rather than tempura batter or breadcrumbs, to protect the ice cream from the hot oil, and can be made with any flavour of ice cream you prefer.

deep-fried ice cream

Put a large plate or metal tray in the freezer to chill. When it is very cold, use an ice cream scoop to form mounds of the ice cream of your choice, and place them on the cold plate or tray, keeping them well separated. Return the plate or tray to the freezer, and leave until the ice cream is rock-hard. When ready to proceed, take 8 sheets filo pastry, stack them on top of each other, and cut into 15cm (6in) squares. Heat enough oil for deep-frying to 180°C/350°F. Working quickly, place a portion of ice cream in the centre of each pastry square, gather up the sides of the pastry and pinch to seal into a parcel, wetting the edges with a brush so that they stick together and completely enclose the ice cream. Fry in the hot oil until the pastry is lightly golden. Drain thoroughly, and serve immediately with a drizzle of caramel, chocolate, golden syrup or maple syrup sauce, if desired.

green tea ice cream

Remove 400g (14oz/2 cups) vanilla ice cream from the freezer, and allow to soften but not melt in a large mixing bowl. Meanwhile, in a saucepan, bring 150ml (⅔ cup) full-fat milk to the boil, then turn off the heat. Stir in 1 tbsp powdered green tea, and set aside to steep for 20 minutes. Blend the milky tea with the softened vanilla ice cream, beating vigorously with a wooden spoon until well combined. Transfer to a freezerproof plastic container, and freeze for several hours before serving.

india, pakistan and sri lanka

Cooking on the Asian subcontinent has been influenced by Greek, Mongol and Persian invaders, spice-hungry Arab traders, and periods of British, Portuguese and French rule. The civilization stretches back some 5000 years. When coupled with the area's sweeping geographical differences, it is not surprising that the kitchens of India, Pakistan and Sri Lanka boast such a varied collection of culinary curiosities.

india, pakistan and sri lanka

Geographically, the Indian subcontinent varies widely, boasting soaring mountain ranges, a dramatic coastline, deserts and the fertile plains of three great river basins. The lay of the land, as well as historical, cultural and religious differences, has produced a fascinating mix of culinary styles.

The Moghul empire fostered a rich and refined cuisine, and imports from the Middle East of dried fruit, almonds and pistachio nuts became integral features of royal banquets. Parsees in India can trace their ancestry back to Persian roots in what is now Iran and, despite the first wave of Parsees leaving Persia back in the first century AD at least, their cooking continues to reflect classic Persian flavours. Well-known Indian sweets such as *kulfi* and *gulab jamun* also have their origins in central Asia. *Gulab* means 'rose', and these sweets are fried balls of curd cheese dipped in rose-scented syrup. *Kulfi*, India's favourite frozen dessert, takes its name from the conical mould in which it is frozen, and was brought to India via Kabul, with the Moghuls. Delicate rice pilafs from Lucknow and rich Hyderabad biryanis were, as they are today, made with the finest long-grain rice, embedded with spiced meat and often touched with saffron, almonds and raisins.

Popular tandoori dishes, which are characterized by spiced yogurt marinades, get their name from the clay oven in which the meat or fish is roasted. Tandoor ovens can be found across much of Asia and are also used for baking flat breads, most notably naan. Although red food colouring may be the hallmark of tandoori curry houses in the West, there are no such artificial additives in traditional tandoori recipes.

While breads are the mainstay of the North Indian diet, southern states are happier with rice. South Indian cooking makes much of locally grown coconuts, curry leaves and tart tamarind flavours, while kitchens in the North Indian state of Punjab embrace their dairy products, preferring to cook favourite dishes in ghee (clarified butter), instead of oil. Recipes from Bengal, East India, are flavoured with nutty-tasting mustard oil, and a fair share of western coastal dishes from Goa brim with a colonial Portuguese influence. Many dishes are surprisingly mild, depending more on the depth of spice blends than brute chilli power. That is not to say that subtlety is the norm for cooking styles across the subcontinent. Tribal dishes from states such as Andhra Pradesh, South India, are loaded with what locals call the *guntur*, or 'flaming chilli', and one bite is all it takes to bring out the fire engines. Contrary to popular impression, authentic Indian cooking does not always involve hours by the grinding stone. A simple fillet of fish wrapped in a banana leaf and baked with a minimum of spices can be enjoyed with as much relish as shellfish simmered in a carefully blended broth of rich coconut milk, pounded chillies, ginger and garlic.

Indian cooks are masters at coaxing maximum flavour from humble vegetables, using deft spicing techniques and winning combinations of contrasting ingredients. Soupy lentils and pulses are served at most meals, and transformed into delicious curries with spices. The blandness of chickpeas (garbanzo beans) may be offset with sour pomegranate, split lentils treated to tangy

OPPOSITE 1 sweet corn **2** plantain **3** aubergine (eggplant) **4** jackfruit **5** coconut **6** mango **7** okra, or bhindi **8** spinach **9** curry leaves
BELOW 1 pistachios **2** basmati rice **3** chapati flour **4** paneer **5** cashew nuts **6** appam flour **7** plain yogurt **8** chickpeas (garbanzo beans) **9** brown lentils

tamarind, and kidney beans simmered with gingery masala. In coastal regions such as Bengal, Kerala and Goa, the many Hindus, who do not usually consume meat, are happy to enliven daily vegetables with tiny fried shrimps and red chillies.

Over and above geographical influences, religious beliefs play a fundamental role in the varied cooking styles of India. Hindus, for example, do not eat beef, and some communities will not touch milk or honey either. Muslims demand that *halal* meat is used in kitchens, which means that animals must be slaughtered according to religious edicts. Kitchen duties are certainly not taken lightly. Many wealthy Brahmins, for example, feel duty-bound to preserve the purity of their high caste by ensuring that the home cooking is overseen by a live-in *maharaj* (head cook), who may enter the kitchen only after bathing and having said daily prayers. The vegetarian Jains follow a faith closely related to Buddhism and will not cook with onions or garlic, in the belief that both of these ingredients increase body temperature and inflame lusty passions, and they also avoid root vegetables. Despite the implied austerity of the phrase 'pure vegetarian cooking', the Jain community is well known throughout India for its tasty own-made pickles, refined milky grain dishes elegantly flavoured with saffron and cardamom, and innovative ways of cooking everyday vegetables.

There are a great many similarities between the cooking of Northwestern India and Pakistan (formerly West Pakistan, from which East Pakistan split to become Bangladesh). In fact it can be difficult to tell them apart because both come under the influence of Punjabi cuisine. While Pakistan is a Muslim country, where Islam eschews the eating of pork, the cuisine features all other meats, especially lamb, and boasts many grand dishes similar to the Moghul culinary ilk. Saffron pilafs, biryanis, samosas and chapatis are as Pakistani as they are Indian, and the dishes range from chilli-hot to mild and subtle.

Much of what is perceived to be Indian cooking in the West, particularly in the United Kingdom, actually hails from Bangladesh. Although separated by a geographical distance of 1500km (890 miles) from Pakistan, the country's cuisine echoes with the same spicy resonance. Bangladesh was once a part of the eastern province of Bengal, and the influences are palpable. The coastline that caresses the Bay of Bengal is blessed with plentiful seafood, and the cooking subsequently features many fish and shellfish dishes, with spices used liberally. Ghee is not used frequently, however, because Bangladeshi chefs tend to prefer neutral-tasting fats such as vegetable, mustard and coconut oils.

Sri Lanka is the 'pearl' that hangs at the tip of the Indian crown. A tiny island of undulating landscape formerly known as Ceylon, it marked a convenient halfway point between Asia's two most active trading empires, and consequently Sri Lanka possesses an incredibly rich culinary heritage. The best cooking is generally based on the highland village traditions. Vegetables, fruits, home-grown meats and poultry feature prominently, and the abundant local seafood enriches every Sri Lankan table.

Much of the cuisine is stamped with the influences of Arab, Indian, Malay, Portuguese, Dutch and British traders and settlers. Many Sri Lankan dishes have marked Portuguese elements, such as the use of red wine vinegar and tomatoes, because these Europeans ruled Sri Lanka for around 150 years during the sixteenth and seventeenth centuries. Sri Lanka's saffron-flavoured rotis are also similar to the flat breads of India, and the cuisine features a mouth-watering range of seafood, beef and poultry curries. The most famous Sri Lankan dishes are undoubtedly the savoury and sweet hoppers (a type of pancake made from fermented rice flour or, in the case of string hoppers, rice noodles), which are eaten mostly at breakfast and lunch, and the spiced rice dish *lamprais*, which is derived from Dutch *lomprijst*.

Fundamentally, the cuisine is very hot and spicy. While similar to South Indian cuisine in its liberal use of chillies, cardamom, cumin, coriander and other spices, it has its own distinctive flavours. This is seen particularly in the use of dried Maldive fish, used in various ways as seasoning and to highlight each spice or curry blend. Many Sri Lankan dishes have the reputation of being high-octane – among the world's hottest in chilli terms. No two Sri Lankans will prepare a dish in the same way, and people from the different regions – highlanders and coastal folk – are fiercely proud of their culinary individuality. This is taken one savoury step further with different ethnic and religious customs coming into play in the Sri Lankan kitchen. Thus, there as many versions of hoppers as there are shreds in a grated coconut. Above all, coconut reigns supreme in Sri Lanka and, when made into coconut sambols enriched with chillies, Maldive fish and lime juice, is ambrosial. Chopped aromatic leaves and shallots are sometimes added and, when ground to a fine paste, it adds delicious zest to plain rice and breads.

OPPOSITE 1 cinnamon sticks **2** whole cloves **3** ground turmeric **4** saffron threads **5** dried red chillies **6** green cardamom pods **7** fennel seeds **8** fenugreek seeds **9** star anise **10** whole black peppercorns **11** coriander seeds **12** cumin seeds

processing spices, herbs and coconut

Food processors have not yet found a place in most Indian kitchens, with many cooks still pledging allegiance to the large household grinding stone and the trusty mortar and pestle. The truth is that pounding the ingredients extracts maximum flavours, and food processors simply do not deliver as good a result. Practical and beautiful implements and storage containers make mixing intricate blends of dried spices, the mainstay of most Indian cooking, a quick, simple process and a joy to perform.

1 COCONUT GRATER

With this sturdy implement, pieces of coconut still in their shells can be grated simply by cranking the handle. An L-shaped metal rod is slotted through a stainless-steel mount, with one end featuring a crosshead with serrated edges and the other a small rubber handle. A lever attached to the rubber suction cap at the bottom of the mount forms a vacuum that secures it to any smooth surface. In South India, where fresh coconut is used daily, some households have a very large version of this contraption that incorporates a stool for sitting.

2 HERB SHREDDER

This stainless-steel gadget with a handy fold-back lid is for shredding fresh herbs and aromatics. When cranked, the handle turns a sharp-toothed spindle that efficiently cuts through the ingredients inside.

3 SQUARE TABLE-SHAPED GRATER

Here, tough aluminium is shaped into a miniature table, and the top is punctured with holes with sharp edges facing upwards to act as a grater. A plate or tray can be placed underneath to catch the shredded food.

4 BRASS AND WOOD COCONUT GRATER

For this tool, a slightly convex brass grater is mounted on a sturdy wooden frame. The protruding teeth are very effective shredders of coconut, gourds and other hard ingredients.

5 STONE MORTAR AND PESTLE

Similar to that used in Southeast Asia and Indochina, this mortar and pestle set is used for grinding fresh aromatic ingredients such as garlic, onions and chillies. It may be granite or marble, and comes in various sizes.

6 BRASS MORTAR AND PESTLE

Freshness is fundamental to spice cookery, and Indian cooks never keep ground spices for long because they lose their flavour and fragrance. Dried whole spices are ground in small amounts as required, in useful little cup-shaped mortars such as this popular brass model with matching pestle.

7 INDIVIDUAL SPICE TIN

This single stainless-steel container is useful for storing large or bulky spices such as cinnamon, bay leaves, green and black cardamom pods, and other dried aromatic ingredients.

8 SPICE BOX

India's most useful and ubiquitous kitchen tool has to be the round stainless-steel spice box known as a *masala dabba*. A tightly lidded tin filled with smaller containers for keeping spices separately, it is used for storing essential spices and holds between five and seven smaller tins. Some have an additional layer for items such as cinnamon sticks to be lain flat.

grinding and tempering spices

Just as important as the spices used in these cuisines is the way in which they are prepared. The spice powder garam masala, which literally means 'hot spice', is a fundamental basic of the regional cuisines of India, Pakistan and Bangladesh. There are countless variations of garam masala found across the Asian subcontinent, as each and every cook has a special recipe with its own proportion of spices to be included. In Sri Lanka, characteristic curry powders lie at the heart of many of this island's dishes.

garam masala

In a dry frying pan, roast each of the following spices separately until just fragrant: 20g (¾oz) black cardamom pods; 20g (¾oz) cinnamon stick, broken into pieces; 20g (¾oz) black peppercorns; 3 heaped tsp cumin seeds, 2 mace blades, 2 tsp cloves and ½ tsp freshly grated nutmeg. Allow to cool. Discard the husks from the cardamom pods, and tip all the spices into a mortar. Grind to a fine powder. Sift to remove any husks or debris, and store in a screw-top glass jar. It will keep for up to 2 months, but is best used as fresh as possible.

xacutti masala

In a dry frying pan over a medium heat, roast the following spices for 30–45 seconds until just fragrant: 6–8 dried red Kashmiri chillies; a 5cm (2in) piece of cinnamon stick; 3 green and 1 black cardamom pods, husks discarded; 2 tbsp coriander seeds; 1 tbsp chopped skinless peanuts; 1 tbsp cumin seeds; 1 tbsp fennel seeds; 1 tbsp white poppy seeds; ½ tbsp sesame seeds; 1 tsp whole cloves; 1 tsp black peppercorns; ½ tsp aniseed; ½ tsp black mustard seeds; ½ tsp fenugreek seeds; ½ tsp ground turmeric; 1 mace blade; and ¼ whole nutmeg, grated. Grind to a fine powder, and use as needed.

dry-roasting and tempering

In the regional cuisines of South Asia, and particularly in South Indian and Sri Lankan cuisine, the dry-roasting and tempering of spices and flavourings are central to achieving the requisite flavour and aroma of dishes. With spice powders such as garam masala, the mixture of whole spices is usually toasted separately in a dry frying pan until fragrant, before being ground together to a powder. Dry-roasting whole spices also makes them easier to grind. If a blend of spices and aromatics such as ginger, chillies or curry leaves is to be used as the basis for a dish, they are 'tempered' by frying them in a little oil over a high heat to bring out their flavour and release their natural oils.

indian spice pastes

Although spices play an integral role in every Indian meal, housewives in India insist on buying whole spices in small quantities because they easily lose their distinctive aromas, especially when exposed to air and kept in hot, humid conditions. Spices may be used raw, but are frequently toasted or fried before further use. When toasting spices, it is preferable to toast them whole and grind them afterwards. Good Indian cooks are skilled at blending ingredients for spice pastes, and individual households take pride in handing family recipes down through the generations. The pastes are best made just prior to cooking, not in bulk, to maximize freshness and flavour.

paste for mutton curry

To make a curry paste (top left) for 750g (1lb 10oz) cubed mutton or lamb, soak 6 dried chillies in a little warm water until soft, then pound them to a paste using a mortar and pestle. Add 1 tbsp grated fresh root ginger, and grind until well incorporated. In a small bowl, combine 2 tbsp finely chopped onion, 1 tbsp ground coriander, 2 tsp ground cumin, 2 tsp ground turmeric and ½ tsp ground cinnamon with 1 tbsp tamarind juice to make a paste. Stir in 8 fresh curry leaves, 4 whole cardamom pods (seeds only), 2 tsp salt and the chilli and ginger paste. To use, heat 4 tbsp vegetable oil in a karahi over a low heat. Gently fry the paste for 5 minutes until fragrant and the oil is released.

paste for grilled chicken

This paste (top right) is suitable for rubbing into 4 skinless chicken joints for grilling. Using a mortar and pestle, grind 1 tbsp grated fresh root ginger and 3 garlic cloves until fine. Add ½ tsp pounded black peppercorns and 1 tsp chilli powder. Heat 1 tbsp ghee in a karahi over a low heat, and gently fry the paste for 4 minutes. Add 1 tsp salt, 1 tsp sugar and 1 tbsp freshly squeezed lemon juice. Remove from the heat, leave to cool, then rub the spice paste over the chicken pieces.

paste for pork vindaloo

Soak 6 dried red chillies in hot water until soft; drain. In a mortar, pound the chillies, 5 garlic cloves and 30g (1oz) fresh root ginger to a paste. In a dry frying pan, toast 3 cardamom pods (seeds only), 1 tbsp coriander seeds, 1 tsp cumin seeds, 10 black peppercorns, ½ tsp freshly ground nutmeg, 4 whole cloves and a 5cm (2in) piece of cinnamon stick over a low heat for about 30 seconds until fragrant. Grind the spices to a powder, before blending with the onion and garlic paste. Heat 2 tbsp vegetable oil in a karahi over a low heat. Fry the spice mixture, stirring continuously, for 4 minutes or until oil comes to the surface. Add 2 tsp salt and 2 tbsp palm vinegar or white wine vinegar. Stir over a low heat until the paste (bottom left) thickens.

paste for goan fish curry

Soak 5 dried chillies in a little water to soften. In a mortar, grind 1 tbsp coriander seeds and 1 tsp cumin seeds until fine. Blend in 1 tbsp paprika and ½ tsp ground turmeric. Remove from the mortar, then grind the soaked chillies with 1 large chopped onion, 3 garlic cloves and 1 tbsp grated fresh root ginger. Add the spice mix, 1 tsp salt and 3 tbsp water. To use, heat 4 tbsp vegetable oil in a karahi over a low heat. Fry the paste (bottom right) for 4 minutes, then add 750g (1lb 10oz) fish.

pork vindaloo

Viindaloo is typical of the cooking of Goa on the western seaboard of India, and many dishes are heavily influenced by earlier French and Portuguese colonials. Pork dishes are best when cooked with lean pork that has a little marbled fat, as much of the intense flavour comes from this.

SERVES 4–6   PREPARATION TIME: 1 HOUR, PLUS 2–3 HOURS' MARINATING

TOOLS
Cleaver
Chopping board
Heavy saucepan and ladle
Vegetable knife

INGREDIENTS
1 quantity vindaloo paste
    (see page 129)
175ml (¾ cup) palm vinegar
    or white wine vinegar
1 tsp paprika
1kg (2¼lb) boneless pork,
    with a little marbled fat, cut
    into 3cm (1¼in) cubes
3 tbsp ghee or vegetable oil
½ star anise
1 large onion, sliced
1 tsp sugar

1 In a bowl, mix together the vindaloo paste, vinegar and paprika. Add the pork, and stir to coat the pork in the spices. Leave to marinate in the refrigerator for 2–3 hours.

2 Heat the ghee or oil in a heavy saucepan, and toss in the star anise. Swirl it around for a few seconds before adding the onion. Reduce the heat to low, cover the pan, and fry for 5 minutes until soft and starting to caramelize.

3 Drain the marinade liquid from the pork; reserve. Tip the pork into the pan, and cook, stirring, for about 10 minutes until the pork is well browned.

4 Sprinkle over the sugar, and pour in the reserved marinade, sprinkle over the sugar and simmer, covered, for about 40 minutes until the pork is tender and the sauce is nearly dry. If you need to top up with a little more liquid, add hot water and adjust with a little more vinegar for the required acidity.

5 Serve hot with plain basmati rice or naan (see page 145).

DAS SREEDHARAN okra thoran

Thorans, an essential element of Keralan meals, are dishes of crunchy stir-fried vegetables flavoured with coconut and curry leaves. Das Sreedharan of Rasa Restaurants says his favourite school lunch was a tiffin of rice, yogurt, pickles and a crisp thoran dish such as this one. Any combination of firm vegetables can be substituted for the okra.

SERVES 4   PREPARATION TIME: 20 MINUTES

TOOLS
Small knife
Chopping board
Karahi
Colander

INGREDIENTS
5 tbsp vegetable oil
1½ tbsp mustard seeds
10 curry leaves
2 dried red chillies
1 onion, finely chopped
1 tsp ground turmeric
200g (7oz) okra, chopped
   into 1cm (½in) pieces
50g (½ cup) freshly grated
   or unsweetened
   desiccated
   (shredded)
   coconut
salt

1 Heat the oil in a karahi, and add the mustard seeds. As they begin to pop, add the curry leaves and chillies, then the finely chopped onion.

2 Cook, stirring, for 5 minutes until the onion softens, then stir in the turmeric and a little salt, and stir-fry for 2 minutes. Add the chopped okra, and cook for another 3–4 minutes.

3 Remove the pan from the heat, and stir through the coconut. Mix well, then serve hot.

ROOPA GULATI spiced lamb with almonds

Not all Indian dishes call for hours by the grinding stone, yet even the simplest recipes can offer dramatic flavours, says food writer, broadcaster, restaurant critic and television chef Roopa Gulati. Simple dry dishes such as this one have their origins in the desert, where fresh vegetables are hard to find and water is a precious resource.

SERVES 4   PREPARATION TIME: 1 HOUR

TOOLS
Knife
Chopping board
Lidded pot
Small karahi

INGREDIENTS
500g (1lb 2oz) boned leg of
   lamb, cut into 2cm (¾in) cubes
200ml (scant 1 cup) Greek-style
   yogurt
3 onions, finely sliced
4 garlic cloves, finely sliced
2cm (¾in) piece of fresh root
   ginger, finely sliced
2cm (¾in) piece of cinnamon
   stick
2 small bay leaves
3 whole cloves
¼ tsp black peppercorns
1 tsp cumin seeds
6 tbsp vegetable oil
1 mace blade
2 dried red chillies, split
   and deseeded
4 tbsp flaked almonds
2 tbsp fresh coriander
   (cilantro) leaves
a few drops of pandan leaf
   essence (optional)

1 In a pot, combine the lamb, yogurt, 2 of the sliced onions, garlic, ginger, cinnamon, bay leaves, cloves, peppercorns, cumin seeds and 4 tbsp of the oil. Mix well, add a little salt and bring to a simmer. Cover tightly, reduce the heat and cook gently for about 40 minutes until the meat is tender.

2 Once the meat is cooked, heat the remaining 2 tbsp oil in a small karahi, and add the rest of the sliced onion, plus the mace and red chillies. Reduce the heat, and gently fry the onions until they are very soft in texture and a nutty golden colour.

3 Stir the onion mixture and flaked almonds into the meat. Season to taste with salt, and reheat the lamb as necessary. Sprinkle with the coriander (cilantro) leaves and a little pandan leaf essence (if using) just before serving hot.

VIVEK SINGH breast of pigeon with spiced kebabs and black lentils

Although pigeons are eaten throughout the subcontinent, you rarely see them on restaurant menus. The Cinnamon Club's renowned chef Vivek Singh simply loves the taste and texture of good-quality pigeon, which he sees as unusual and a lot more interesting than the regular chicken you find on all menus. This recipe uses most of the flesh on the squab, but requires a friendly butcher to take the pain out of preparation. The breast of the pigeon receives the tandoor treatment, while the rest is minced into a stunning kebab. Many people are put off eating such a small bird because of dealing with the bones, but this is a very user-friendly way of presenting pigeon. You can serve this with a little salad as an accomplished starter or appetizer, or with small quantities of black lentils and rice pilaf as a stunning main course.

SERVES 4 AS A STARTER OR 2 AS A MAIN   PREPARATION TIME: 1 HOUR 30 MINUTES, PLUS OVERNIGHT SOAKING

TOOLS
Knife
Chopping board
Nonstick frying pan or skillet
Heavy saucepan or pot

INGREDIENTS
For the squab
1st marination
2 pigeons, breasts boned and skin
   on, and leg, liver and heart minced
   (ground) (to be used for kebabs)
1 tsp fresh ginger purée
1 tsp fresh garlic purée
½ tsp salt
1 tsp chilli powder
juice of ½ lemon
2nd marination
½ onion, chopped, fried until crisp
   and blended to a paste
1 tbsp Greek-style yogurt
½ tsp garam masala (see page 128)
1 tbsp vegetabe oil

For the kebabs
1 tbsp vegetable oil, plus extra for deep-frying
¼ tsp royal cumin
1 finely chopped onion
1 small raw beetroot (red beet), boiled,
   peeled and finely chopped
¼ tsp chilli powder
¼ tsp ground dry-roasted cumin seeds
1cm (½in) piece of fresh root ginger,
   finely chopped
2 fresh green chillies, chopped
sprig of fresh mint leaves, shredded
1 tsp salt
¼ tsp garam masala (see page 128)
1 egg, lightly beaten
toasted breadcrumbs, to coat

For the black lentils
250g (9oz) whole urad dal (black
   lentils or black gram), soaked in
   lukewarm water overnight
1 tsp fresh ginger purée
1 tsp fresh garlic purée
1 tsp chilli powder
1 tsp salt
2 tbsp concentrated tomato
   purée (paste)
150g (5½oz/about 1½ sticks) lightly
   salted butter, cut into rough cubes
1 tsp garam masala (see page 128)
½ tsp ground fenugreek
½ tsp sugar
2 tbsp single (light whipping) cream

1 First, make the black lentils. Boil the drained soaked lentils in 1 litre (4 cups) water until thoroughly cooked but not mushy – this takes about 1 hour.

2 Add the ginger and garlic purées, chilli powder and salt, and boil for a further 10 minutes. Reduce the heat slightly, add the tomato purée and butter, and gently simmer for a further 15 minutes or until the lentils are thick, taking care that the emulsion does not split – that is, the butter does not separate.

3 Stir in the garam masala, fenugreek and sugar, and check the seasoning. Stir in the cream, and keep warm until needed.

4 Meanwhile, to make the squab, preheat the oven to 200°C/400°F/Gas 6. Pat dry the pigeon breasts with kitchen paper, and put in a non-reactive shallow dish. Mix together the ginger purée, garlic purée, chilli powder, salt and lemon juice, and use to marinate the pigeon for 20 minutes.

5 Heat a nonstick heavy frying pan or skillet over a medium-high heat until hot but not smoking. Put the breasts in the pan skin-side down. Sear for 3–4 minutes until the skin is starting to crisp and

brown, and the fat is starting to render; turn over and sear on the other side for a further 2 minutes.

6 Mix together all the ingredients for the second marination. Transfer the breasts to a roasting dish, coat with the marinade, and finish in the oven for 5 minutes; the meat should still be pink.

7 To make the spiced kebabs, heat the oil in a pan, add the royal cumin seeds and, when they start to crackle, add the chopped onion and sauté until golden brown. Add the minced pigeon and beetroot (beet), and sauté for a further 3 minutes, then add the chilli powder and ground cumin. Continue cooking until the mixture is almost dry. Add the ginger, green chilli, mint, salt and garam masala, and stir through. Remove from the heat, and allow to cool.

8 Shape the mixture into 4 cakes. Dip them in the beaten egg, then roll each one in breadcrumbs. Deep-fry until golden brown on both sides, and keep warm to serve alongside the breast.

9 To serve, cut the breasts into slices lengthways. Spoon the black lentils onto individual serving plates. Arrange the spiced kebabs and breasts on top, and serve immediately.

pots, pans and griddles

An Indian kitchen is designed to stand up to the toughest of tasks. Catering for extended families calls for cavernous karahis and enormous pots that are often large enough to feed a family of fourteen in one sitting. It is best to choose pans that are made from heavy-gauge metal; a lightweight pan cannot hope to hold its own against the often-involved stages of frying and scraping spice pastes.

2 SMALL KARAHI
A familiar sight in restaurants, these can be brought directly to the table.

3 BLACK TERRA-COTTA CURRY POT
Used throughout the subcontinent for thousands of years, terra-cotta or clay pots often have a thick rim and are used for simmering curries and stews on charcoal-burning braziers. The model seen here is matt black with the patina of age, having been handed down over several generations.

4 TAWA
One of the most important utensils in the Indian kitchen, these griddles are made from cast iron and commonly have a long handle. Tawas are used for cooking breads such as parathas and chapatis. In South India, they are used for frying *dosas*, pancakes made from ground rice and lentils. Good heat conductors, they cook breads evenly without scorching and are also ideal for roasting spices. Tawas come in many sizes; smaller ones are no more than 10 cm (4 in) in diameter; others may be as large as a bicycle wheel.

1 KARAHI
Also known as a *kadai* or *cheena chatti*, this utensil is not very different in shape from the Chinese wok, but most karahis are smaller in size. In India, they usually have a rounded base; however, most karahis available in the West have flat bottoms that enable them to sit straight on electric hobs. They usually have two handles and are made of cast iron, aluminium, enamel or stainless steel. The enamel karahi shown here is effectively a nonstick pot that can be scrubbed without fear of chipping the surface. The handles are made of the same metal as the bowl section, which means that they can get quite hot while on the stove and therefore care must be taken when moving the pan. The karahi is used for frying spices and pastes, and making vegetable dishes. Large models can be used for deep-frying.

5 STRAIGHT-SIDED ALUMINIUM POT

Known as a *patila* in India, this is an all-purpose pot for rice and curries. Care must be taken not to cook dishes of an acidic nature in this type of pan because the aluminium will react with the food. It has no handles and comes with a flat, tight-fitting lid.

6 STAINLESS-STEEL POT

Many cooks are fond of using stainless-steel pots because they are durable and easy to clean. This round-bottomed stewing pot with a copper base has a fat belly that tapers towards the lip, and is used for simmering curries and boiling liquids.

8 STAINLESS-STEEL YOGURT MAKER

Yogurt is a staple food in homes across the subcontinent, and most cooks make their own on a daily basis, using a spoonful of the previous day's yogurt to set a new batch. Stainless-steel makers are more durable than their terra-cotta counterparts and are available in many sizes.

9 TERRA-COTTA YOGURT MAKER

Terra-cotta crocks are thought to be the best for setting yogurt because they give a superior texture and the porous material helps to keep the yogurt cool during the hot months of summer.

7 IDLI PAN

A staple breakfast dish of South India, *idlis* are steamed cakes made from a fermented mixture of rice and lentil flours. The batter is cooked in a steamer that resembles a large egg poacher and is made from stainless steel or aluminium. This round-bottomed steamer has two decks (some have as many as four) with moulds for four idlis on each layer. The moulds are fixed to a central rod, and the idlis are cooked by the steam produced by the simmering water in the bottom of the pan. The rod allows easy removal.

CYRUS TODIWALA roast chicken madurai masala

Madurai, a town in the South Indian state of Tamil Nadu, is noted for its mild dishes, of which this chicken recipe is typical. It comes from top chef Cyrus Todiwala of London's Café Spice Namasté. The ingredients list may seem rather long, but the dish is in fact very simple to make.

SERVES 4   PREPARATION TIME: 1 HOUR

TOOLS
Knife
Chopping board
Lidded pot
Basting spoon

INGREDIENTS
4 chicken thighs, skin on
2 tsp salt
½ tsp ground turmeric
3 tbsp vegetable oil
10 curry leaves
½ tsp cumin seeds
½ tsp fennel seeds
3 bay leaves
200g (7oz) onions, finely sliced
    (about 1¼ cups)
1 tbsp fresh ginger purée
1 tbsp fresh garlic purée
150g (5½oz) tomatoes, halved
1 tsp ground coriander
½ tsp chilli powder
1 tbsp chopped coriander
    (cilantro) leaves
10 fresh mint leaves, shredded

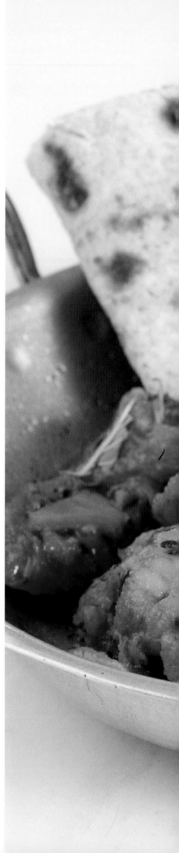

1 Clean the chicken thighs, removing any excess fat. Rub with the salt and ground turmeric, and set aside.

2 Heat the oil in a pot over a medium to medium-high heat. Add the curry leaves and cumin and fennel seeds, and fry for a few minutes until brown and fragrant, shaking the pan vigorously to prevent burning.

3 Add the bay leaves and onions, and sauté for 6–8 minutes until the onions are lightly golden. Add the ginger and garlic purées, and cook, stirring, for 1 minute. Tip in the tomatoes, and continue to cook until almost dry.

4 Mix the ground coriander and chilli powder with a little water to make a paste, and add to the pan. Cook, stirring, for 1 minute, then push the fried paste aside.

5 Lay the chicken thighs in the pan skin-side down, and spread the paste all over them, rubbing it in well. Cover, reduce the heat and allow the chicken pieces to brown for a few minutes on the skin side. Add 2 tbsp water to create steam and facilitate the cooking.

6 Turn the chicken thighs over, and continue cooking for 15 minutes or until done. To test whether the chicken is cooked, pierce the thickest part of one thigh with a metal skewer; if the juices that run out are clear, the chicken is ready.

7 Sprinkle over the fresh coriander (cilantro) and mint leaves, cover the pan and remove from the heat, ready for serving hot with some flat bread or basmati rice.

ATUL KOCHHAR grilled sea bream with spice rub

When Michelin-starred chef Atul Kochhar entertains at home, he also wants to be able to sit and chat with his friends – making the recipe given here, *bhuni machchi*, from Atul's book *Fish, Indian Style*, very much his kind of dish. He loves coming up with new combinations of spices, and the spice rub here is a particular favourite. Many other spice blends work well, so adapt it and use whatever you fancy – it's as easy as that.

SERVES 4   PREPARATION TIME: 30 MINUTES

TOOLS

Mortar and pestle
Grill (broiler)
Frying pan or skillet

INGREDIENTS

8 small or 4 large red bream
    fillets (or use red snapper,
    John dory, sea bass, tilapia
    or barramundi)
lemon wedges, to serve

For the spice rub

3 tbsp walnut or olive oil
4 tbsp chopped coriander
    (cilantro) leaves
2 garlic cloves, crushed
1 tsp coriander seeds,
    crushed
1 tsp cumin seeds, crushed
1 tbsp freshly squeezed
    lemon juice
1 small fresh green chilli, very
    finely chopped

For the tomato salad

4 plum tomatoes, chopped
1 tbsp chopped coriander
    (cilantro) leaves
1½ tsp walnut or olive oil
1 tbsp shelled walnuts, toasted
    in a dry frying pan, then lightly
    crushed
sea or kosher salt and freshly
    ground black pepper

1 Mix together all the ingredients for the spice rub, and season with salt. Line a baking sheet with foil, and arrange the fish fillets on it, skin-side down. Brush the spice rub over the fish.

2 Place the tray of fish under a hot grill (broiler) for 6–8 minutes, until the fish is cooked through and lightly golden. Remove from the heat, and keep warm.

3 Meanwhile, mix together all the ingredients for the tomato salad. Serve the fish with the salad and some lemon wedges for squeezing over.

xacutti chicken

A speciality hailing from Goa in southern India, *xacutti* is a distinctive masala packed with spices. This is a slightly modified dish, where you can use store-bought garam masala to save time, or experiment with either the xacutti masala or garam masala on page 129. Traditionally, Goan chefs always grind their xacutti masala from scratch, and pair it with roasted coconut to impart xacutti's characteristic flavour.

SERVES 4–6   PREPARATION TIME: 1 HOUR

TOOLS
Cleaver
Chopping board
Small karahi or wok
Lidded pot
Vegetable knife

INGREDIENTS
1 whole chicken, about 1.5kg
   (3¼lb)
2 tbsp unsweetened desiccated
   (shredded) coconut
1 tbsp vegetable oil
2 large onions, finely chopped
1 tbsp tomato purée (paste)
4 whole fresh red chillies

½ tsp ground cloves
2 tbsp xacutti or garam masala
   (see page 129)
1 cinnamon stick, about 8cm
   (3in) long
chopped coriander (cilantro) leaves,
   to garnish
lime wedges, to serve
For the marinade
1 tbsp fresh garlic purée
1 tbsp fresh ginger purée
2 tbsp finely chopped coriander
   (cilantro) leaves
1 tbsp tamarind concentrate
½ tsp ground turmeric
1 tsp chilli powder

1 Blend together the marinade ingredients in a shallow glass or ceramic dish. Joint and cut the chicken into about 12 bite-sized pieces; trim off and discard any excess fatty skin. Add the chicken pieces to the marinade, cover with cling film (plastic wrap) and leave to marinate in the refrigerator for at least 30 minutes.

2 Heat a karahi or wok without oil over a medium heat, and toast the coconut for a few minutes until golden brown, being careful not to scorch it. Remove and set aside.

3 Now heat the oil in a clean saucepan over a medium heat, and fry the onions for about 5 minutes until soft and starting to caramelize and turn golden. Return the roasted coconut to the pan with the tomato purée (paste), chillies, ground cloves, xacutti or garam masala, and cinnamon stick. Stir well for a minute or two to blend and allow the flavours to mingle.

4 Add the chicken pieces, together with their marinade, and keep stirring around the pan over a high heat for 5 minutes. Pour over 500ml (2 cups) water, and bring the mixture to the boil. Reduce the heat to low, and leave to simmer, covered, for 25 minutes until the chicken is tender and the sauce is thick. Serve garnished with the chopped coriander (cilantro) and the lime wedges for squeezing over.

bread-making implements

Many centuries ago, the Moghuls brought fine-textured breads to the subcontinent, and royal kingdoms took pride in the skill of their cooks. Even in rice-eating areas, most homes have a rolling pin and chapati board, and prospective brides' culinary skills are often judged by the standard of their bread making.

2 3 CHAPATI ROLLING PINS
These special rolling pins are usually made from hardwood, and are narrow, with tapered ends. Chapati boards and rolling pins can be found as sets in Indian stores and at street bazaars.

1 CHAPATI BOARD
It is not imperative that top-quality hardwood is used for a chapati board because it is used only as a base for rolling out dough. Some cooks prefer to use a stone base instead. Round marble slabs, although heavy and expensive, are really useful when rolling out delicate breads. The cool marble surface is oiled to keep rich doughs from sticking during the hot summer months.

4 CHAPATI PRESSER
There are two types of chapati: one baked in a tandoor; the other cooked on a *tawa*, or griddle. A chapati presser is used for tawa-baked chapatis. Once the bread is partially cooked, it begins to rise and puff with hot air. Gentle pressure is applied with this tool to help the chapati to rise uniformly, without expelling the air, in order to create a light texture.

MEHERNOSH MODY *naan*

An authentic naan needs to be cooked in an authentic tandoor. The technique involves rolling out the dough, opening the lid of the tandoor and literally sticking the bread to the wall of the oven. Nevertheless, this recipe from Mehernosh Mody, of London's Franco-Indian restaurant La Porte des Indes, should give good results with a domestic oven.

SERVES 14   PREPARATION TIME: 40 MINUTES, PLUS 2 HOURS' RISING

TOOLS
Sifter
Rolling pin
Tawa
Baking sheets

INGREDIENTS
900g (2lb) plain (all-purpose)
   flour (about 7¼ cups)
1 tbsp baking powder
1 tsp sugar
1 egg, lightly beaten
300ml (1¼ cups) milk, boiled and
   cooled to lukewarm
300ml (1¼ cups) lukewarm water
4 tbsp vegetable oil
2 tbsp sesame seeds
melted butter, for brushing
salt

1 Sift the flour into a large bowl with the baking powder, sugar and some salt. Make a well in the centre, and gradually add the egg, milk and lukewarm water. Stir to blend into a dough.

2 On a floured work surface, knead the dough until firm. Return the dough to the bowl, cover with a warm, damp cloth and leave to rise for 30 minutes.

3 Knead the oil into the risen dough, then leave to rise again, covered with a warm damp cloth, for 1 hour or until the dough has doubled in size.

4 Punch down (knock back) the dough. Divide into 14 equal-sized balls, and place them on a floured tray. Cover once again with a warm, damp cloth, and set the tray of balls aside to rise for 30 minutes.

5 Heat the oven to 240°C/475°F/Gas 9, and place 2 baking sheets in it to get hot. On a lightly floured surface, roll out each ball into a teardrop shape about 5mm (¼in) thick, and sprinkle each one with the sesame seeds.

6 Grease the hot baking sheets and, working in batches, place the naans on them and bake for 5–6 minutes each until golden brown and puffed. Brush with a little melted butter before serving warm.

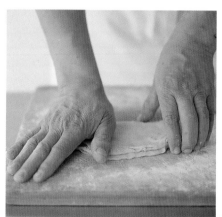

paratha

There are many different types of paratha, some as simple as a dough made from wholemeal (whole-wheat) flour and water, enriched with oil or ghee. It is primarily the way the dough is worked that distinguishes this flat bread from other popular options such as chapati and naan.

SERVES 8   PREPARATION TIME: 40 MINUTES

TOOLS	INGREDIENTS
Chapati board	150g (5½oz) ghee, plus extra for greasing
Rolling pin	500g (4 cups) plain (all-purpose) flour
Tawa	2 tsp sugar
Brush	1 tsp baking powder
	2 eggs
	250ml (1 cup) milk or water
	salt

1 Melt the 150g (5½oz) ghee, and mix with the flour, sugar, baking powder and a good pinch of salt in a large bowl. Lightly beat together the eggs and milk, and add to the bowl. Stir to blend the ingredients into a dough.

2 Turn out the dough onto a lightly floured work surface, and knead for at least 10 minutes until a soft dough forms. Wrap in a clean damp tea towel or kitchen cloth, and allow to stand for at least 2 hours.

3 Divide the dough into 8 portions, and shape into balls. While you work with one, keep the others covered with the damp cloth.

4 Flatten the ball (top left), and roll out on lightly floured board into a thin circle. Fold over once to make a half-moon (second from top left), then again to make a curved-edge triangle (second from bottom left). Roll out again until twice the size, and dust with a little flour.

5 Fold all the edges inwards to make a rough circle again, and roll out for the last time into a circle about 5mm (¼in) thick.

6 Heat the tawa, and grease with a little ghee. Place one of the paratha on the tawa, and cook until bubbles appear. Flip over, and cook the other side (bottom left), brushing the bread with a little more melted ghee. When done, the paratha should be golden brown. Continue until all the parathas are cooked. Serve warm.

moulds and presses

India is a nation of munchers, where crunchy snacks are distiguished by their varied shapes and textures. Many tools for snack making have remained unchanged for thousands of years, and people are often surprised that the complex spirals of spicy bites such as *murukku* have actually been created by a simple-looking press.

3 KULFI MOULDS

These cone-shaped moulds with screw-top lids are used for making *kulfi*, India's famous frozen dessert. Aluminium is a popular material for moulds because it cools more quickly than plastic when placed in ice. *Kulfi* were originally made in clay pots sealed with dough. In many old quarters, these traditional ices continue to be frozen in the same type of pot today.

1 SEVIYA PRESS

This little brass cylinder with a crank handle incorporates a selection of perforated plates, each with small holes or gashes, chosen according to the shape of snacks required. The press is used for making Sri Lankan string hoppers, South Indian *murukkus* and other sweet and savoury snacks. Dough is pressed into the cylinder, then the top lid of the press is wound down into place. When the handle is turned, it pushes the dough out in the desired shape, ready for steaming or deep-frying.

4 VADAI MAKER

Vadai are round, savoury rice flour cakes that look like exotic doughnuts; they originate from South India, but are popular throughout the country. The plunger on this stainless-steel gadget forces out the vadai dough in a ring shape that is ready for frying.

2 STAINLESS-STEEL RICER

In the West, this tool is most commonly used for mashing cooked potatoes. In South India and Sri Lanka, ricers may be employed to help shape string hoppers. Made of stainless steel, the ricer has a hinged lid that presses the dough through the perforated base when force is applied. This is done over oiled plates, or banana leaves, so that the piles of string hoppers that are created are ready for steaming.

string hoppers

Indian *appam* (*idiappam* in South India), Sri Lankan *appe* and string hoppers are from the same family. Basic recipes vary with regional differences, but rice flour and coconut milk are the main ingredients, and they can be savoury or sweet. To make string hoppers, a batter is forced through a metal mould into a tangle of thin threads, or noodles, which is steamed before serving. Most Indian and Sri Lankan stores sell appam flour ready-mixed for cooking.

SERVES 4   PREPARATION TIME: 35 MINUTES

TOOLS
Ladle
Steamer
Seviya mould
Heatproof steaming plate

INGREDIENTS
300g (10oz/scant 2 cups)
    appam flour
150ml (⅔ cup) coconut milk
½ tsp salt
soft brown sugar or demerara
    sugar, for sprinkling
vegetable oil for greasing

1 Sift the appam flour into a bowl, and pour in the coconut milk and salt. Beat until the mixture forms a smooth batter with a creamy consistency.

2 Meanwhile, bring some water to a boil in a steamer, and place a lightly oiled heatproof plate in the pan. Cover tightly, to allow the steam to build up.

3 To make the string hoppers, use a seviya mould fitted with a perforated disc that has notches the diameter of matchsticks cut out from it. Pour the appam batter into the mould.

4 Rotate the handle of the seviya mould over the plate in the steamer, making small mounds of appam threads. Repeat until there are enough piles to fill the plate, making sure that the sides do not touch.

5 Cover and steam for 10–15 minutes until the hoppers are fluffy and fragrant. Transfer to a serving plate, and sprinkle with the sugar before serving hot.

ROOPA GULATI sweet mango chutney

Simple to make and packed with fruity flavour, this chunky chutney from food writer and television chef Roopa Gulati is a class apart from store-bought varieties. For best results, buy green mangoes from a specialist grocer, and don't be afraid to give them a squeeze – steer clear of any that feel even slightly squishy; the firmer, the better.

MAKES 800ML (26FL OZ)   PREPARATION TIME: 30 MINUTES

TOOLS
Vegetable knife
Chopping board
Stainless-steel saucepan

INGREDIENTS
1kg (2¼lb) firm green mangoes
1 tsp ground turmeric
1 tsp salt
2 tbsp vegetable oil
¾ tsp nigella seeds
1 tsp fennel seeds
½ tsp dried red chilli flakes
    (red pepper flakes)
4cm (1½in) piece of fresh root
    ginger, chopped
200g (7oz/scant 1 cup packed)
    jaggery or light muscovado
    sugar

1 Peel the mangoes, remove the central stones and cut the flesh into 3cm (1¼in) chunks. In a bowl, combine the mangoes with the turmeric and salt.

2 Heat the oil in a medium saucepan, and toss in the nigella seeds, fennel seeds and chilli flakes. After about 30 seconds, add the mangoes, and fry over a medium heat, stirring occasionally, for 5 minutes. Pour in 500 ml (16 fl oz) water, and simmer until the fruit has softened and cooked down.

3 Stir in the jaggery or sugar until it has dissolved. Cook over a medium heat, stirring occasionally, for a further 15 minutes until the chutney has thickened. To test whether setting point has been reached, spoon a teaspoonful of hot chutney onto a chilled plate or saucer, then return the plate to the refrigerator for a minute – the surface of the chutney should wrinkle when you push a finger or teaspoon through it.

4 When the chutney has cooled, spoon it into sterilized jars, and seal tightly. Store in a cool, dark place until needed. It should keep for 2–3 months; refrigerate after opening.

ROOPA GULATI tomato chutney

This bold, gingery chutney is so moreish that Roopa Gulati likes to use it as the base of a meal: for a quick on-the-go lunch, she suggests that you serve it warm with a heap of fluffy rice, halved hard-boiled eggs and a sprinkling of chopped coriander (cilantro) leaves.

MAKES 500ML (16FL OZ)   PREPARATION TIME: 25 MINUTES

TOOLS
Vegetable knife
Chopping board
Stainless-steel saucepan

INGREDIENTS
3 tbsp vegetable oil
2 tsp mustard seeds
½ tsp nigella seeds
1 tbsp fennel seeds
2 red onions, diced
2 garlic cloves, finely chopped
3cm (1¼in) piece of fresh
    root ginger, finely chopped
2 large fresh green chillies,
    deseeded and chopped
2 x 400g (14oz) cans chopped
    tomatoes
100g (3½oz/about ⅔ cup) pitted
    and chopped dates
3–4 tbsp caster (superfine)
    sugar
100ml (scant ½ cup) white
    wine vinegar

1 Heat the oil in a medium saucepan set over a medium heat. Add the mustard seeds, and fry for a few seconds until they stop popping. Stir in the nigella and fennel seeds, and fry for another 10 seconds until fragrant.

2 Reduce the heat, and add the remaining ingredients. Simmer, uncovered, for 10–15 minutes until thickened. The chutney should have a sweet–sour taste; add more sugar if needed. Serve warm or at room temperature.

sri lankan pickles and sambols

Pickles and sambols are staples of Sri Lankan cuisine, and appear at almost every meal from morning to night. You will find them served with savoury hoppers for breakfast or as part of a selection of dishes served at the table for people to pick and choose what they want. The key to combining dishes successfully in Sri Lankan cuisine is to remember always to balance the hot and fiery with something cooling such as a salad, so mix and match – and enjoy.

aubergine pickle

Using a mortar and pestle, coarsely grind 2 tsp black mustard seeds, 2 tsp cumin seeds, 2 tsp coriander seeds and 1 tsp fennel seeds. Trim off and discard the stalk ends of 500g (1lb 2oz) aubergines (eggplants). Cut the aubergines into thin slices, and heat a heavy pan over a medium-high heat. Add a little vegetable oil, and fry the aubergine slices for 2 minutes on each side until golden brown. Cook in batches so that you don't crowd the pan. Remove and drain on kitchen paper. Using the same pan, gently cook 1 large finely sliced onion for about 5 minutes until soft and translucent. Add 3 finely sliced garlic cloves, and cook for 30 seconds until just turning white. Sprinkle in 1 tsp sugar, and cook for another couple of minutes until starting to caramelize. Push the onion to one side of the pan, and add a little more oil. Tip in the coarsely ground spices with ½ tsp ground turmeric. Fry the spices for a minute until fragrant, then mix through the onion. Add 3 deseeded and finely chopped fresh green chillies, 3 tbsp palm vinegar or white wine vinegar, 1 tsp tamarind concentrate and the aubergine slices. Mix together, and season well with sea or kosher salt and freshly ground black pepper. Cook for a further 8–10 minutes until the flavours have combined. Serve at room temperature as an accompaniment.

onion sambol

To temper the spices, heat 4 tbsp vegetable oil in a medium heavy pan over a high heat. When the oil is hot, add 6–8 curry leaves, 2 tsp chilli powder, 1–2 tsp dried red chilli flakes (red pepper flakes), 5 whole cloves, 5 lightly crushed green cardamom pods, a 5cm (2in) piece of cinnamon stick, 1 tsp Maldive fish flakes, ½ tsp brown mustard seeds and ¼ tsp ground turmeric, and fry for about 1 minute, stirring frequently, until fragrant. Tip in 4 finely chopped large red onions, then sprinkle over 1–2 tsp sugar. Cook for another minute or so, stirring, until starting to soften. Season with sea or kosher salt and 1 tsp tamarind concentrate. Cover the pan, and reduce the heat to low. Cook gently for 8–10 minutes, stirring occasionally. Increase the heat slightly, and continue cooking for another few minutes until the onions are soft, caramelized and a rich golden colour. Serve warm or at room temperature, sprinkled with some crisp-fried shallots.

tomato sambol

Preheat a charcoal grill or a ridged cast-iron grill pan or griddle until very hot. Char-grill 3 or 4 ripe plum tomatoes for a few minutes until the skins are charred and blistered, but the tomatoes are still holding their shape. Leave to cool for about 15 minutes, then cut into 1cm (½in) dice. Put in a nonreactive bowl, and set aside. Heat 1½ tsp coconut oil in a small heavy pan over a high heat. Add ¾ tsp dried red chilli flakes (red pepper flakes) and 1–2 finely chopped garlic cloves, and season with a little sea or kosher salt. Fry for about 30 seconds, stirring constantly, until the chilli starts to crisp and brown. Transfer to the bowl with the tomatoes, and stir through. Add 1 small finely sliced red onion, 1 tbsp thick coconut milk (coconut cream), ¾ tsp Maldive fish flakes, coarsely ground, and 1 finely chopped fresh green chilli. Mix together, and squeeze over the juice of ½–1 lime. Taste, and season with more salt if needed. Leave to rest for 5–10 minutes to allow the flavours to develop. Serve immediately.

white vegetable curry

This version of the basic Sri Lankan white curry is made with potato, pumpkin and okra, but you can choose any sort of vegetables you like to make this – courgettes (zucchini), green beans, asparagus, aubergines (eggplants) and bitter gourd all make good choices.

SERVES 4–6   PREPARATION TIME: 45 MINUTES

TOOLS
Vegetable knife
Chopping board
Karahi or large heavy pan

INGREDIENTS
1 tbsp vegetable oil
1 onion, finely chopped
6 curry leaves
6–8 fenugreek seeds
½ tsp ground turmeric
6 whole black peppercorns
¼ tsp brown mustard seeds
1–2 fresh green chillies,
    deseeded and split
    lengthways
2 garlic cloves, finely sliced
300g (10oz) potatoes, peeled
    and cut into chunks (about
    2 cups prepared)
300g (10oz) pumpkin, peeled
    and cut into chunks (about
    2 cups prepared)

150g (5½oz/about 1½ cups)
    fresh okra, halved
5cm (2in) piece of
    cinnamon stick
½ tsp finely grated fresh ginger
1 stalk lemon grass, tough outer
    layer removed (optional)
750ml (3 cups) coconut
    milk
250ml (1 cup)
    coconut cream

1 Heat the oil in a karahi or large heavy pan over a high heat. Add the onion, curry leaves, fenugreek seeds, turmeric, peppercorns, brown mustard seeds, chillies, garlic and ginger. Fry for about 30 seconds until fragrant and the mustard seeds have popped.

2 Add the cinnamon stick, lemon grass (if using) and coconut milk, and simmer gently, uncovered, for about 10 minutes.

3 Now add the potatoes and pumpkin, and season with salt. Simmer gently for 10–15 minutes until the vegetables are just tender, then tip in the okra. Pour in the coconut cream, and simmer for a further 5 minutes. Serve with flat bread or plain rice.

sri lankan crab curry

Practically an iconic dish, this is a real festive offering if you can find the type of crabs that have mottled grey-green shells. Some Asian supermarkets sell them frozen if the fresh ones are not available. These are smallish crabs, each about the size of a hand and with a very sweet flavour. You can also use cooked crabs such as Dungeness, but the flavour will not be as rich, or try making this curry with soft-shell crabs, as here.

SERVES 4   PREPARATION TIME: 30 MINUTES

TOOLS
Cleaver
Chopping board
Saucepan and ladle
Karahi or frying pan or skillet

INGREDIENTS
8 small soft-shell crabs
600ml (scant 2½ cups) coconut milk
2 large onions, finely chopped
5 garlic cloves, coarsely ground
2 tbsp grated fresh root ginger
½ tsp ground fenugreek
10 curry leaves or fresh sweet
   basil leaves
5cm (2in) piece of cinnamon stick
1 tsp chilli powder
1 tsp ground turmeric
2 tbsp salt
juice of 3 limes
2 tbsp unsweetened desiccated
   (shredded) coconut

1 If you are not using soft-shell crabs, remove the outer large shell of each crab, and discard the fibrous tissue found under each shell. Cut each crab into 2 pieces, and separate the large claws from the body. Trim off the flat ends of legs; they contain no meat. Wash and drain.

2 Put the coconut milk in a saucepan with the onions, garlic, ginger, fenugreek, curry or basil leaves, cinnamon, chilli powder, turmeric and salt. Bring to the boil. Simmer for 20 minutes until all the flavours are well incorporated.

3 In a separate, small dry frying pan or skillet, toast the coconut for a few minutes until golden brown, being careful not to scorch, then remove from the heat and set aside.

4 Add the crab pieces to the coconut milk mixture, and gently simmer for 8 minutes. Add the salt, lime juice and toasted coconut at the last minute, and serve hot with plain rice or flat bread.

ROOPA GULATI saffron chicken tikka

Besides adding a tropical flavour, fresh pineapple contains an enzyme that acts as a natural meat tenderizer and also helps to cut down on cooking time. These delectable morsels have a deliciously smoky wisp of a crust and make marvellous cocktail snacks.

SERVES 4   PREPARATION TIME: 45 MINUTES, PLUS OVERNIGHT MARINATING

TOOLS
Mortar and pestle
Grill (broiler)
Bamboo skewers

INGREDIENTS
½ tsp saffron threads
1 tsp cardamom seeds
125ml (½ cup) Greek-style
    yogurt
2 tbsp thick double
    (heavy whipping) cream
4cm (1½ in) piece of fresh root
    ginger, finely grated
1 tbsp ground almonds
125g (4½oz/¾ cup) fresh
    pineapple chunks
600g (1lb 5oz) skinless
    chicken thigh fillets, cut
    into 3cm (1¼ in) cubes
about 1 tbsp butter, melted
juice of 1 lime
To garnish
lime wedges
sprigs of fresh coriander
    (cilantro)

1 Put the saffron threads in a small bowl with 1 tbsp warm water. Leave to soak for at least 30 minutes until the liquid turns a deep auburn.

2 Using a mortar and pestle, pound the cardamom seeds to a fine powder and whisk them into the yogurt. Stir in the cream, ginger and ground almonds.

3 Finely chop the pineapple, or blend to a paste in a small food processor. Using your hands, squeeze out any excess juice, and add the pulp to the spiced yogurt.

4 Add the chicken to the yogurt mixture. Pour over the saffron and its soaking liquid, and stir through well. Cover with cling film (plastic wrap), and leave to marinate in the refrigerator overnight.

5 The next day, soak the bamboo skewers in cold water for at least 30 minutes to prevent scorching. Preheat the grill (broiler) to its highest setting.

6 Drain the chicken pieces from the yogurt, and thread onto the skewers. Pour a little melted butter over each skewer, and cook the chicken near the top of the hot grill for about 5 minutes on each side, until cooked through and beginning to char a little at the edges.

7 Sharpen the chicken with the lime juice, and serve hot garnished with wedges of lime and sprigs of coriander (cilantro).

YOGESH ARORA palak paneer

Most homes in India make their own paneer by adding enough vinegar to boiling milk to separate the curds from the whey. The curds are then pressed for about 30 minutes, or longer if a firmer texture is preferred, to give a nutritious form of protein that is important to India's many vegetarians. In the West, ready-made paneer is now available in many supermarkets. This recipe comes from Yogesh Arora of the famous Tiffin Room at Raffles Hotel in Singapore.

SERVES 4   PREPARATION TIME: 10 MINUTES

TOOLS
Knife
Chopping board
Karahi

INGREDIENTS
2 tbsp vegetable oil
1 small onion, chopped
1 tsp chopped or minced garlic
1 tsp chopped or minced
   fresh root ginger
1 large fresh green chilli,
   chopped

600g (1¼lb) spinach
   leaves, chopped
2 tbsp butter
2 tbsp single (light whipping)
   cream
¼ tsp ground white pepper
pinch of ground cardamom
pinch of garam masala (see
   page 128)
200g (7oz) paneer (Indian curd
   cheese), cubed
salt

1 Heat the oil in a saucepan over a medium heat, and sauté the onion for a few minutes until soft and golden brown. Add the garlic, and sauté for a further 1 minute, then add the chopped ginger and green chilli, and cook for a further 2 minutes.

2 Add the spinach, then the butter, cream, pepper, cardamom, garam masala and some salt.

3 Mix in the paneer, and stir over a medium heat for about 2 minutes until the cheese is heated through. Adjust the seasoning to taste, and serve immediately.

ROOPA GULATI watermelon curry with mint

Fresh and invigorating, this fruity curry from food writer and television chef Roopa Gulati is as healthy as it is tasty. Spiked with chilli and sweetened with toasted fennel seeds, it is best served with a mound of white rice.

SERVES 4   PREPARATION TIME: 30 MINUTES

TOOLS

Vegetable knife
Blender or food processor
Large karahi or saucepan

INGREDIENTS

½ small watermelon, about
  2kg (4½lb)
1 tsp paprika
¼ tsp ground turmeric
½ tsp dried mint
½ tsp garam masala (see
  page 128)
1 fresh green chilli, deseeded
  and chopped
3cm (1¼in) piece of fresh root
  ginger, chopped
2 tbsp vegetable oil
2 tsp fennel seeds
juice of ½ lime
1 tbsp shredded mint leaves

1 Cut the skin and pith away from the watermelon, remove any seeds and roughly cube the flesh.

2 Put half of the watermelon in a blender or food processor, and add the paprika, turmeric, dried mint, garam masala, green chilli and ginger. Blend until smooth, and set aside.

3 Heat the oil in a karahi or large saucepan set over a medium heat. Toss in the fennel seeds, and swirl around in the oil for a few seconds until they darken. Add the spiced watermelon purée. Bring to a boil, reduce the heat slightly and simmer for about 10 minutes until syrupy.

4 Add the remaining watermelon cubes to the hot sauce, and warm through. Sharpen with the lime juice, and scatter over the shredded mint.

tiffins and serving items

Mumbai is famous for its tiffins. After vegetables and curries have been cooked, lunches are carried in tightly lidded stacked tins to offices across the city. When it comes to tableware, stainless steel is the preferred material. Although relatively expensive, it does not react to the acid in tangy Indian pickles.

1 TIFFIN CARRIERS

The term 'tiffin' was coined by the British while they were in India and was used to denote a light midday meal that may have included shepherd's pie and trifle for dessert. Today, tiffin boxes are a stacked tower of stainless-steel containers filled with home-made chapatis or rice, lentils, vegetable curry and perhaps a meat dish. Tiffin deliveries in Mumbai have grown into a lucrative business. After lunches have been made at home, meals are collected by tiffin boys, who then deliver thousands of hot meals to offices in the city. So successful is the industry that the delivery boys have formed their own trade union.

2 3 LUNCH BOXES

Many school children take these small boxes to school because they are just the right size to hold a midmorning snack. They often have built-in trays for holding pickles and relishes. Although plastic boxes are gaining popularity, these steel boxes continue to be chosen in India for their durability.

4 PICKLE SERVER

These stainless-steel sets with tiny accompanying spoons are a familiar sight in curry houses, where they are used for serving pickles and sauces. In India, dry spices such as toasted cumin and pounded chillies may be served in them, too, for sprinkling over dishes.

5 THALI AND KATORI SETS

At Indian meals, different dishes are served together on a *thali* (steel plate), in separate *katoris* (bowls). *Katoris* come in many sizes and are ideal for serving individual portions of lentils, curries, sweets and yogurt. Ceremonial *thalis* may be ornately designed and made from copper or silver, but everyday versions are usually stainless steel or aluminium.

6 7 RICE SCOOPS

Common in all Indian homes, these metal scoops are used for serving rice at the table.

small cooking tools

Implements used in an Indian kitchen are rarely chosen for their good looks; cooks are far more concerned with durability. Many of the tools pictured here are handcrafted, so appearance and quality vary with each piece. Street markets are the best places to buy such equipment at affordable prices.

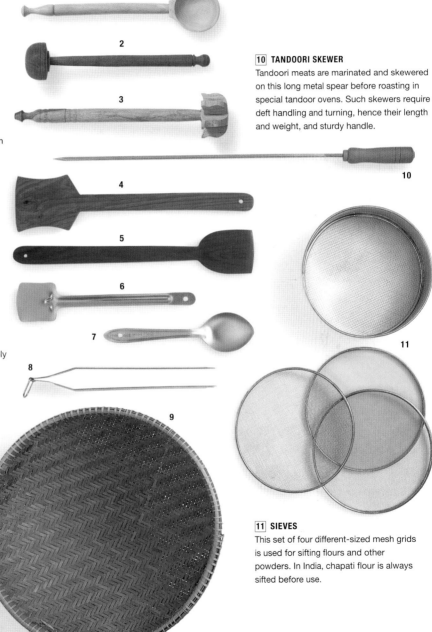

1 LONG-HANDLED SCOOP
This long wooden scoop is ideal for stirring gravies and serving soupy lentils into small dishes. As in Southeast Asia, empty coconut shell halves are used in South India as ladles and, like this model, have a stick attached that acts as the handle.

2 3 LARGE WOODEN MASHERS
Cooked vegetables such as spinach, aubergine (eggplant) and potatoes are often mashed with these fearsome-looking wooden tools. The club-shaped heads are usually grooved along the sides, which also makes them invaluable churners for yogurt-based drinks such as *lassi*, and home-made butter.

4 5 WOODEN SPATULAS
These flat wooden tools are a versatile addition to the kitchen, and may be used in the same manner as wooden spoons.

6 STEEL SPATULA
A very thin flat spatula, this tool is good for turning fried eggs and flipping delicate *dosa*.

7 STEEL BASTING SPOON
Some Indian chefs favour these comparatively flat spoons for cooking curries.

8 TONGS
Many cooking pots such as *patilas* do not have handles, so tongs are often used to remove them from the stove top. A pair of tongs is also an invaluable tool for turning chapatis while they cook on a griddle.

9 ROUND WINNOWING BASKET OF WOVEN PALM LEAVES
In rural India, rice and other grains are winnowed after harvesting to separate the chaff from the grain. Small amounts are placed in the basket (or a flat tray of similar materials), and gently tossed in the air.

10 TANDOORI SKEWER
Tandoori meats are marinated and skewered on this long metal spear before roasting in special tandoor ovens. Such skewers require deft handling and turning, hence their length and weight, and sturdy handle.

11 SIEVES
This set of four different-sized mesh grids is used for sifting flours and other powders. In India, chapati flour is always sifted before use.

ROOPA GULATI keralan fish curry

The sun-kissed toasted spices, creamy coconut milk and aromatic curry leaves in Roopa Gulati's homely curry celebrate the flavours of traditional South Indian cooking. Serve with a mound of fluffy basmati rice and spoonfuls of a lemony pickle.

SERVES 4   PREPARATION TIME: 45 MINUTES

TOOLS

Knife
Chopping board
Mortar and pestle
Griddle or small frying pan
    or skillet
Karahi or heavy saucepan

INGREDIENTS

2 tsp paprika
¾ tsp ground turmeric
juice of 1 lime
600g (1¼lb) turbot or other
    firm white fish fillets, cut into
    4cm (1½in) cubes
1 tsp whole black peppercorns
1 tsp coriander seeds
¼ tsp fenugreek seeds
3 dried red chillies, soaked for
    20 minutes in hot water
60ml (¼ cup) vegetable oil
1 tsp mustard seeds
2 tbsp curry leaves
1 onion, finely chopped
4 garlic cloves, shredded
4cm (1½in) piece of fresh root
    ginger, shredded
250ml (1 cup) coconut milk
To garnish
1 tbsp toasted cashew nuts
1 tbsp toasted unsweetened
    shredded coconut

1 Combine the paprika, turmeric and lime juice in a large bowl. Add the turbot, then stir to coat the fish in the marinade; leave to marinate while you make the curry base.

2 Heat a flat griddle or small frying pan over a medium heat. Toast the peppercorns, coriander seeds and fenugreek for about 1 minute until they give off a warm, spicy aroma.

3 Using a mortar and pestle, pound the toasted spices until they are finely ground. Add the soaked chillies and 2 tbsp of the soaking water; continue pounding until you have a paste. Set aside.

4 Heat the vegetable oil in a sturdy pan set over a medium heat. Toss in the mustard seeds, followed by the curry leaves. Swirl everything around for about 30 seconds, then reduce the heat to low.

5 Add the onion and soften, without colouring, for 5 minutes. Stir in the spice paste, garlic and ginger, and continue to fry for 2–3 minutes.

6 Add the fish to the pan, along with any spiced lime juice. After a minute, pour in the coconut milk. Bring to a simmer, and cook for about 5 minutes until the fish is tender.

7 Scatter the cashew nuts and coconut over the curry before serving.

lamb samosas

Perhaps the best ambassador for Pakistani and Indian cuisine abroad, samosas are versatile street snacks that may contain a variety of meat and vegetarian fillings and lend themselves to experimentation. Indian and other South Asian grocers sell ready-made samosa wrappers, but if necessary you will find that filo pastry is an acceptable substitute. Tiny samosas make great cocktail snacks.

SERVES 8   PREPARATION TIME: 45 MINUTES

TOOLS	INGREDIENTS
Small knife	400g (14oz) samosa wrappers
Chopping board	vegetable oil for deep-frying
Small pot	**For the filling**
Colander	150g (5½oz/1 small) potato
Karahi	150g mutton curry paste
Wire mesh ladle or slotted spoon	(see page 129)
	400g (14oz) lamb mince (ground lamb)

1 To make the meat filling, peel the potato, and cut into 1cm (½in) cubes; you will end up with about 1 cup. Bring a pan of water to the boil, and cook the potato for 10 minutes. Drain well, and set aside in a bowl to cool.

2 Heat the curry paste in the karahi, and stir in the lamb mince (ground lamb). Cook for 10–20 minutes over a low heat, then add the cooked potato. Stir for another 2 minutes, then transfer to a plate to cool.

3 To shape the samosas, place about 1 tbsp of meat mixture in the middle at the end of a pastry strip (above left). Dampen the edges with a little water to help them to seal. Fold a corner of the pastry over the mixture to form a triangle (above centre), then continue folding in alternate directions to give a triangular parcel (above right). Continue in this way until all the wrappers and filling have been used; keep the finished samosas covered with a clean damp cloth while you work with the remainder, to keep them moist.

4 Heat enough oil for deep-frying in the karahi. When the oil is hot, working in batches so that you don't crowd the pan, deep-fry the samosas for a few minutes until crisp and golden brown on both sides. Remove with a wire mesh ladle or slotted spoon, and drain on kitchen paper. Serve hot.

ROOPA GULATI lamb biryani

According to Roopa Gulati, true biryanis are the ultimate party dish and showcase the very best of Moghul cooking. This elegant North Indian classic combines the fragrance of basmati rice with home-ground garam masala and meltingly tender pieces of lamb.

SERVES 6–8 PREPARATION TIME: 2 HOURS, PLUS 1 HOUR'S MARINATING

TOOLS

Knife
Chopping board
Mortar and pestle
Food processor
Grater
2 large casseroles
Large saucepan
Colander

INGREDIENTS

½ tsp saffron threads
¾ tsp cardamom seeds
2 mace blades
4 onions
90ml (⅓ cup) vegetable oil,
    plus extra for deep-frying
8cm (3½in) piece of fresh root
    ginger, peeled
6 garlic cloves, finely chopped
1 tsp chilli powder
juice of 1 lime
750g (1lb 10oz) boneless
    lamb shoulder, cut into 4cm
    (1½in) cubes
6 green cardamom pods
6 black cardamom pods
5cm (2in) piece of
    cinnamon stick
½ tsp whole cloves
2 dried bay leaves
1 tsp garam masala (see
    page 128)
3 fresh green chillies, split
    lengthways, deseeded and
    shredded
200ml (scant 1 cup) Greek-style
    yogurt
450g (2½ cups) basmati rice
handful of fresh mint leaves
30g (2 tbsp) butter

1 Soak the saffron threads in 2 tbsp hot water, and set aside until ready to use.

2 Using a mortar and pestle, pound the cardamom seeds and mace to a powder, then set aside; you'll need this later when layering up the rice and meat.

3 Slice 2 of the onions, then sprinkle them with salt and set aside for 20 minutes. Squeeze out any excess water from the onions, and pat dry with kitchen paper. Deep-fry the sliced onions in hot oil until golden, and drain on kitchen paper. Set half aside for garnishing the biryani.

4 Transfer the remaining fried onions to a food processor. Pour in 3 tbsp hot water, and purée; you should have about 2 tbsp onion paste.

5 Finely grate half of the ginger, and combine with the garlic, chilli powder and lime juice in a large bowl. Stir in the onion paste, and add the lamb. Mix everything together, and leave to marinate in the refrigerator for 1 hour.

6 Dice the 2 remaining onions. Heat the 90ml (⅓ cup) oil in a large flameproof casserole set over a medium heat, and gently fry the diced onions for 5 minutes until soft but not coloured.

7 Slice the remaining ginger into fine strips, and set aside. Add the green and black cardamom pods, cinnamon, cloves and bay leaves to the pan. Fry for about 30 seconds until you get a warm, spicy aroma.

8 Tip in the meat and its marinade, and add the garam masala, green chillies and ginger strips. Bring to a simmer, and gradually add the yogurt, a tablespoon at a time. Cover, and simmer for about 45 minutes until the lamb is tender and the masala thickened; the sauce should be well reduced and almost clinging to the meat.

9 Meanwhile, cover the rice with cold water and leave to soak for 20 minutes. Preheat the oven to 160°C/325°F/Gas 3. Ten minutes before the meat is ready, bring a large pan of salted water to the boil. Drain the rice, add to the pan and cook for 5 minutes – it should be half-cooked and still have bite to it. Drain the rice in a colander.

10 Put half of the hot meat in the bottom of a large clean casserole. Cover with half of the freshly boiled rice, and sprinkle with half of the ground cardamom and mace spice mixture and half of the mint.

11 Top with the remaining meat and rice. Scatter over the rest of the spice mix, mint leaves and the sliced browned onions that you fried in step 3. Dot the surface with the butter, and drizzle over the saffron and its soaking liquid. Cover the biryani with dampened greaseproof paper or baking parchment, and a tight-fitting lid.

12 Bake in the oven for 40 minutes until the rice is perfumed and perfectly cooked. Gently fluff up the grains with a fork, and serve the biryani hot straight from the pan.

ROOPA GULATI cinnamon masala koftas

Punjabi comfort food doesn't get better than this – meatballs spiked with astringent chillies and aromatic coriander (cilantro) are complemented by the appealing warmth of toasted cinnamon in a spicy tomato masala. Serve with plain rice or warm flat bread.

SERVES 4   PREPARATION TIME: 1 HOUR 20 MINUTES

TOOLS
Knife
Chopping board
Grater
Flameproof casserole

INGREDIENTS
3 onions
7cm (2¾in) piece of fresh root
    ginger, finely chopped
2 fresh green chillies,
    finely chopped
4 tbsp chopped coriander
    (cilantro) leaves
½ tsp ground cinnamon
500g (1lb 2oz) lamb mince
    (ground lamb)
1 egg, lightly beaten
90 ml (⅓ cup) vegetable oil
2 x 3cm (1¾in) pieces of
    cinnamon stick
1 tsp ground turmeric
¾ tsp garam masala (see
    page 128)
1 x 400g (14oz) can chopped
    tomatoes
2 tbsp Greek-style yogurt

1 To make the koftas, finely dice one of the onions and 3cm (1¼in) of the ginger. Mix the onion and ginger with the chillies, 3 tbsp of the coriander (cilantro), cinnamon and lamb. Mix in the egg to bind everything together.

2 Using wet hands, shape the spiced lamb into meatballs about 3cm (1¼in) in diameter. Set on a tray and chill, covered, for 30 minutes.

3 Heat the oil in a large flameproof casserole set over a medium heat. Fry the meatballs in batches for 3–5 minutes until sealed and browned. Remove from the casserole, and set aside on a plate while you make the masala.

4 Grate the 2 remaining onions. Add the cinnamon sticks to the casserole, still over a medium heat, and after about 30 seconds stir in the grated onions. Reduce the heat a little, and soften for 5 minutes.

5 Finely grate the remaining ginger, and add to the casserole with the turmeric and garam masala. Fry for a minute before tipping in the tomatoes. Pour in about 200ml (scant 1 cup) hot water, and bring to the boil.

6 Return the meatballs to the casserole along with any juices, reduce the heat and gently simmer for 20 minutes until cooked through.

7 Drizzle the yogurt over the koftas, and garnish with rest of the chopped coriander before serving.

vadai with green coconut chutney

Vadai are a South Indian speciality, and come in several variations ranging from semolina and potato *vadai* to the urad dal–based *vadai* given here. Rather like savoury doughnuts, their cake-like texture and earthy flavours are set off perfectly here by the accompanying fresh coconut chutney.

SERVES 4–6   PREPARATION TIME: 30 MINUTES, PLUS 2 HOURS' SOAKING

TOOLS
Colander
Mortar and pestle
Karahi or heavy frying pan
Blender or food processor
Vadai maker (or shape by hand)
Heavy pot

INGREDIENTS
200g (1 cup) skinned and split urad dal (white lentils or skinned and split black lentils)
1 tbsp vegetable oil, plus extra for deep-frying
3 fresh green chillies, deseeded and finely chopped
2 garlic cloves, finely chopped
2 onions, finely chopped
10–12 curry leaves

300g (10oz/scant 2 cups) cooked chickpeas (garbanzo beans), rinsed and drained
1 small bunch of fresh coriander (cilantro) leaves, chopped, plus extra, to garnish
100g (⅔ cup) rice or chickpea flour (besan or gram flour)
2 tsp garam masala (see page 128)
1 tsp asafoetida powder
½ tsp baking powder
sea salt and freshly ground black pepper
Green coconut chutney
6 tbsp grated fresh coconut or 8 tbsp flaked coconut
4 tbsp fried gram dal (chana dal), picked over and rinsed

6 fresh green chillies
1 small bunch of fresh coriander (cilantro) leaves
1cm (½in) piece of fresh root ginger, finely shredded
marble-sized piece of tamarind pulp, seeds removed
sea salt
For tempering
2 tsp vegetable oil
1 tbsp brown mustard seeds
1 tsp cumin seeds
1 tsp skinned and split urad dal (white lentils or skinned and split black lentils), picked over and rinsed
1 fresh red chilli, sliced
½ tsp asafoetida powder
a few curry leaves

1 To make the *vadai*, put the urad dal in a bowl, cover with cold water and soak for 2 hours. Drain in a colander, then rinse under cold running water. Leave to drain again completely.

2 Meanwhile, make the green coconut chutney. Using a mortar and pestle, pound the coconut, fried gram dal, chillies, coriander, ginger and tamarind to a rough paste, adding a little water – just enough to loosen the paste. Alternatively, use a blender or food processor. Season with salt, and transfer to a small serving bowl.

3 To temper the spices for the chutney, heat the oil in a karahi or heavy frying pan over a high heat. Add the spices, chilli and curry leaves, and fry until the mustard seeds start to pop. Add to the chutney paste, and mix thoroughly. Set aside until needed.

4 To finish making the *vadai*, heat the 1 tbsp oil in a clean karahi or heavy pan over a medium-high heat. Fry the green chilli for about 2 minutes until fragrant, then add the garlic and cook for another 30 seconds or so. Add the onion and curry leaves, and continue to fry for 4–5 minutes until the onion is soft and starting to caramelize. Remove from the heat.

5 Put the drained urad dal, chickpeas (garbanzo beans), onion mixture, and half the coriander (cilantro) in a blender or food processor. Blend until almost smooth, but still with a little texture. Transfer to a bowl. Add the rice or chickpea flour, garam masala, asafoetida, baking powder and the remaining chopped coriander. Mix together, and season with salt and black pepper. The batter should be very thick, to stand up to shaping and deep-frying.

6 If you do not have a *vadai* maker, you can shape the *vadai* with your hands. Working as quickly and lightly as possible, take a ladleful of batter, and place it on the palm of one hand. Wet your other hand with a little water, and use to flatten the batter slightly; you should end up with a disc about 4cm (1¾in) in diameter. Continue until you have used all the batter, placed each uncooked vadai on a sheet of cling film (plastic wrap) as you go. Press a hole in the centre of each ball with your little finger, so that it shaped like a doughnut.

7 In a large heavy pan, heat enough oil for deep-frying to 180°C/350°F. Test that the oil is hot enough by dropping in a little of the batter – it should sizzle immediately and turn brown within about 40 seconds. If you are using a *vadai* maker, simply fill it with the batter, and press down on the plunger to make the individual *vadai*. Cooking in batches and making sure not to crowd the pan, deep-fry the *vadai* for 2–3 minutes until crisp and golden brown on the outside. Serve hot with the fresh coconut chutney in a small bowl on the side.

fruit-flavoured lassi

More than just a drink, Indian lassi is a real coolant, a yogurt beverage similar to a milkshake, and the best way to quell the fire of a hot spicy curry. Plain versions (usually diluted with chilled water) come salted or sweet, with a hint of cardamom, but fruit-flavoured lassi made with yogurt is increasingly popular. If you prefer not to make your own yogurt, choose a mild live yogurt such as bio-yogurt, which is good for the digestive system. Most Indian and other Asian stores sell ready-puréed mango, and whole jackfruit and lychees canned in their own juice are available in Asian grocers.

To make enough mango, jackfruit or lychee lassi for 4 people, purchase at least 650g (1¼lb) canned fruit in its own juice. Set aside a few small pieces of fruit to use as a garnish, then purée the remaining fruit with the juice from the can. In a large bowl, whisk 500ml (2 cups) plain yogurt until creamy, then blend in the fruit purée. Chill thoroughly. To serve, pour into tall glasses, add a little crushed ice, dilute with a little milk (if liked) and garnish with the reserved fruit. For a tangy variation common in South India, use buttermilk in place of yogurt.

CAMELLIA PANJABI saffron and cardamom kulfi

A favourite Indian dessert, kulfi is an ice cream traditionally made by reducing the milk over a gentle heat for a very long time; however, it is also easy to make with evaporated milk. This recipe comes from Camellia Panjabi, who is one of India's most respected restaurateurs and cookery writers, as well as a director of the United Kingdom's prestigious Masala Zone group.

SERVES 4   PREPARATION TIME: 45 MINUTES, PLUS FREEZING TIME

TOOLS
Kulfi moulds
Small heavy pot
Wooden spoon

INGREDIENTS
2 x 410g (14oz) cans
    evaporated milk
4 tbsp sugar
3 green cardamom pods

12 saffron threads
3 tbsp double (heavy whipping)
    cream
2 sheets silver leaf,
    to decorate (optional)

1 Pour the evaporated milk into a heavy saucepan. Add the sugar and cardamom pods, and cook over a low heat for 10 minutes, stirring and scraping the sides and bottom of the pan continuously with a wooden spoon.

2 Remove the pan from the heat, and discard the cardamom pods before adding the saffron. Mix well, and leave to cool before stirring in the cream.

3 Fill the kulfi moulds, cover and freeze for 4–5 hours.

4 To remove the kulfi from the moulds, briefly dip each one into hot water, and press out the kulfi. Decorate with silver leaf, if liked, for festive occasions.

indochina

including thailand, vietnam, laos, burma and cambodia

The Buddhist culture of Indochina has Hindu roots and dates back over some 3000 years to the days when India began trading with China after the Silk Road and spice routes opened. With the inevitable intermarriages among Indian, Chinese and local peoples, the resulting culinary mix has become an intriguing blend of hot, sweet, sour, aromatic and savoury flavours – often all in one dish.

indochina including thailand, vietnam, laos, burma and cambodia

For Thai cooking, in particular, the keynote is the artful blend of fresh herbs and other aromatics, which are often ground to a paste and cooked in a little oil before being combined with coconut milk, tamarind juice or stock. In addition to the world-renowned green and red curries, which have evolved from early Indian influences into uniquely light concoctions, typical dishes of Thailand include satay, fish and prawn cakes, tantalizing soups and salads zesty with lime and lemon grass. And when it comes to presentation, the Thais are masters at transforming fruits and vegetables into glorious works of sculptured edible art.

Cambodian or Khmer cuisine echoes Chinese and Thai elements, and, like Laotian cooking, tends to ride stickily on glutinous rice. The Mekong River, which runs through the region, yields abundant fish and shellfish, and these, along with vegetables, are the key ingredients, but will be augmented by free-range chickens, duck, pigeons and tiny paddy-field birds. Pork and beef are rarely used, and lamb figures rarely outside the cities, where the imported meat has a ready market in tourists. At every Cambodian meal there is a pungent dip of chillies and fish sauce. Noodle dishes are the staple fare of the rural folk, but will be enriched with fish, chicken, venison and spices. Wild mushrooms and jungle greens turn up in salads, while coconut milk is the basis of simple desserts that usually employ bananas, mangoes and other tropical fruits.

The cornerstone of Burmese meals is perfectly fluffy rice, around which is served many pickles and dips. A typical family meal will consist of rice, a hot and sour soup, fish and chicken curries, cellophane noodles, salads of leaves and indigenous greens, and always a dip of *balauchaung*, made of shrimp paste, chillies, lime juice and dried shrimp. Many dishes require little cooking; raw salads and pickles predominate.

The cuisine of Vietnam, a country which was once a French enclave, is a curious amalgam of Chinese, Thai and French cooking, with rice and rice noodles as the foundation, although French baguettes are often served with stir-fried dishes! Vietnamese fish sauce, called *nuoc mam*, is more pungent than the Thai version. The country's famous beef soups are richly aromatic with Chinese five-spice blends, but it is the noodles that truly mark Vietnamese cuisine. They feature in *pho bo*, the definitive beef noodle dish, which includes a broth that is rich with cinnamon, coriander, pepper and other fine spices. Like the Thais, the Vietnamese are extremely fond of salads, but these are certainly not boring plates of lettuce leaves. Cabbage, carrots, celery, fruits and steamed chicken, for example, will be tossed in aromatic

dressings of sesame oil, lime juice and sugar, and strewn lavishly with peanuts, mint, fresh coriander (cilantro) and chillies to give wonderfully healthy dishes bursting with vibrant, pungent flavours.

OPPOSITE 1 galangal 2 Thai mango 3 lemon grass 4 coriander (cilantro) 5 Thai holy basil (*bai kaprao*) 6 red chillies 7 coconut 8 limes 9 Thai aubergines (eggplants) 10 kaffir lime leaves 1 green bird's-eye chillies
BELOW 1 rice paper wrappers 2 black rice 3 coconut milk 4 fish sauce 5 shrimp paste 6 peanuts 7 dried shrimp 8 rice noodles 9 palm sugar

natural leaves and containers

In many parts of Asia, ingenious use is made of the local plant life in the form of wrappers, skewers, plates, containers and other natural utensils. These 'tools' are fundamental to the rustic flavour of the cuisines. A wonderfully sustainable resource, they play the dual role of being functional and imparting subtle fragrance to the food prepared. With so many Western countries now home to burgeoning Asian communities, once-exotic ingredients are now easier to find; however, they have been used in this way since long before metal made its first glimmer.

1

1 BANANA LEAVES

As large as umbrellas, subtly perfumed and extremely pliable, banana leaves are excellent for wrapping large items of food, usually whole fish for steaming, braising and grilling. Thick enough to use as disposable plates, they are used widely as such in India and Indochina, as well as the rest of Southeast Asia. Specialist stores sell them trimmed and folded; they need only a quick dip in hot water before use. Store away from cold air; otherwise they will turn yellow and brittle within a few days.

2 PINEAPPLE HALVES

Thai chefs are particularly adept at playing with this succulent tropical fruit, using the flesh as an ingredient and the shell as a highly fragrant serving dish. The remaining half of the shell is used as a lid to keep the food warm during the meal. The natural juices still in the fruit shell enhance the dish in a magical way.

3 LEMON GRASS

These grasslike plants have a heady and pervasive scent, especially at the root end. They are generally about 1cm (⅛in) thick, but when really lush can grow to twice this girth. The thin 15cm (6in) long leaves are usually discarded. Whole stems make natural lemon-scented skewers around which minced meat and seafood can be wrapped. When bruised and shredded at the root end, lemon grass becomes a basting brush with natural citric flavour. The plant's thick roots can be split and stuffed with minced food before grilling. The bottom 4cm (1¾in) or so at the root end is typically ground with other spices and herbs to make curry pastes.

2

3

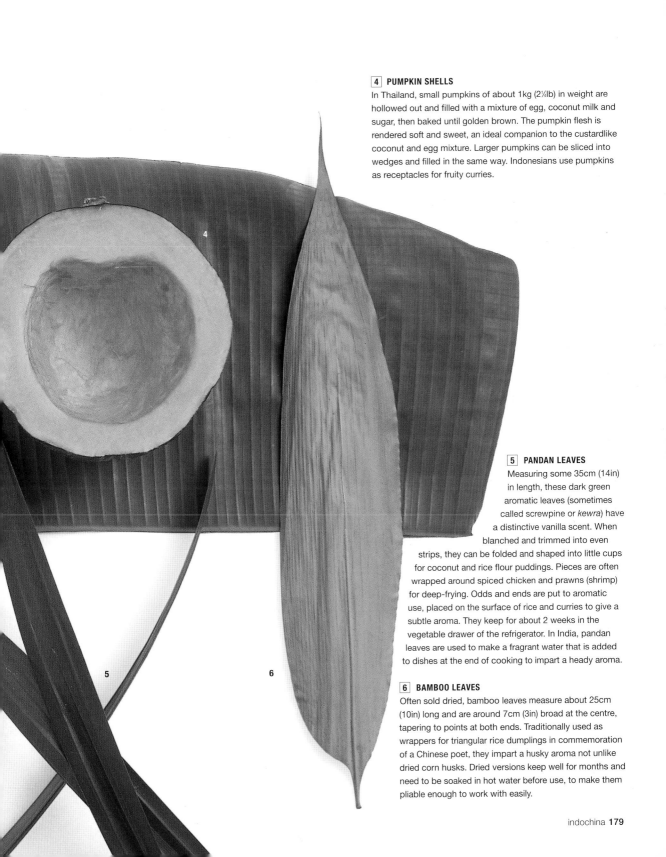

4 | PUMPKIN SHELLS

In Thailand, small pumpkins of about 1kg (2¼lb) in weight are hollowed out and filled with a mixture of egg, coconut milk and sugar, then baked until golden brown. The pumpkin flesh is rendered soft and sweet, an ideal companion to the custardlike coconut and egg mixture. Larger pumpkins can be sliced into wedges and filled in the same way. Indonesians use pumpkins as receptacles for fruity curries.

5 | PANDAN LEAVES

Measuring some 35cm (14in) in length, these dark green aromatic leaves (sometimes called screwpine or *kewra*) have a distinctive vanilla scent. When blanched and trimmed into even strips, they can be folded and shaped into little cups for coconut and rice flour puddings. Pieces are often wrapped around spiced chicken and prawns (shrimp) for deep-frying. Odds and ends are put to aromatic use, placed on the surface of rice and curries to give a subtle aroma. They keep for about 2 weeks in the vegetable drawer of the refrigerator. In India, pandan leaves are used to make a fragrant water that is added to dishes at the end of cooking to impart a heady aroma.

6 | BAMBOO LEAVES

Often sold dried, bamboo leaves measure about 25cm (10in) long and are around 7cm (3in) broad at the centre, tapering to points at both ends. Traditionally used as wrappers for triangular rice dumplings in commemoration of a Chinese poet, they impart a husky aroma not unlike dried corn husks. Dried versions keep well for months and need to be soaked in hot water before use, to make them pliable enough to work with easily.

spiced steamed fish in banana leaf

Usually served as an appetizer, these Thai fish cakes are a wondrous bundle of intoxicating flavours that could also form part of a main meal. They look impressive served in their banana leaf cups and can also be baked or barbecued.

MAKES 8   PREPARATION TIME: 35 MINUTES

TOOLS
Cleaver or sharp knife
Chopping board
Food processor
Mortar and pestle
8 fresh banana leaves, each
    about 25cm (10in) square
Cocktail sticks or toothpicks
Steamer
Heatproof steaming plate

INGREDIENTS
450g (1lb) white fish fillet, such as cod
    or halibut
2 tbsp fish sauce such as *nam pla*
2 tbsp freshly squeezed lime juice
1 tsp sugar
2 eggs, lightly beaten
4 tbsp thick coconut milk or coconut cream
sliced cucumber, to serve

For the paste
1 tbsp grated fresh root ginger
2 fresh red chillies, deseeded if liked
1 tsp ground turmeric
1 onion
2 stalks lemon grass, 5cm (2in) root end, peeled
1 tbsp ground coriander
1 tsp shrimp paste

To garnish
4 tbsp coconut cream
2 kaffir lime leaves, shredded
1 fresh red chilli, finely sliced

To make banana leaf cups   1 Using a saucer or cardboard template about 15cm (6in) in diameter, mark out a circle on each banana leaf; cut out. **2** Fold in one-side of the banana leaf circle, and turn in the corner. Secure with a cocktail stick or toothpick. **3** Fold in the next two sides, turn in the corners and secure with cocktail sticks or toothpicks. **4** Fold in the remaining side to make an open box with a flat base and tapered top. Secure with a cocktail stick or toothpick.

1 Chop the fish meat, then blend in a food processor for a few minutes to make a paste.

2 Using a mortar and pestle, grind together the paste ingredients until the texture of thick cream, then blend with the fish.

3 Transfer the mixture to a bowl, and add the fish sauce, lime juice and sugar. Stir well until combined, before adding the beaten egg and coconut milk or cream. Mix together until evenly combined.

4 Trim off and discard the hard rind on the banana leaves, and blanch the banana leaves in boiling water for 1 minute to make them more pliable; drain well. Shape the banana leaves to make 8 cups following the instructions above. Put 2 tbsp of the fish mixture in the centre of each banana leaf cup.

5 Put the parcels on a lightly oiled plate in a steamer, making sure that they do not touch each other, and steam for 10 minutes until cooked through. You may need to cook the parcels in batches.

6 To finish, drizzle a little coconut cream over each fish cake, and garnish with the kaffir lime leaves and chilli. Serve with the sliced cucumber.

Cook's tip If banana leaves are unavailable, put the fish mixture in lightly oiled ramekins, cover with foil and steam for 15 minutes. You can use 2 tbsp yellow curry paste (see page 186) instead of the spice paste, if preferred.

CHEF CHANG pineapple fried rice

The Blue Elephant restaurants, tropical hothouses of orchids and other heady blooms, are known as much for their evocative ambience as for the quintessentially Thai menu. Use the largest pineapple you can find for this recipe based on royal fried rice by Chef Chang, whose grandmother was a lady-in-waiting at the Thai royal court. His original dish uses a rather complex sauce, which can be substituted, as it has been here, with a stock (bouillon) cube.

SERVES 2 PREPARATION TIME: 35 MINUTES, PLUS OVERNIGHT CHILLING FOR RICE

TOOLS
Rice cooker
Cleaver
Small all-purpose knife
Chopping board
1 fresh pineapple for 'container'
Wok and ladle

INGREDIENTS
200g (1⅛ cups) jasmine rice
4 tbsp groundnut (peanut) or
   other vegetable oil
2 large eggs
60g (2oz) mixed red, yellow and
   green sweet peppers,
   deseeded and finely diced
   (about ½ cup chopped)

2 tbsp finely diced Spanish,
   yellow or red onion
2 tbsp finely diced carrot
60g (2oz) peeled and deveined
   cooked prawns (shrimp)
60g (2oz) picked crabmeat
1 tsp salt
½ tsp ground white pepper
½ tsp sugar
1 fish or vegetable stock
   (bouillon) cube, dissolved in
   2 tbsp water
2 spring onions (scallions),
   finely sliced
2 tbsp finely chopped cucumber
2 tbsp chopped fresh ripe
   tomato
fresh coriander (cilantro) leaves,
   to garnish (optional)

1 Cook the rice in a rice cooker. Drain, allow to cool quickly and leave to chill overnight.

2 Cut the pineapple in half lengthways. With a small knife, cut deep into the sides of each half, about 1cm (½in) in from the skin. Cut all around the fruit and right down the middle core, keeping 1cm (½in) away from the skin. Make small cuts across, and lift out chunks of the pineapple flesh. (You can reserve the chunks for another use or simply eat fresh.) Scoop out the remaining bits of flesh with a spoon, leaving a smooth oval-shaped container.

3 Rake the cold cooked rice for a few minutes to loosen the grains. Heat the oil in a wok until very hot. Break in the eggs, and scramble lightly. Add the rice, and stir-fry for 2 minutes.

4 Add the diced peppers, onion, carrot, prawns (shrimp) and crabmeat, and stir-fry for 1 minute. Add the seasonings, sugar and stock, and mix well. Toss in the spring onions (scallions), and stir briefly, then remove the wok from the heat.

5 Carefully spoon the fried rice mixture into the pineapple shells, and scatter with the cucumber and tomato. Garnish with some fresh coriander (cilantro) leaves, if liked, before serving.

bamboo leaf dumplings

Originating in China, these dumplings have become staple snack fare throughout Indochina, each region and food vendor having their own version of the spicy filling. Dried bamboo leaves are sold in Asian grocers and food stores, and need to be blanched in boiling water before use to make them pliable.

SERVES 4   PREPARATION TIME: 2 HOURS, PLUS OVERNIGHT SOAKING FOR RICE

TOOLS

Cleaver
Chopping board
Small pot
Colander
Mortar and pestle
Wok and ladle
Bamboo leaves
Kitchen string
Large pot
Pair of wooden tongs

INGREDIENTS

400g (14oz) lean boneless pork,
    cut into 1cm (½in) cubes
3 tbsp finely chopped onion
2 tbsp finely chopped garlic
2 tbsp groundnut (peanut) or
    other vegetable oil
2 tbsp ground coriander
1 tbsp ground cumin
1 tbsp sugar
2 tsp salt
800g (4 cups) glutinous
    rice, soaked overnight

1 Put the pork in a pot of boiling water for 1–2 minutes to part-cook. Drain.

2 Using a mortar and pestle, grind the onion and garlic to a purée. Heat the oil in a wok over a medium heat, and fry the purée for 4 minutes. Add the drained pork, and stir-fry for 2 minutes.

3 Sprinkle in the coriander, cumin, sugar and salt, and stir-fry for 2 minutes. Add 200ml (scant 1 cup) water, and cook over a high heat until the mixture is almost dry but still moist. Transfer to a plate, and allow to cool.

4 Blanch the bamboo leaves in a pot of boiling water to soften, then drain. Drain the glutinous rice.

5 Fold a bamboo leaf in two, making a triangular container with a long back from 2 leaf ends. Place 1 tbsp rice on the bamboo leaf, press on 1 tbsp pork mixture and cover with another 1 tbsp rice. Fold over both leaf ends to make a pyramid-shaped dumpling. Hold each dumpling firmly while wrapping a piece of kitchen string twice around it, and tie firmly to secure. Leave a tail of string at least 20cm (8in) long, to make it easier to remove the cooked dumplings from the pot using a pair of tongs.

6 Bring a large pot of water to the boil, add the dumplings and simmer for 1 hour; lift out and drain. To serve, cut the string from the dumplings and discard. Take the dumplings to the table still in their wrappers, where diners can unwrap the leaves themselves to get to the dumplings inside.

spiced chicken in toei leaves

Toei leaves, as they are called in Thailand, are known as pandan leaves elsewhere in tropical Asia and the botanical name is screwpine leaf. They are available fresh in most Chinese and Thai supermarkets, and their fragrance is faintly reminiscent of vanilla. They also yield a rich jade-green juice when ground.

MAKES 15   PREPARATION TIME: 20 MINUTES, PLUS 30 MINUTES' MARINATING

TOOLS
Sharp knife
Chopping board
About 8 *toei* leaves
Cocktail sticks or toothpicks
Wok and slotted spoon

INGREDIENTS
500g (1lb 2oz) skinless chicken
   breast fillets
2 tbsp yellow curry paste
   (see page 186)
2 tbsp fish sauce such as *nam pla*
1 tbsp freshly squeezed lime juice
1 tsp sugar
groundnut (peanut), corn or other
   vegetable oil, for deep-frying

1 Cut the chicken into fifteen 4cm (1¾in) cubes. Mix together the curry paste, fish sauce, lime juice and sugar in a shallow glass or ceramic dish, add the chicken and turn until coated in the marinade. Cover the dish, and leave to marinate in the refrigerator for 30 minutes.

2 Trim each *toei* leaf so that you end up with 15 strips in total, each about 15cm (6in) long and 4cm (1¾in) wide. Wrap a *toei* leaf around each piece of chicken, overlapping once. Tuck in the end firmly to make a triangular shape, and secure with a cocktail stick or toothpick. Trim off any excess leaf.

3 Heat enough oil for deep-frying in a wok. When the oil is hot, cooking in batches, fry the chicken parcels for 5–6 minutes until cooked. Remove using a slotted spoon, and drain on kitchen paper.

4 Serve the chicken parcels in their leafy wrappers, allowing diners to unwrap them at the table, or remove the leaves and arrange the spicy chicken on a warm serving plate.

grinding implements

These mortar and pestle sets are different not merely for aesthetic reasons; each has specific purposes. Indochina's uniquely shaped terra-cotta model is meant for processing delicate fresh herbs and spices for salad making. The stronger granite version is the one needed for pounding pungent curry pastes from firm fresh ingredients such as candlenuts, galangal, garlic and chillies.

1 GRANITE MORTAR AND PESTLE

A granite mortar can withstand the heavy pounding needed to produce fine fresh curry pastes. To use, prepare all the ingredients, and put them in individual bowls, ensuring that the foods are dry to the touch. Start with drier items such as candlenuts and garlic, before moving on to those that will splatter. Always grind a small amount at a time. With a regular thumping and circular motion, grind the spices on the bottom and sides of the mortar. Keep a spoon handy to scrape down the bits that rise up the sides of the mortar and, when done, use a spoon to scrape up every last bit of paste.

2 TERRA-COTTA MORTAR AND PESTLE

The pestle accompanying the tall terra-cotta mortar is a large wooden club, about 30cm (12in) long. It does a gentle bashing job, rather than grinding foods, so it is not effective for pounding hard ingredients to a paste or powder; however, the mortar's depth and size mean that, after a salad dressing has been made in it, the other salad ingredients can be tossed and turned there, too, without the need for a separate bowl. Wash in hot soapy water, then turn upside down and leave to dry before storing. Looked after properly, one of these will last several lifetimes.

1

2

thai curry pastes

The principles behind the preparation of Indochinese spice pastes remain constant – only the ingredients differ. These pastes, the basis of all curries and spicy side dishes, are ground to the required consistency using a granite mortar and pestle. Unlike an electric blender or food processor, this rustic tool can be manipulated at will for coarse, fine or puréed pastes. Grinding by hand naturally takes longer, but gives a curry of delicious toothsome quality and allows the cook to adjust specific quantities of fresh ingredients bit by bit, according to their fragrance.

masaman curry paste

This paste combination hails from southern Thailand, where many Thai Muslims live, and has evolved from a mix of Thai-Malaysian origins.

MAKES ABOUT 200G (7OZ) PASTE

(illustrated on page 187)

Cook's tip When using, 1 tbsp fresh curry paste is sufficient for 450g (1lb) meat, poultry or seafood.

INGREDIENTS

2 tbsp ground coriander
1 tbsp ground cumin
1 tsp ground turmeric
1 tbsp chilli powder
2 tbsp chopped onions
4 garlic cloves, chopped
4 thin slices galangal, chopped
1 tbsp shrimp paste
120ml (½ cup) vegetable oil

1 In a dry frying pan, roast the coriander, cumin, turmeric and chilli powder over a low heat for 8 minutes until fragrant.

2 Using a mortar and pestle, grind the onions, garlic, galangal and shrimp paste until fine and creamy in consistency. Mix with the roasted spices.

3 Heat the oil in a frying pan, and fry the paste over a medium-low heat for 10 minutes, stirring continuously. The paste will absorb most of the oil during frying; when the oil begins to separate again, the paste is ready.

4 Remove from the heat, and allow to cool. Transfer to an airtight jar, and use as needed. Keep any excess refrigerated, well covered with cling film (plastic wrap) or a tight-fitting lid.

green curry paste

Thai green curry is practically a national dish, winning fans across the world with its aromatic blend of herbs and spices that marry well with meat, chicken and seafood.

MAKES ABOUT 200G (7OZ) PASTE

INGREDIENTS
2 stalks lemon grass, tough
   outer layer removed, roughly
   chopped
2 slices galangal, about 5mm
   (¼in) thick, chopped
4 fresh green chillies,
   roughly chopped
1 tsp whole black peppercorns

3 tbsp chopped coriander
   (cilantro) roots, stalks and
   leaves
1 tbsp shrimp paste
3 kaffir lime leaves
2 tbsp chopped onions
4 garlic cloves, chopped
120ml (½ cup) vegetable oil

1 Using a mortar and pestle, grind the lemon grass, galangal, chillies and coriander (cilantro) to a paste. Gradually add the remaining ingredients, except the oil, a little at a time so as not to overcrowd the mortar. Keep grinding until you have a fine, almost creamy paste.

2 Heat the oil in a wok or frying pan, and fry the paste over a medium-low heat for 10 minutes, stirring continuously. The paste will absorb most of the oil during frying; when it begins to separate again, the paste is ready.

3 Remove from the heat, and allow to cool. Transfer to an airtight jar, and use as needed, keeping any excess in the refrigerator, well covered with cling film (plastic wrap) or a tight-fitting lid.

yellow curry paste

This distinctive paste clearly shows close ties with Malaysian and Burmese curries in its use of turmeric.

MAKES ABOUT 220G (8OZ) PASTE

INGREDIENTS
6 dried red chillies
2 tbsp ground coriander
1 tsp ground cumin
50g (1¾oz) fresh turmeric
   or 1 tsp ground
1 large onion, sliced
2 stalks lemon grass, tough
   outer layer removed,
   roughly chopped

1 tbsp chopped galangal
4 garlic cloves, chopped
1 tbsp shrimp paste
1 tsp salt
120ml (½ cup) vegetable oil

1 Soak the dried chillies in hot water until softened, then drain and slice. Meanwhile, roast the coriander and cumin in a dry frying pan over a low heat for about 8 minutes until fragrant.

2 Using a mortar and pestle, grind all the other ingredients, except the salt and oil, as you would for the green curry paste, until the paste is fine and creamy in consistency. Mix with the roasted spices and salt.

3 Heat the oil in a frying pan, and fry the paste over a medium-low heat for 10 minutes, stirring continuously. The paste will absorb most of the oil during frying; when the oil begins to separate again, the paste is ready.

4 Remove from the heat, and allow to cool. Transfer to an airtight jar, and use as needed, keeping any excess in the refrigerator, well covered with cling film (plastic wrap) or a tight-fitting lid.

red curry paste

This well-known spice paste's versatility means that it lends itself to meat, seafood and vegetables alike.

MAKES ABOUT 220G (8OZ) PASTE

INGREDIENTS
10 dried red chillies
2 tbsp ground coriander
1 tsp ground cumin
1 tsp whole black peppercorns
1 onion, sliced
2 stalks lemon grass, tough
   outer layer removed, chopped
1 tbsp chopped galangal

4 garlic cloves, chopped
4 kaffir lime leaves, sliced
1 tbsp shrimp paste
1 tsp salt
120ml (½ cup) vegetable oil

1 Soak the dried chillies in hot water until softened, then drain and slice. Meanwhile, roast the coriander and cumin in a dry frying pan over a medium-low heat for about 8 minutes until fragrant.

2 Using a mortar and pestle, grind the soaked chillies, peppercorns, onion, lemon grass and galangal to a paste. Add the garlic, kaffir lime leaves and shrimp paste, a little at a time. Keep grinding until you have a fine, almost creamy paste. Mix with the roasted spices and salt.

3 Heat the oil in a wok or frying pan, and fry the paste over a low heat for 10 minutes, stirring constantly. The paste will absorb most of the oil during frying; when the oil begins to separate again, the paste is ready

4 Remove from the heat, and allow to cool. Transfer to an airtight jar, and use as needed. Keep any excess in the refrigerator, well covered with cling film (plastic wrap) or a tight-fitting lid.

Green curry paste

Masaman curry paste

Yellow curry paste

Red curry paste

DAVID THOMPSON
green curry with fish dumplings and aubergine

Having first come to prominence at his former Sydney restaurant Darley Street Thai, David Thompson is today recognized by the Thai government as one of the world's leading experts on Royal Thai cuisine. His knowledge is manifest in his menu at Nahm, Europe's first Michelin-starred Thai restaurant, in London's Halkin Hotel, where this mouth-watering dish features. You can use an oilier fish to make the dumplings, but will need to adjust the flavour balance of the sauce.

SERVES 4   PREPARATION TIME: 30 MINUTES

TOOLS
Cleaver
Chopping board
Mortar and pestle
Large pot
Wire mesh strainer
Saucepan

INGREDIENTS
For the fish dumplings
3 coriander (cilantro) roots, chopped
pinch of salt
1 tbsp chopped wild ginger
5 white peppercorns
200g (7oz) pike or walleye, or monkfish fillets
2 tbsp fish sauce such as *nam pla*, or light soy sauce
a little palm sugar
1 stalk lemon grass, crushed
For the curry
500ml (2 cups) coconut cream
3 tbsp green curry paste (see page 186)
a little chicken stock or extra coconut milk
fish sauce such as *nam pla*, to taste
fresh chillies such as bird's-eye, finely chopped, to taste
500ml (2 cups) coconut milk
3–4 Thai or apple aubergines (eggplants), quartered
2 kaffir lime leaves
a few long fresh green and red chillies, deseeded and cut into julienne, to garnish
a handful of fresh Thai basil leaves
a little shredded wild ginger

1 To make the fish dumplings, using a mortar and pestle, pound the coriander (cilantro) roots with the pinch of salt, wild ginger and peppercorns until fine in texture. Transfer to a large bowl, and clean out the mortar.

2 Put the fish in the mortar, and pound until smooth. Add to the bowl, and work the mixture into a ball. Pick up the ball, and throw it back into the bowl. Repeat several times to develop the flavour and firm up the flesh. Season with fish sauce or light soy sauce, and some palm sugar.

3 Roll and pinch portions of the fish mixture between your fingertips to give dumplings of about 2cm (¾in) in diameter. Bring a pot of salted water to the boil, and add the crushed lemon grass. Reduce the heat and, working in batches if necessary, gently poach the dumplings for about 2 minutes. Drain and set aside.

4 Meanwhile, in a saucepan, bring the coconut cream to a boil, and boil until it separates. Reduce the heat to medium, and add the green curry paste. Cook for 4 minutes, adding some chicken stock or extra coconut milk if needed, until the curry looks like scrambled eggs. Add a little fish sauce and chillies to taste.

5 Stir in the coconut milk, and return to the boil. Add the aubergines (eggplants), and cook for 3 minutes. Just before serving, add the fish dumplings, kaffir lime leaves, julienned green and red chillies, Thai basil and wild ginger. Serve hot.

chicken and lemon grass curry

In the tradition of Thai yellow curries, this dish is highly aromatic, thanks to the addition of lemon grass, basil and kaffir lime leaves. It is also extremely easy to prepare.

SERVES 4   PREPARATION TIME: 25 MINUTES

TOOLS
Cleaver
Chopping board
Wok and ladle

INGREDIENTS
2 skinless chicken breast fillets, about 250g (9oz) in total
2 tbsp groundnut (peanut) or other vegetable oil
2 stalks lemon grass, tough outer layer removed, thinly sliced
1 large onion, thinly sliced
400ml (1⅔ cups) coconut milk
2 tbsp tamarind paste
1 tbsp palm sugar
2 tbsp yellow curry paste (see page 186)
3 kaffir lime leaves

1 Cut the chicken into bite-sized pieces, discarding any fatty skin and gristle.

2 Heat half of the oil in a wok, and sauté the chicken over a high heat for 3 minutes until golden. Drain on kitchen paper, and set aside to keep warm.

3 Heat the remaining oil in the wok, and stir-fry the lemon grass and onion for 2 minutes until soft and fragrant.

4 Stir in the coconut milk, tamarind paste, palm sugar and yellow curry paste, and simmer gently for 5 minutes. Return the sautéed chicken to the wok, and simmer the curry for a further 10 minutes. Serve hot with noodles or jasmine rice.

Cook's tip Sautéing the chicken separately first is a traditional cooking method, but you can omit this step with only a marginal difference to the taste of the finished dish. Simply add the chicken in step 3, and cook for 3 minutes.

masaman lamb curry

Often called Muslim curry (the word *masaman* is thought to derive from an older Thai word meaning 'Muslim'), this dish is typical of southern Thai cooking, where the region nudges northern Malaysia. Here, the population is largely Muslim and, over centuries, has had influence upon the culinary mores of its neighbour. Malaysian cuisine has itself been heavily influenced by early Indian, Arab and Persian traders.

SERVES 4   PREPARATION TIME: 45 MINUTES

TOOLS
Cleaver
Chopping board
Wok and ladle

INGREDIENTS
2 tbsp groundnut (peanut) oil
1 large onion, sliced
2 tbsp masaman curry paste
  (see page 185)
500ml (2 cups) coconut milk
500g (1lb 2oz) lean boneless
  lamb, cut into bite-sized cubes
2 tbsp fish sauce such as
  nam pla
2 tbsp freshly squeezed
  lime juice
1 tsp sugar
100g (3½oz) Thai or ordinary
  aubergines (eggplants)
  (or use a mixture of Thai
  and pea aubergines)
2 tbsp chopped Thai basil,
  plus extra leaves,
  to garnish

1 Heat the oil in a wok over a low heat, and fry the onions for about 5 minutes until soft but not coloured. Blend the curry paste with a little of the coconut milk, and add to the wok. Increase the heat to medium, and fry for 1 minute until fragrant.

2 Now add the lamb, and stir-fry vigorously for 3 minutes. Reserve 1 tbsp of the coconut milk for garnishing, and tip the rest into the wok with the fish sauce, lime juice and sugar. Reduce the heat to low, and leave to simmer for 20 minutes.

3 If using Thai aubergines (eggplants), slice each aubergine in half; if using large purple ones, cut into 1cm (½in) wide half-moon pieces. Pea aubergines can be left whole. Add to the wok, and simmer for 5 minutes over a high heat.

4 Just before serving, sprinkle over the basil. As a typical Thai flourish, pour the reserved coconut milk in a swirl on top of the curry, garnish with some extra basil leaves and serve immediately.

DARANEE COBHAM hot and sour fish curry

Monaco's Royal Thai has won itself many devotees since opening as the first Thai restaurant in the principality. It draws a celebrity clientele, including Prince Albert of Monaco and the singer Shirley Bassey. Daranee Cobham has steered the restaurant to its success with her distinctive menu of mainly Royal Thai dishes. This recipe, known as *kaeng som*, is typical of southern Thailand and is a richer cousin of the popular *tom yam kung* (hot and sour seafood soup).

SERVES 4   PREPARATION TIME: 30 MINUTES

TOOLS
Cleaver
Chopping board
Mortar and pestle
Medium pot

INGREDIENTS
4 sea bass or other meaty
    fish fillets
1 tsp salt
2 tbsp freshly squeezed
    lemon juice
1 tbsp tamarind concentrate
1 tbsp fish sauce such as
    nam pla
1 tsp sugar
1 stalk lemon grass (use 5cm
    (2in) of the root end), bruised
200g (7oz) fresh pineapple,
    cut into cubes (about
    1¼ cups chopped)

For the spice paste
2 garlic cloves, roughly chopped
5 dried red chillies
½ tsp salt
30g (1oz) fresh turmeric,
    roughly chopped
2 stalks lemon grass, tough
    outer layer removed, roughly
    chopped
40g (1½oz) shrimp paste

To garnish
fresh Thai sweet basil leaves
finely chopped fresh red chilli

1 Rinse the fish fillets, and pat dry with kitchen paper. Rub all over with the salt, and set aside. Blend together the lemon juice, tamarind concentrate and 200ml (scant 1 cup) water. Pour into a medium pot.

2 To make the spice paste, using a mortar and pestle, grind the garlic, red chillies, salt, turmeric, lemon grass and shrimp paste to a fine smooth paste. Add to the pot with the fish sauce, sugar and bruised lemon grass. Bring to the boil, reduce the heat slightly and simmer for 5 minutes.

3 Lastly, add the fish fillets and pineapple, and simmer for 5–8 minutes until done. Check the seasoning, and serve hot, garnished with basil leaves and red chilli.

scaling, shredding and carving

Many small jobs in the Indochinese kitchen are not small in importance because the way an ingredient is prepared has a major impact on the texture and presentation of a dish. This is most evident in Thai cooking, where salads may be given an artful touch by shredding or carving the ingredients so that the dish both looks and tastes glorious. Good cooks also prefer to do their own processing of fresh seafood, and this is performed with specific tools to make the job much easier.

1 FISH SCALER
This simple but effective tool comprises a wooden handle attached at one end to a serrated metal blade, which is bent into a U-shape. The sharp teeth make short work of scaling fresh fish.

2 DUAL-PURPOSE SLICER AND SHREDDER
Mounted on a wooden handle, this tool makes a fine job of cutting wafer-thin slices of firm fruits and vegetables; the serrated edge on the blade is used for producing fine shreds.

3 VEGETABLE SHREDDER
Suitable for either right- or left-handed people, this swivel-bladed gadget makes fine strands of fruits and vegetables, as well as very thin slices.

4 FRUIT AND VEGETABLE CARVING SET
Looking rather like a tool kit for dentists or surgeons, this collection of specialized blades is available in various sizes in Thai stores and supermarkets. Once the preserve of the royal kitchens, the carving of fruit and vegetables into intricate floral shapes is a skill of which Thai chefs are particularly proud, and the results of their labours are often found adorning lavish buffet tables. The tips of these tools may be either curved or pointed to near-needle sharpness, for making the necessary nicks in melons and root vegetables that are meant to mimic the delicate petals of a flower. Dexterity is enhanced by holding the tools close to the blade while carving. The sharp ends can be poked into a cork for safety when not in use.

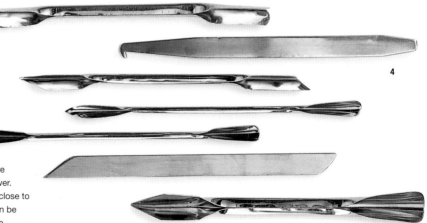

shaped cutters and moulds

The special moulds and other tools for making the bewildering range of Indochinese sweetmeats and snacks have evolved over centuries. Originally made from natural materials such as wood or bamboo, they are today available in light metals. Many are shaped to echo the symbolism rife in ancient Asian cultures, or are designed to make intricate patterns of great beauty.

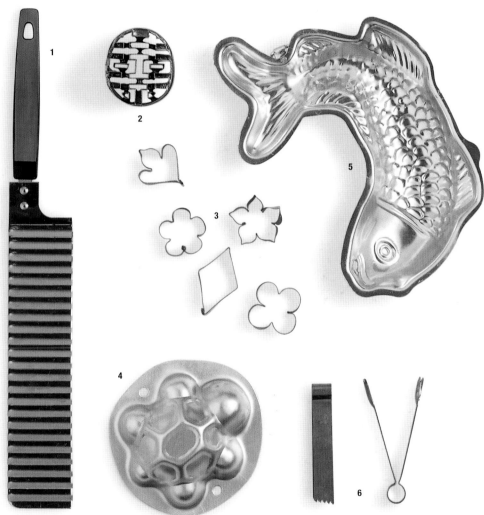

1 LONG SERRATED CUTTER

The jellies eaten in Indochina are not of the wobbly gelatinous type known in Western countries. Most are firm and made from agar agar, a seaweed by-product. In Asia, agar agar is usually sold in long translucent strips; however, in the West it is readily available in granule form. Agar agar has the advantage of being able to set without refrigeration, which is a real benefit in hot climates. Often enriched with coconut cream, the jellies are moulded and turned out, but are rarely served whole. They may be cut into diamonds or triangles with a regular knife, of course, but this serrated cutter easily produces slices of jelly that are then served from a plate.

2 VEGETABLE CUTTERS

Metal cutters such as these, formed into outlines of Chinese characters, flowers or animals, are used to stamp out shapes from slices of carrot, radish and other hard root vegetables. The shapes are then used to decorate dishes of noodles and salads. These cutters are also commonly used in China.

3 BRASS-SHAPED CUTTERS

Strips of brass are bent into floral or heraldic cutters for little rice flour biscuits (cookies).

4 5 TURTLE AND FISH MOULDS

Animals, birds and plants all have their place in ritualistic practices. These moulds are probably derived from those used by European colonials in earlier times, but are now used extensively in Indochina to make a wide range of sweet puddings.

6 TWEEZERS

Even the smallest rice flour cake will be lovingly designed and crimped to take on pretty floral forms. These tweezers, available large and small, are for pinching designs and attractive rimmed edges on cakes, cookies and pastries.

spicy salads

Luscious ripe papayas and mangoes are often thought of as a sweet fruit; however, in Asia, both papayas and mangoes are frequently used when they are green or unripe, in savoury dishes such as salads and curries. In this case, they are thought of more as a vegetable. The green papaya salad from Thailand featured below is known as *som tam* and made almost entirely in a large terra-cotta mortar. Beneath it is a raw fish salad from Cambodia. This is also an intriguing dish, very similar to the South American *ceviche*, although its origins probably go back to China, where raw fish was, and still is, eaten to symbolize rebirth. In Mandarin, the words for raw fish are *yu sang*, which sound exactly like the term for 'rebirth', but are written differently in the Mandarin script. You could also use prawns (shrimp) for this dish; whatever seafood you do use, make sure that it is absolutely fresh.

green papaya salad

Soak 1 tbsp dried shrimp in a little water until soft, then drain. In a large mortar, grind 2 fresh green chillies and 4 garlic cloves until fine, then add the softened shrimps. Peel 1 large green papaya, and shred directly into the mortar. Dissolve 1 tbsp palm sugar in 2 tbsp hot water, and add to the mortar with 2 tbsp fish sauce such as *nam pla* and 2 tbsp freshly squeezed lime juice. Add 2 tbsp torn coriander (cilantro) leaves and 12 halved cherry tomatoes, and gently toss the salad. Transfer to a bowl or serving dish, and serve immediately.

cambodian raw fish salad

Wash 600g (1lb 5oz) skinned fresh tuna or salmon fillet, and pat completely dry with kitchen paper before cutting into chunks. Put in a bowl, squeeze the juice from 6 limes all over the fish, stir well and chill for 2 hours. In a mortar, grind 4 garlic cloves, 6 shallots, 3 slices of fresh root ginger, 2 stalks lemon grass, tough outer layer removed, and 4 fresh green chillies until fine. Dissolve 1 tbsp palm sugar in 2 tbsp hot water, and add to the mortar with 1 tbsp fish sauce and 2 tbsp finely shredded Thai sweet basil. To serve, toss the marinated fish in the dressing, and garnish with some more sweet basil leaves.

MARLENA SPIELER vietnamese cabbage salad

This is a crisp, refreshing salad that goes well with barbecued meats or Vietnamese spring rolls, and makes a refreshing light starter. The recipe comes from Marlena Spieler, who has produced many top-selling cookbooks and is European food correspondent and roving food columnist for the *San Francisco Chronicle*.

SERVES 8–10   PREPARATION TIME: 25 MINUTES, PLUS 30 MINUTES' SWEATING

TOOLS

Cleaver
Mandolin
Chopping board
Vegetable shredder
Large bowl
Large sieve or colander

INGREDIENTS

1 cabbage
1 cucumber
2 carrots
1 bunch of spring onions
   (scallions)
5 garlic cloves
1–2 tbsp shredded or chopped
   fresh root ginger
6 tbsp sugar

3 tbsp white wine vinegar
juice of 2 limes or lemons
2–3 tbsp sesame oil
½ tsp dried red chilli flakes (red
   pepper flakes) or ½ fresh red
   chilli, chopped
2 tsp light soy sauce or fish
   sauce such as *nuoc mam*
3 tbsp chopped coriander
   (cilantro) leaves
1 tbsp chopped mint leaves
   (optional)
6–8 tbsp skinless raw peanuts,
   roasted and coarsely chopped
salt and freshly ground
   black pepper

1 Using a mandolin or cleaver, core and thinly slice the cabbage. Slice the cucumber into julienne, and shred the carrots. Thinly slice the spring onions (scallions), and chop the garlic.

2 In a large bowl, combine the cabbage, cucumber, carrots, spring onions, garlic and ginger, and season generously with salt. Set aside for at least 30 minutes to sweat, then drain in a colander and squeeze out the excess liquid, handfuls at a time.

3 Return to a clean bowl, and add all the remaining ingredients, except the peanuts. Season with salt and black pepper, then cover with cling film (plastic wrap) and refrigerate.

4 Before serving, drain the salad again, and adjust the seasonings to taste. Serve garnished with the peanuts.

burmese vegetable salad

Burmese salads can be very complex and contain as many as a dozen different greens. The dressing is a usually a cooked affair, very aromatic and fragrant with spices and herbs. It is a blank canvas, really, as you can use whatever vegetables you fancy. The traditional recipe calls for yard-long (snake) or runner beans, okra, bamboo shoots, cucumber, spring onions (scallions) and beansprouts.

SERVES 4   PREPARATION TIME: 20 MINUTES

TOOLS
Vegetable knife
Chopping board
Wok and ladle
Large pot and perforated ladle
Colander

INGREDIENTS
100g (3½oz) yard-long (snake),
    green or runner beans
100g (1 cup) fresh okra
100g (1 cup) canned bamboo
    shoots, rinsed and drained
4 spring onions (scallions)
100g (1 cup) beansprouts
½ cucumber
2 tsp salt
2 tbsp toasted sesame seeds,
    to garnish
crisp-fried garlic and shallots,
    to garnish
For the dressing
2 tbsp vegetable oil
10 shallots, finely chopped
6 garlic cloves, sliced
2 tbsp sesame oil
1 tsp ground turmeric
2 tbsp rice wine vinegar
1 tsp salt
½ tsp sugar

1 To make the dressing, heat the oil in a wok, and fry the shallots and garlic until golden brown. Remove from the wok, and drain on kitchen paper. Add the sesame oil to the remaining oil in the pan, and stir in the turmeric over a low heat.

2 Add the rice vinegar, salt and sugar, and stir well. Keep warm while you prepare the vegetables.

3 Cut the beans into 5cm (2in) lengths. Trim the okra, and cut each one into two. Cut the spring onions (scallions) into 5cm (2in) lengths on the diagonal. Slice the cucumber in half lengthways. Remove the soft core and any seeds, and cut on the diagonal into diamond shapes.

4 Bring 1 litre (4 cups) water to the boil, and add the salt. Blanch the vegetables, a handful at a time, for 1–2 minutes. Remove with a slotted ladle, and drain in a colander.

5 Serve cold or warm with the sesame and turmeric dressing dribbled over the top and sprinkled with the toasted sesame seeds and fried garlic and shallots (or serve these in small bowls at the table, so that people can sprinkle them over as they like).

stir-fried morning glory

Morning glory is a vegetable indigenous to most of Southeast Asia, and in Thailand it grows vigorously. It features not only in Thai cooking, but Chinese, Malay and Indonesian cuisine as well. Also known as water convolvulus and water spinach, it is rich in nutrients and crisp and crunchy when stir-fried. Spinach makes a decent substitute.

SERVES 4   PREPARATION TIME: 10 MINUTES

TOOLS
Vegetable knife
Chopping board
Colander
Lidded wok and ladle

INGREDIENTS
200g (7oz) water convolvulus
2 tbsp groundnut (peanut) or
    other vegetable oil
2 garlic cloves, sliced
1 tbsp red or yellow curry paste
    (see page 186)
1 tsp sugar

1 Slice the stalks of the water convolvulus into 5cm (2in) pieces, and roughly shred the leaves. Wash and drain thoroughly.

2 Heat the oil in a wok, and stir-fry the garlic for 1 minute until lightly golden, then add the curry paste and sugar. Stir-fry for another minute.

3 Add the water convolvulus and 100ml (scant ½ cup) water. Cover the wok, and cook over a high heat for about 3 minutes until the convolvulus is tender. Serve immediately.

fried squid with garlic

The term 'local dish' usually refers to a recipe that is home-cooked using local ingredients, and one that is not ubiquitous in restaurants. It is essentially a simple and rustic dish, as exemplified in this Thai recipe.

SERVES 4   PREPARATION TIME: 15–20 MINUTES

TOOLS
Cleaver
Sharp knife
Chopping board
Wok and ladle

INGREDIENTS
500 g (1 lb 2 oz) fresh squid
    (calamari), cleaned
2 tbsp groundnut (peanut) or
    other vegetable oil
2 tbsp chopped garlic
1 small onion, thinly sliced
1 tsp crushed black
    peppercorns
1 tbsp oyster sauce
1 tbsp fish sauce such as
    nam pla
To garnish
fresh Thai sweet basil leaves
green peppercorns

1 Cut the squid (calamari) into 5cm (2in) pieces. With a sharp knife, lightly score a crisscross pattern on each piece of squid so that, when cooked, they curl up in a pretty way.

2 Heat the oil in a wok, and stir-fry the garlic for 1 minute until lightly golden, taking care that it does not burn. Add the onion, and stir-fry for a further 1 minute.

3 Now add the peppercorns, squid, oyster sauce and fish sauce, and stir-fry vigorously for 2 minutes. Serve garnished with basil leaves and green peppercorns.

Cook's tip If you can get hold of fresh green peppercorns from a Thai or other Southeast Asian grocer or supermarket, they give the dish an authentic peppery fillip.

mee krob

Mee krob, which literally means 'crispy noodles', is practically a national dish in Thailand, where each village or region has its own variation. This particular recipe comes from the capital city of Bangkok and typifies the cooking of the country's south.

SERVES 4   PREPARATION TIME: 15–20 MINUTES

TOOLS
Knife
Chopping board
Wok and ladle

INGREDIENTS
groundnut (peanut) or other
    vegetable oil for deep-frying
300g (10oz) dried rice vermicelli
2 tbsp chopped garlic
150g (5½oz) picked fresh or
    canned white crabmeat
250g (9oz) peeled and deveined
    raw prawns (shrimp)
3 spring onions (scallions), cut into
    thin strips about 5cm (2in) long
2 tbsp chilli paste
2 tbsp fish sauce such as
    nam pla
2 tbsp freshly squeezed
    lime juice
1 tsp sugar
200g (2 cups) beansprouts

1 Heat enough oil in a large wok to deep-fry the vermicelli. When the oil is hot, deep-fry a few handfuls of vermicelli at a time until they puff up and turn a pale golden colour. When cooked, drain on kitchen paper and set aside.

2 Pour off all but 2 tbsp of the oil, and fry the garlic until lightly golden. Add the crabmeat, prawns (shrimp) and spring onions (scallions), and stir-fry for 2 minutes.

3 Add the chilli paste, fish sauce, lime juice and sugar, then stir through. Add the crisp vermicelli, and toss gently. Turn off the heat, and toss in the beansprouts (they should be practically raw). Serve immediately.

fried mushrooms

In Laos, rural dwellers gather wild mushrooms to use in many different dishes. This is a rustic Laotian dish that can use any kind of mushrooms, particularly if they are fresh. Use a combination of straw, field and oyster mushrooms for interesting textures and tastes. Pork or chicken is often added for a little extra flavour.

SERVES 4   PREPARATION TIME: 20 MINUTES

TOOLS
Pair of tongs
Vegetable knife
Chopping board
Wok and ladle

INGREDIENTS
2 spring onions (scallions)
2 tbsp groundnut (peanut) or
    other vegetable oil
2 garlic cloves, chopped
200g (7oz) mixed fresh
    mushrooms, sliced
    (about 3 cups sliced)
120g (4½oz) belly pork, cut
    into strips
2 tbsp fish sauce such as
    nam pla
½ tsp freshly ground black pepper

1 Using a pair of tongs, roast each of the whole spring onions (scallions) over a naked flame (or use a ridged cast-iron grill pan or griddle) for a couple of minutes until softened and starting to char. Chop finely, and set aside.

2 Heat the oil in a wok, and fry the garlic until golden brown. Add the chopped spring onions, and stir-fry for 30 seconds.

3 Tip in the pork, and stir-fry over a medium-high heat for 1 minute, then add the fish sauce and black pepper. Increase the heat to high, and cook for a further 3 minutes.

4 Add the mushrooms, and continue stir-frying over a high heat for 3 minutes until the mixture is nearly dry. Serve with plain rice.

beef with sesame sauce

Some four centuries ago, a wave of people migrated south into Vietnam from South China. Although over time they assimilated into Vietnamese culture, adopting the local customs and traditions, and the Vietnamese language, they kept many classical Chinese dishes such as this one.

SERVES 4   PREPARATION TIME: 30 MINUTES

TOOLS
Cleaver
Chopping board
Wok and ladle

INGREDIENTS
300g (10oz) boneless sirloin
    or rump steak, sliced into
    thin strips
1 tbsp dark soy sauce
2 tbsp Chinese rice wine such
    as Shaoxing
2 tbsp groundnut (peanut) or
    other vegetable oil
3 garlic cloves, coarsely crushed
1 tbsp shredded fresh root
    ginger
1 tbsp sesame paste
½ tsp salt
1 tsp cornflour (cornstarch)
2 spring onions (scallions),
    cut into 5cm
    (2in) lengths

1 Marinate the beef with the soy sauce and wine for 20 minutes.

2 Heat the oil in a wok over a medium-high heat. Add the garlic and ginger, and fry for 30 seconds until fragrant. Tip in the beef, together with its marinade, and stir-fry over a high heat for 1 minute. Add the sesame paste and salt, and quickly toss through.

3 Blend 125ml (½ cup) water with the cornflour, and add to the pan. Cook until the sauce is thick and glossy, then toss in the spring onions (scallions). Stir-fry for 30 seconds until well coated and starting to soften.

4 Serve hot with plain rice or noodles.

simple dipping sauces

Dipping sauces are an integral part of every Thai meal, as indeed they are across Indochina. Vietnam, for instance, has its chilli dipping sauce *nuoc cham*, or *nuoc mam cham* (see page 208), among others. These dips are usually an ingenious blend of aromatics such as lemon grass, garlic, galangal, ginger, kaffir lime leaves and basil that work in harmony with the chilli and dried spices.

chilli dipping sauce

This pungent dip, with its fiery dose of chillies, is ubiquitous throughout Thailand as a perfect accompaniment for steamed, fried and grilled foods.

MAKES ABOUT 200G (7OZ) SAUCE

INGREDIENTS
15 large fresh green chillies, stalks removed
6 garlic cloves, peeled but left whole
9 Thai or other shallots, peeled but left whole
½ tsp shrimp paste
½ tsp salt
1 tbsp fish sauce such as *nam pla*
3 tbsp freshly squeezed lime juice
1 tsp sugar

1 Roast the chillies in a dry frying pan over a low heat for about 5 minutes, turning occasionally, until they are slightly blackened. Remove from the pan, and repeat with the garlic and shallots, again for 5 minutes, until they are slightly seared and blackened.

2 Using a mortar and pestle, grind the chillies until crushed. Next, add the garlic and continue to grind.

3 Add the shallots and grind again, followed by the shrimp paste and salt. Continue grinding until the ingredients form a fairly smooth paste. Stir in the fish sauce, lime juice and sugar.

shrimp paste with lime leaf

A zesty dip for fried seafood, this can also be mixed with warm cooked rice to make a quick savoury dish. The traditional dip does not contain lime leaves, but they do add a delicious fragrant tang.

MAKES ABOUT 150G (5OZ) SAUCE

INGREDIENTS
piece of shrimp paste, about 4cm (1¾in) square and 1cm (½in) thick
6 fresh red chillies
4 kaffir lime leaves, sliced
1 tbsp hot water
pinch of salt
juice of 3 limes

1 Wrap the shrimp paste in foil, and toast over a gas flame for about 3 minutes until slightly charred. The easiest way to do this is to mould the shrimp paste over the tip of a bamboo or metal skewer, then toast and turn until done.

2 Using a mortar and pestle, grind the chillies until fine, then add the toasted shrimp paste and lime leaves. Continue grinding until it forms a thick paste, then stir in the hot water, salt and lime juice.

Cook's tip The shrimp paste can also be wrapped in foil and grilled or broiled, turning halfway during cooking, for 8 minutes.

dried shrimp, chilli, lime juice and basil

This is a versatile condiment that can be used as a dipping sauce or as a spice paste for fried dishes.

MAKES ABOUT 200G (7OZ) SAUCE

INGREDIENTS
3 tbsp dried shrimp
4 fresh red chillies
juice of 3 limes
2 tsp sugar
1 tsp fish sauce such as *nam pla*
1 tsp finely chopped Thai sweet basil

1 In a small bowl, soak the dried shrimp in 125ml (½ cup) hot water until softened, then drain thoroughly.

2 Using a mortar and pestle, grind the shrimps until fine, then add the chillies. Continue grinding until mixed together.

3 Mix together the lime juice, sugar, fish sauce and basil. Combine with the ground ingredients, and add 2 tbsp water.

Chilli dipping sauce

Shrimp paste with lime leaf

Dried shrimp, chilli, lime juice and basil

CORINNE TRANG crispy rice flour crêpes with sprouts and mushrooms

Banh xeo, as they are called in Vietnamese, is the onomatopoeic name derived from the sizzling sound the batter makes when it hits the hot surface of the crêpe pan. These delicate lacy and crispy crêpes, from Corinne's *Noodles Every Day*, can be filled with all sorts of ingredients – as is the case with all dumplings and spring rolls, almost any filling works. The batter comprises coconut milk, rice flour and a hint of bright yellow turmeric for colour. The sweet and sour fish dipping sauce is made spicy with chillies and garlic, while freshly squeezed lime or lemon gives it a sour edge. Called *nuoc cham* or *nuoc mam cham* in Vietnamese, it is the ubiquitous condiment of the Vietnamese table. Drizzle it over grilled meat set atop thin rice noodles tossed with shredded vegetables for refreshing fare, perfect for summer.

MAKES ABOUT 12 CREPES   PREPARATION TIME: 45 MINUTES

TOOLS
Vegetable knife
Chopping board
Wok and ladle
Crêpe pan

INGREDIENTS
1 tbsp plus more groundnut
    (peanut) or other vegetable oil
10 medium to large fresh shiitake
    mushrooms, stems discarded,
    caps cut into julienne
225 g (8 oz) rice flour
pinch or two of ground turmeric
125 ml (4 fl oz) unsweetened
    coconut milk
200g (2 cups) mung beansprouts
1 large Boston or butterhead
    lettuce, leaves separated
2 medium to large carrots,
    finely julienned
1 English cucumber, peeled
    (optional), halved lengthways
    and finely sliced crossways
sea or kosher salt and freshly
    ground black pepper

Sweet, sour and spicy fish sauce
125ml (½ cup) fish sauce such
    as *nuoc mam*
115g (½ cup) sugar
125ml (½ cup) freshly squeezed
    lime or lemon juice
1 large garlic clove, thinly sliced
    or very finely chopped
1–2 fresh Thai red chillies such
    as bird's-eye, stemmed,
    deseeded and thinly
    sliced or very finely chopped
1 shallot, peeled, thinly sliced,
    rinsed and drained (optional)

1 To make the dipping sauce, in a medium bowl, whisk together the fish sauce and sugar until the sugar is completely dissolved. Stir in the lime or lemon juice, and add the garlic and chillies. Let steep for 20 minutes or so before serving. It will keep refrigerated in an airtight container for up to 1 week.

2 Heat the 1 tbsp oil in a wok over a high heat, and stir-fry the mushrooms for 1–2 minutes until wilted. Add the beansprouts, lightly toss and transfer to a plate to cool.

3 To make the crêpes, whisk together the flour, turmeric and coconut milk in a bowl until smooth.

4 Heat a crêpe pan over a medium-high heat and add 60ml (¼ cup) batter, while swirling the pan to distribute the batter across the surface of the pan evenly. Cook for about 5 minutes until set and crispy. Once the edges start lifting up, the crêpe is just about ready. Scatter about a handful of stir-fried mushrooms and mung beansprouts on one half of the crêpe and fold over the other half, as you would when making an omelette. Slide onto a plate. Make only as many crepes as there are guests. Make seconds fresh, once the first round of crêpes has been eaten.

5 Garnish each crêpe with freshly torn lettuce leaves and mint, carrots and cucumber, and serve with the dipping sauce on the side. Instruct guests to drizzle about 2 tsbp dipping sauce over their crêpe.

6 An alternative way to serve this crêpe is to break off a piece of it and wrap it, along with some fresh mint, carrots, and cucumber, in a whole lettuce leaf. Held between your fingers, this lettuce roll can then be dipped in the sauce.

Cook's note As your pan gets hot, you may have to sacrifice the first couple of crêpes, offering them up to the kitchen gods. Using a 25cm (10in) crêpe pan, if you have beginner's luck, you may actually get 14 or 15 finished crêpes.

TOM KIME pho bo

Pho has near cult status across Vietnam. This recipe come from chef and author Tom Kime, and he counts the beef noodle soup *pho bo*, with its deliciously pungent aroma, among his favourite of all dishes. As he says, 'If steam had a taste, it would be *pho*.' The soup is not complicated to make and is definitely worth the effort. Traditionally eaten for breakfast, it makes a hearty meal, with its sweet, rich stock and the toasted aromas of the spices.

SERVES 4   PREPARATION TIME: 2 HOURS

TOOLS
Sharp knife
Chopping board
Mortar and pestle
Heavy saucepan or stockpot
Fine sieve or strainer

INGREDIENTS
For the stock
3 star anise
2 cinnamon sticks
2 tbsp coriander seeds
1 tsp salt
40g (1½oz) fresh root ginger, peeled (use the peelings and trimmings for the stock; reserve flesh for the garnish)
1 head of garlic, cloves separated and peeled
½ medium-hot fresh red chilli, halved and deseeded
4 stalks of fresh coriander (cilantro), including roots
2 tbsp groundnut (peanut) oil

2 carrots, roughly chopped
2 celery sticks, roughly chopped
5 shallots, unpeeled and roughly chopped
1kg (2¼lb) beef bones, roasted until golden brown
salt and freshly ground black pepper
For the soup and garnish
250g (9oz) wide rice noodles
2 limes
20 fresh Thai sweet basil leaves
20 fresh mint leaves
30 fresh coriander (cilantro) leaves (use leaves reserved from the stock)

2 large handfuls of peppery mixed leaves such as rocket (arugula), watercress and mustard cress
fish sauce such as *nuoc mam*, to taste
light soy sauce, to taste
250g (9oz) beef sirloin, thinly sliced
4 spring onions (scallions), finely chopped
1 fresh red chilli, deseeded and finely chopped
3 shallots, finely sliced
100 g (1 cup) mung beansprouts

1 To make the stock, put the whole dried spices and salt in a mortar, and bruise with a pestle to release the oils (you do not need to pound until smooth – just enough that you release the perfumes – because they are strained out of the final soup). Add the ginger peelings, head of garlic, chilli and coriander roots and stalks (reserve the leaves for the garnish), and continue to pound.

2 Heat the oil in a high-sided heavy saucepan or stockpot over a medium-high heat. Add the spice mix, and fry for 3–4 minutes until aromatic. Tip in the carrots, celery and shallots, and continue to cook over a medium-high heat for about 8 minutes until caramelized. Reduce the heat to medium if the vegetables are catching. Add the beef bones, cover with 2 litres (4 cups) water and bring to the boil. Reduce the heat slightly, and simmer for 1½ hours, skimming off any scum that rises to the surface.

3 Prepare the other ingredients: soak the rice noodles in warm water to soften. Finely slice the reserved ginger flesh, then restack and cut into a fine shred. Quarter 1 of the limes, and put in the centre of the table. Pick and wash all the herbs and leaves, and also put in a bowl in the centre of the table.

4 When ready to serve, strain the stock and skim off any excess fat. Taste and adjust the seasoning. Add a litle fish sauce, a squeeze of lime juice and lots of black pepper. It should be savoury, sweet and not too bland. Add more fish sauce or light soy sauce if needed. Return to the heat and bring to the boil.

5 Drain the noodles, and blanch in the hot stock: they will take only about a minute to cook, so make sure that you do it right at the end when everything else is ready.

6 Put a little chilli, spring onion, shallot and ginger in each of 4 serving bowls. Add a splash of lime juice and fish sauce (about 1 tsp of each). Fill each bowl one-third full with the cooked rice noodles. Arrange some sliced beef on top, then a handful of beansprouts. Ladle the hot stock over the bowl, and serve; put the remaining garnish ingredients in small bowls on the table with the leaves and lime quarters.

7 Allow each guest to fine-tune their own dish by adding any extra elements they choose: more sour, hot or salty. The stock and the beef provide the sweet elements. Take a few of each type of leaf, and tear them into the bowl, to release their distinctive zesty perfumes and oils. When your bowl is complete with lime juice, fish sauce and the herbs, stir from the bottom to combine all the flavours, and enjoy.

Cook's note You can use the remains of a Sunday roast for the beef bones needed for the stock, or buy some beef bones from your butcher and roast or grill them for about 30 minutes until golden brown.

vietnamese summer rolls

Goi cuon, or summer rolls, are a fresh and zingy alternative to deep-fried spring rolls; their name literally means 'mixed salad roll' in Vietnamese. The flavours of the filling shine through the uncooked rice wrappers, and these are an ideal snack on a hot summer's day or as part of a selection of foods for an informal meal on a balmy evening. They are traditionally served with a dipping sauce made with ground hoisin sauce and fermented soya beans, mixed with fried garlic, tamarind water and coconut water; a variation based on this, minus the soya beans, is given below.

SERVES 4–6   PREPARATION TIME: 30 MINUTES

TOOLS

Sharp knife
Chopping board
Wok and ladle

INGREDIENTS

100g (3½oz) rice vermicelli
1 tbsp groundnut (peanut) or rapeseed (canola) oil
250g (9oz) fresh shiitake mushrooms, stems discarded and caps cut into 2.5cm (1in) pieces
60ml (¼ cup) rice vinegar
2 tbsp light soy sauce
2 tsp hoisin sauce or fish sauce such as *nuoc mam*, to taste
1 tsp toasted sesame oil
12–16 cooked medium prawns (shrimp), peeled, deveined and roughly chopped
2 spring onions (scallions), finely sliced
2.5cm (1in) piece of fresh root ginger, finely grated

1 carrot, cut into julienne
½ English cucumber, peeled, deseeded and cut into julienne
handful of fresh mint leaves
handful of fresh sweet basil leaves, preferably Thai
handful of fresh coriander (cilantro) leaves
juice of 1 lime or 1 tbsp tamarind concentrate, or to taste
16 Vietnamese rice paper (*banh trang*) wrappers
sea salt and freshly ground black pepper

For the peanut dipping sauce
2 garlic cloves, peeled but left whole
1 tbsp groundnut (peanut) or other vegetable oil

1 small fresh bird's-eye chilli, deseeded and finely chopped
2cm (1in) piece of fresh root ginger, finely grated
100ml (scant ½ cup) chicken stock or water
1 tsp sugar
2 tsbp natural peanut butter or finely ground roasted skinless peanuts, or more to taste
3 tbsp coconut cream
3 tbsp hoisin sauce
1 tbsp fish sauce such as *nuoc mam*
juice of 1 lime or 1 tbsp tamarind concentrate
3–4 tbsp roasted skinless peanuts, coarsely ground or chopped, to garnish

1 To make the dipping sauce, using the back of a knife, crush the garlic with a little sea salt on a wooden chopping board. Heat the oil in a wok, and add the garlic, chilli and ginger and chilli. Fry for a couple of minutes until the garlic is lightly golden.

2 Add the stock or water, sugar, peanut butter, coconut cream and hoisin sauce, and whisk to dissolve the sugar. Bring to the boil. Reduce the heat, and simmer gently for 5–10 minutes. Remove from the heat, and allow to cool. Squeeze over the lime juice, add the chopped peanuts and stir through. Garnish with the coarsely ground or chopped peanuts. Set aside until needed.

3 Put the vermicelli in a medium bowl. Pour over enough hot water to cover by about 5cm (2in); leave to soak for 10 minutes. Drain, and rinse under cold water. Set aside.

4 Heat the groundnut (peanut) or rapeseed (canola) oil in a clean wok set over a high heat. Add the mushrooms, and stir-fry until they are tender and have released most of their liquid. Add the vinegar, soy sauce, hoisin or fish sauce, and sesame oil; stir-fry for about 1 minute more. Season with salt and black pepper. Transfer to a small bowl, and allow to cool to room temperature.

5 In a bowl, mix together the mushroom mixture, prawns (shrimp), spring onions (scallions), ginger, carrot, cucumber, mint, basil, coriander (cilantro) and lime juice or tamarind concentrate.

6 Fill a shallow dish with warm water. Working with 1 rice paper wrapper at a time, soak in water for 30 seconds; immediately lay flat on a work surface. Put some mixture on the bottom third, leaving a 1cm (½in) border. Fold the bottom of wrapper over filling; roll over once, tuck in the sides, and finish rolling. Sit the finished roll on a plate; cover with a clean damp cloth or piece of dampened kitchen paper. Repeat the process with the remaining ingredients. Serve with the peanut dipping sauce.

grill racks

Grilled and barbecued foods figure prominently in Indochina. Everywhere in the cities and towns from Bangkok to Ho Chi Minh City, street vendors ply their wares from makeshift carts that contain no more than a charcoal brazier and various implements for grilling meats and seafoods. Racks such as these hold the food tightly yet openly, allowing the cook to baste the food liberally with marinade using a brush or a bruised stalk of lemon grass, which will add its own distinctive flavour.

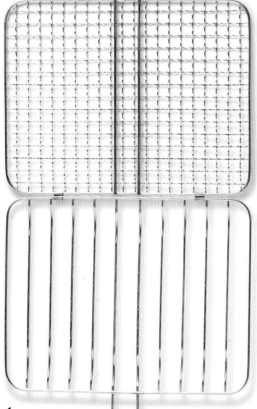

1

2

1 LARGE WIRE RACK

These wire racks are a modern take on rustic bamboo ones and can cradle a whole fish, spatchcocked chicken or wild bird, large squid and split jumbo prawns (shrimp). The handles allow frequent turning for effective grilling. As they are made of metal, the handles get extremely hot during cooking, so it is advisable to wrap a damp towel around them or to use a thick oven glove. After use, scrub the racks vigorously to remove stuck-on bits of charred food and stubborn stains.

2 SMALL WIRE RACK

A wire rack of this size is ideal for grilling smaller items such as spiced patties and shellfish, and helps to prevent flavourings such as garlic, onions and herbs falling away.

lemon grass prawn satay

Lemon grass is used as a herb throughout Southeast Asia, but here it is ingeniously employed as a skewer. You don't actually eat the lemon grass stalk because it is too fibrous, but the citrus tang it imparts to the barbecued minced prawn (shrimp) paste is delicious.

SERVES 4   PREPARATION TIME: 40 MINUTES

TOOLS
Cleaver
Chopping board
Mortar and pestle
Charcoal barbecue or grill

INGREDIENTS
450g (1lb) fresh raw prawns
  (shrimp), peeled and deveined
3 spring onions (scallions),
  roughly chopped
3 fresh red chillies, roughly
  chopped
2 garlic cloves, roughly chopped
2 eggs
juice of 2 limes
2 tbsp fish sauce such as
  nam pla or *nuoc mam*
1 tbsp cornflour (cornstarch)
1 tsp freshly ground
  black pepper
1 tsp sugar
10–12 stalks lemon grass,
  about 12cm (5in) long
2 tbsp groundnut (peanut)
  or other vegetable oil

1 Preheat a charcoal barbecue or grill until hot and the flames have died away. Mince the prawns (shrimp) with the cleaver, and set aside.

2 Using the mortar and pestle, grind the spring onions, chillies and garlic until very fine. Add the minced prawns, and continue to grind until the mixture resembles pâté.

3 Transfer the mixture to a bowl, and add the eggs, lime juice, fish sauce, cornflour (cornstarch), black pepper and sugar. Mix well, kneading until the mixture is thick and doughlike in consistency.

4 Take about 2 tbsp of the mixture, and shape it around a lemon grass stalk. Repeat with the remaining mixture and lemon grass stalks until all are used. Brush lightly with the oil.

5 Grill the satay skewers for 5–8 minutes, turning frequently, until slightly charred. Serve warm.

coriander and garlic marinated chicken

This is a signature dish of many Thai restaurants, but there are numerous regional variations. The Thai penchant for using fresh coriander (cilantro), roots and all, is simple culinary ingenuity.

SERVES 4   PREPARATION TIME: 40 MINUTES, PLUS 30 MINUTES' MARINATING

TOOLS
Cleaver
Chopping board
Mortar and pestle
Charcoal barbecue or grill
Basting brush

INGREDIENTS
4 whole chicken legs on the
    bone (thighs and drumsticks)
4 garlic cloves, roughly chopped
2 tbsp fresh coriander (cilantro),
    including roots and stalks
1 tbsp fish sauce such as
    nam pla
2 tbsp freshly squeezed
    lime juice
1 tbsp palm sugar
1 tsp freshly ground
    black pepper

1 Make deep slits along the thickest part of each chicken leg. Set aside.

2 Using a mortar and pestle, pound the garlic and coriander (cilantro) until finely minced, and mix together with the fish sauce, lime juice, palm sugar and black pepper.

3 Put the chicken in a shallow nonreactive dish, and pour the marinade over. Marinate the chicken in the refrigerator for at least 30 minutes.

4 For best results, barbecue or char-grill the chicken for 20–30 minutes over hot coals, turning occasionally and basting with the marinade, until cooked through. Alternatively, put the chicken on a grill rack, and cook under a preheated medium grill (broiler) for 20–25 minutes, turning once or twice, and basting as you do so.

ALAN DAVIDSON north vietnamese fish brochettes

There was once a road in Hanoi called *Phõ hàng chà cá*, named in celebration of this dish, *cha ca nuong*, but now it has another name. Yet this recipe – the version here is from the renowned seafood expert and food historian Alan Davidson – is still among the most celebrated in North Vietnam. You can use any sea fish with firm flesh, and for authenticity choose the Vietnamese fish sauce nuoc mam.

SERVES 4   PREPARATION TIME: 20 MINUTES, PLUS 2–3 HOURS' MARINATING

TOOLS
Cleaver
Chopping board
Bamboo skewers
Wok and ladle
Barbecue or charcoal grill
Grill rack
Basting brush
Mortar and pestle

INGREDIENTS
500g (1lb 2oz) firm white fish
4 streaky bacon rashers
  or pancetta slices
3 tbsp groundnut (peanut)
  or other vegetable oil
2 spring onions (scallions),
  chopped
5–6 tbsp roasted
  skinless peanuts
For the marinade
3 tbsp groundnut
  (peanut) or other
  vegetable oil
3 tbsp fish sauce
  such as *nuoc mam*
2 tbsp rice wine
pinch of ground
  turmeric
2 tsp chopped
  wild ginger
2 tsp shrimp paste

1 Clean the fish, remove any bones and skin, and cut the flesh into 3cm (1¼in) cubes.

2 In a large bowl, combine the ingredients for the marinade, add the cubed fish and turn gently to coat. Leave to marinate for 2–3 hours.

3 Soak the bamboo skewers in cold water for at least 30 minutes. Cut the bacon or pancetta into 3cm (1¼in) squares, and thread the skewers with alternating pieces of fish and bacon. Sit on a plate, cover with cling film (plastic wrap) and chill until needed.

4 Meanwhile, heat the oil in a wok, and fry the spring onions (scallions) until soft. Transfer the spring onions and their oil to a small bowl.

5 Heat a barbecue or charcoal grill until hot. Put the skewers on the grill rack, close the rack and place on the barbecue or grill. Baste the fish during cooking with the spring onion (scallion) oil.

6 Meanwhile, using a mortar and pestle, roughly pound the peanuts, and sprinkle them over the fish brochettes just before serving.

fried shrimp cakes

Tod man goong, or fried shrimp cakes, are a close relative of Thailand's famous spicy fish cakes, but are more savoury because of the richness provided by the prawn (shrimp) meat. These make excellent finger food for special occasions, and freeze well if you make a large batch.

SERVES 4   PREPARATION TIME: 30 MINUTES

TOOLS
Cleaver
Chopping board
Wok and slotted spoon
Mortar and pestle

INGREDIENTS
500g (1lb 2oz) raw prawns
   (shrimp), peeled, deveined
   and chopped
1 egg, lightly beaten
2 tsp cornflour (cornstarch), plus
   extra, to dust
2 spring onions (scallions),
   finely chopped
1 tbsp lard
1 tbsp fish sauce such as *nam pla*
1 tsp sugar
1 tbsp crushed garlic
½ tsp freshly ground black
   pepper
groundnut (peanut) or rapeseed
   (canola) oil for deep-frying

1 Using a mortar and pestle, grind the chopped prawns (shrimp) until very fine. Mix with the egg, cornflour (cornstarch), spring onions (scallions), lard, fish sauce, sugar, garlic and black pepper, and blend until well combined.

2 With floured hands, shape the mixture into round flat cakes about 5cm (2in) in diameter and 1cm (½in) thick. Pat firmly, and dust with a little extra cornflour.

3 Heat enough oil for deep-frying in a wok over a medium-high heat. Deep-fry the shrimp cakes for a few minutes until lightly golden brown on both sides, and serve with a diced cucumber and chilli dip.

natural basketware

Various types of palm frond are dried and woven into a range of functional and decorative containers for food storage and presentation in Indochina. Thai and Laotian meals, in particular, often feature sticky rice that is served in these small baskets, and they do double duty as containers for rice crackers, prawn (shrimp) wafers, spiced nuts and vegetable crudités.

1 STEAMING BASKET
Here, a large palm basket with sloping sides sits over a metal pot. Portions of food, usually rice, are placed in the basket, and the pan is filled with water, then the whole device is set over a heat source. A separate cover is put on top, so that the food cooks in the steam generated in the base.

2 LARGE STORAGE BASKET
Made of very fine bamboo weave, square at the bottom and round at the top, this type of basket is traditionally used for storing dry grain. This is not advisable in kitchens today; grain products should be stored in robust sealed containers to deter pests.

3 WATER BUCKET
In remote areas where modern plastic products are a rarity, large dried leaves are fashioned into buckets such as this one used for collecting fresh water.

4 LIDDED BASKET
A clever design featuring broad bands of bamboo interwoven with finer strips, this attractive basket has a lid attached by a string and stands securely on its integral crossbar feet. In Indochina, a basket such as this would be used for serving cooked rice.

5 SMALL ROUND BASKET
Almost a replica of the Chinese rice bowl, this type of basket, with its very fine weave, is widely used for serving condiments, vegetable crudités and dry snacks.

6 7 SMALL LIDDED BASKETS
A tiny variation of the taller lidded basket shown left, these are used in Thailand for serving small bites or snacks. The baskets may be plain or decoratively woven, as in the star-shaped box below, with lids entirely separate, or attached by a small cord.

coconut wood tools

The coconut palm provides more than just food in the tropics. Its leaves and trunk are used in building, the hair covering the mature shells is made into matting, and the oil is made into cosmetics. Coconut shells are never without purpose in Asia and, even without being crafted into utensils, they make handy water scoops, all-purpose containers and serving bowls.

1 5 COCONUT SHELL LADLES
The natural curve of coconut shells makes them ideal ladles when a handle is attached. Similar tools are found in most coconut-growing regions, including South India. The long-handled ladles are ideal for serving soups and curries, while shorter ones can be used as rice scoops, or for serving salads and desserts.

2 PERFORATED SPOON
Coconut wood may seem rustic, yet this humble material can be shaped, perforated or carved to function just like any modern kitchen implement. This one is a useful straining or draining tool.

3 SPATULA
This tool is finely honed to work as efficiently as the modern equivalent for flipping and stirring.

4 SLOTTED SPOON
Like the perforated spoon, this tool is useful for lifting saucy foods from the wok.

6 SALAD SERVERS
Salads are a key feature of Indochinese cuisines. Here, fine craftsmanship transforms the coconut shell into a salad set comprising a large fork and spoon with smooth, rounded handles.

pork-stuffed squid

Stuffing squid with minced or ground pork is a fairly common culinary practice throughout Southeast Asia, and these often end up in soups as well. This is a typical Vietnamese version that is served dry as a main course or appetizer. Cellophane noodles are variously called glass noodles, transparent vermicelli or mung bean noodles.

SERVES 4   PREPARATION TIME: 25 MINUTES

TOOLS
Vegetable knife
Cleaver
Chopping board
Cocktail sticks or toothpicks
Large pot and slotted spoon
Wok or frying pan

INGREDIENTS
12 medium squid (calamari),
    each about 8cm (3in) long
5 canned Chinese mushrooms,
    drained
200g (7oz) pork mince
    (ground pork)
2 garlic cloves, minced
2 spring onions (scallions),
    finely chopped
1 tbsp chopped coriander
    (cilantro)
2 tbsp fish sauce such as
    nuoc mam
½ tsp freshly ground
    black pepper
30g (1oz) glass or cellophane
    noodles, soaked until soft
3 tbsp groundnut (peanut) or
    other vegetable olive oil

1 Wash and gut the squid (calamari) if this has not already been done for you. Remove the tentacles, and slice off the inky bits. Clean the squid thoroughly, and discard the tentacles (or you can reserve them for another use).

2 Finely mince the mushrooms, and mix with the pork, garlic, spring onions (scallions), coriander (cilantro), fish sauce and black pepper. Finely chop the drained cellophane noodles, and add to the pork mixture. Stir through gently.

3 With a small teaspoon, stuff the body of each squid with the mixture, but be careful not to overfill; the squid will shrink as it cooks, forcing the stuffing out if it has been packed too tightly into its squid casing. Secure the open ends with cocktail sticks or toothpicks, or sew up with a coarse needle and cotton thread.

4 Bring a large pot of water to the boil, and blanch the squid for 3 minutes until the pork is cooked through. Remove from the pot with a slotted spoon, drain and pat dry with kitchen paper.

5 Heat the oil in a wok or frying pan, and shallow-fry a few squid at a time for 2–3 minutes until golden brown. Remove the cocktail sticks or toothpicks, or snip and remove the thread. Serve immediately.

golden rice

As in other Asian countries, rice is the focal point in every Burmese meal. Usually, rice is cooked au naturel, but occasionally, when there is a festive reason, rice receives special treatment such as this. The 'golden' tag comes from the use of ground turmeric, a favourite Burmese condiment. Saffron is a posh variation of this, or you can use both for extra oomph. It can be served with a whole range of dishes, including meat and poultry curries or sambals.

SERVES 6–8   PREPARATION TIME: 30 MINUTES

TOOLS
Vegetable knife
Chopping board
Wok and ladle
Large pot

INGREDIENTS
3 tbsp groundnut (peanut) or
    other vegetable oil
6 garlic cloves, finely sliced
4 shallots, chopped
250g (1½ cups) long-grain or
    basmati rice
2 tsp ground turmeric
1 tsp saffron threads
2 tsp salt

1 Heat the oil in a wok, and fry the garlic and shallots until crisp and golden brown; set aside on kitchen paper. Rinse the rice, drain in a colander and put in a large pot. Add enough fresh water to cover the rice to 2.5cm (1in) above the level of the rice.

2 Swirl in the saffron and turmeric, and stir well. Cover, and cook over a medium heat for about 12 minutes, checking now and then to reduce the heat to low while keeping the rice on a simmer, to prevent scorching. A Japanese automatic rice cooker is ideal for this without the need for checking.

3 Add the salt in the last few minutes of the cooking time, and stir through well. To serve, check the seasoning, sprinkle the fried garlic and shallots over the rice, and serve hot.

shredded chicken soup

I once had the privilege of learning Lao cooking from a Lao student who lived in our family boarding house for two years. On weekends, Samly would cook up a storm, having learned from his mother, who was an excellent cook. Lao cuisine uses a lot of spring onions (scallions), which are toasted, then ground, for smoky flavour. When fresh coriander (cilantro) is used, the roots are not discarded, but ground up as well.

SERVES 4   PREPARATION TIME: 30 MINUTES

TOOLS
Cleaver
Chopping board
Large pot
Wok and ladle
Slotted spoon

INGREDIENTS
4 skinless chicken thigh or
   breast fillets
5 whole cloves
1 small bunch of fresh coriander
   (cilantro), including roots
3 spring onions (scallions)
2 tbsp groundnut (peanut) oil
5 shallots, sliced
3 garlic cloves, finely sliced
1 tbsp fish sauce such as
   nam pla
½ tsp freshly ground
   black pepper

1 Bring 1 litre (4 cups) water to the boil in a large pot, and add the cloves and coriander (cilantro). Reduce the heat slightly so that the water is shimmering, and poach the chicken for 20 minutes. Remove the chicken from the pot with a slotted spoon and, when it is cool enough to handle, shred the meat and set aside. Discard the cloves and coriander, and skim off any fatty bits in the stock.

2 Toast the spring onions (scallions) over a gas flame for a few minutes until starting to soften and slightly charred (or use a hot unoiled ridged cast-iron grill pan or griddle); chop finely, and set aside. Heat the oil in a wok, and fry the shallots and garlic for a few minutes until crisp and golden brown. Remove from the wok, and drain on kitchen paper.

3 Return the soup to the boil, and add the chopped spring onion, chicken, fish sauce and black pepper. Check the seasoning, and serve the hot soup in individual bowls, garnished with a sprinkling of the fried garlic and shallot.

moulded rice

Not much is known about Cambodian cuisine outside its borders as a result of the country's isolation in the past, but historically it is closely related to both Lao and northeast Thai (Isaan) cooking styles, with spicy overtones. Rice is often cooked with meat and spices, and moulded much like Thai sticky rice.

SERVES 4   PREPARATION TIME: 25 MINUTES

TOOLS
Cleaver
Chopping board
Pot or electric rice cooker
Wok and ladle
Small rice bowls

INGREDIENTS
300g (1¾ cups) jasmine rice
2 tbsp lard or vegetable oil
2 garlic cloves, finely chopped
2 spring onions (scallions),
    finely sliced
1 tbsp fish sauce such as *nam pla*
½ tsp freshly ground
    black pepper
125g (4½oz) cooked belly
    pork, skin removed, coarsely
    chopped
125g (4½oz) cooked chicken,
    coarsely chopped or shredded
To garnish
flowering Chinese chives
crisp-fried garlic

1 Put the rice in a pot or electric rice cooker. Add 500ml (2 cups) water. The best guide to ratio of rice and water is that the level of water should be about 2.5cm (1in) above the level of the rice, whatever size pot you use. Cook for 15 minutes, covered, and set aside to keep warm.

2 Heat the lard or oil in a wok, and fry the garlic and spring onions (scallions) for a few minutes until golden brown. Add the fish sauce and black pepper. Stir to blend well.

4 Add the rice to this mixture, taste and season with a little salt if needed. Stir well. Transfer to 4 small rice bowls, and press in firmly. Carefully unmould each one onto a serving plate, and serve with other vegetable side dishes or on its own as a one-dish meal, garnished with flowering Chinese chives and crisp-fried garlic.

fish with coconut cream

This is a deliciously mild and aromatic fish dish from Cambodia that uses coconut milk to best advantage. It is the laos root, or galangal, that gives it its characteristic flavour; if this is not available, use fresh root ginger.

SERVES 4   PREPARATION TIME: 30 MINUTES

TOOLS
Cleaver
Chopping board
Wok and slotted spoon
Mortar and pestle

INGREDIENTS
500g (1lb 2oz) meaty fish fillets
    such as monkfish, cod or
    halibut, skinned
5 tbsp groundnut (peanut) or
    other vegetable oil
2 stalks lemon grass, tough
    outer layer removed (use 3cm
    (1¼in) of root end only)
2 slices fresh galangal or fresh
    root ginger
3 fresh red chillies, roughly chopped
4 garlic cloves, halved
200ml (scant 1 cup) coconut milk
1 tbsp fish sauce such as *nam pla*
squeeze of lime juice (optional)
2 tbsp chopped roasted
    skinless peanuts
fresh mint or basil leaves,
    finely sliced, to garnish

1 Slice the fish into thick pieces, and pat dry with kitchen paper. Heat the oil in a wok over a medium-high heat, and shallow-fry the fish for a few minutes on each side until golden brown. Remove from the wok with a slotted spoon, and set aside to keep warm. Remove all but 2 tbsp of oil from the wok, and reduce the heat to low.

2 Using a mortar and pestle, grind the lemon grass, galangal or ginger, chillies and garlic cloves to a paste. Add to the wok, and stir-fry for 5 minutes until fragrant. Pour in the coconut milk, and add the fish sauce. Squeeze over a little lime juice, if you like. Increase the heat slightly, and bubble gently for 5 minutes to reduce the sauce.

3 Return the fried fish to the wok, and sprinkle in the peanuts and fresh mint or basil. Turn the fish once to coat it in the sauce and warm through. Serve with plain boiled rice.

lao pickled greens

When Laotian cooks pickle vegetables, they pull out all the stops and make their fish sauce and pickled vegetables from scratch. Obviously, this is not feasible, so use store-bought fish sauce. Chinese salted vegetable is widely available in Chinese stores. Often, too, Laotian cooks use a hearty beef broth as the dressing base. This is easy enough to replicate with a beef stock (bouillon) cube, as only a little bit is required. This is a modified version using locally available greens.

SERVES 4   PREPARATION TIME: 30 MINUTES

TOOLS
Vegetable knife
Chopping board
Wok or heavy frying pan
Wire-mesh ladle
Mortar and pestle
Colander

INGREDIENTS
1 tbsp vegetable oil
1 aubergine (eggplant), cut into
   thick chip-sized julienne
5 garlic cloves, peeled but
   left whole

4 spring onions (scallions), cut
   into 5cm (2in) lengths
150g (5oz) Chinese salted
   vegetable, sliced into strips
2 tbsp shredded fresh root ginger
1 large Cos (romaine) lettuce,
   finely shredded
100g (3½oz) rice vermicelli,
   soaked in cold water until soft
2 fresh red chillies, deseeded
   and finely sliced
crisp-fried shallots (optional)
For the dressing
1 beef stock (bouillon) cube
1 tbsp fish sauce such as *nam pla*
2 tbsp freshly squeezed lime juice
1 tsp sugar

1 Heat the oil in a wok or heavy pan over a medium-high heat, and fry the aubergine (eggplant) until lightly browned and cooked through. Drain on kitchen paper. Set aside, reserving the oil.

2 Put the whole garlic cloves in a wire mesh ladle. Toast over a naked flame for 30 seconds until slightly charred. Repeat with the white ends of the spring onions (scallions). Using a mortar and pestle, lightly crush both the garlic and spring onions. Set aside.

3 Soak the salted vegetable in cold water for 10–15 minutes, and rinse in a colander to remove some of the saltiness.

4 To make the dressing, dissolve the stock (bouillon) cube in 2 tbsp hot water in a small bowl. Add the remaining dressing ingredients. Blend together well, stirring until the sugar has completely dissolved. Taste and adjust the seasoning as needed.

5 To finish, put all the ingredients, including the reserved oil from cooking the aubergines, in a large bowl, and toss through well. Garnish the pickled greens with some crisp-fried shallots if liked.

burmese chicken noodle curry

Khao swe is a staple of Burmese cuisine, and like several Burmese dishes is served at the table with condiments and garnishes to add to the finished dish. Onions, garlic and fresh ginger provied the base for many Burmese curries. Turmeric is often used to bring spice, heat and colour, but chilli is used sparingly, if at all.

SERVES 4   PREPARATION TIME: ABOUT 1¼ HOURS

TOOLS
Cleaver
Chopping board
Mortar and pestle
Large saucepan

INGREDIENTS
1kg (2¼lb) skinless chicken thigh
    fillets, cut into bite-sized pieces
2 large onions, roughly chopped
5 garlic cloves, roughly chopped
1 tsp finely grated fresh
    root ginger
2 tbsp sunflower or rapeseed
    (canola) oil
½ teaspoon Burmese shrimp
    paste (*ngapi*)
1 x 400ml (14fl oz) can
    coconut milk
1 tbsp medium curry powder
200g (7oz) dried egg noodles
salt and freshly ground
    black pepper

To garnish
chopped coriander (cilantro)
    leaves
finely chopped red onion
fried garlic slivers
sliced fresh red chillies
lime wedges for squeezing over

1 Season the chicken pieces with salt and black pepper, and set aside. Using a mortar and pestle, pound the onion, garlic and ginger until smooth. If necessary, add a little water to assist in blending the mixture. (Alternatively, use a food processor to make the paste).

2 Heat the oil in a large pan over a high heat. Add the onion mixture and shrimp paste, and cook, stirring, for about 5 minutes. Reduce the heat to medium, and add the chicken; cook, turning the chicken pieces, until the chicken has browned.

3 Pour in the coconut milk, and sprinkle over the curry powder. Bring to the boil, reduce the heat and simmer, covered, for about 30 minutes, occasionally stirring the mixture. Uncover the pan, and cook for a further 15 minutes or until the chicken is tender.

4 Meanwhile, cook the noodles according to the packet instructions. Drain in a colander, and divide among 4 large warm serving bowls. Ladle over the curry, and top with the garnishes before serving.

Cook's tip Add a handful of juicy cooked peeled and deveined prawns (shrimp) to the curry for a dinner party or special occasion.

SOMKID BHANUBANDH stir-fried venison with black pepper

Somkid Bhanubandh has the distinction of not only being a first-class chef and restaurateur, but also the wife of a Thai prince, a direct descendant of one of the Thai Chakri kings. Thoroughly schooled in Royal Thai cuisine, a distinctive school within the spectrum of Thai cooking, she has introduced many stars of this cuisine into her menus.

SERVES 4   PREPARATION TIME: 15 MINUTES

TOOLS
Cleaver
Chopping board
Wok and ladle

INGREDIENTS
500g (1lb 2oz) venison fillet, thinly sliced into strips
2 tbsp groundnut (peanut) or other vegetable oil
2 garlic cloves, crushed
1 tbsp oyster sauce
1 tbsp fish sauce such as *nam pla*
½ tsp ground white pepper
½ tsp crushed black peppercorns
2 spring onions (scallions), cut into 2.5cm (1in) lengths
125ml (½ cup) good-quality vegetable stock
1 tsp cornflour (cornstarch)
1 tbsp chopped spring onions (scallions)

1 Use the blunt edge of a cleaver to tenderize the venison a little. Heat the oil in a wok, and fry the garlic for 30 seconds.

2 Throw in the venison slices, and stir-fry over a high heat for 40 seconds. Add the oyster sauce, fish sauce, white pepper and black peppercorns, and continue to stir-fry for a further 30 seconds.

3 Pour in the stock, and bring to a quick boil. Dissolve the cornflour (cornstarch) in a little water to make a paste, and add to the wok. Stir until the sauce has thickened slightly and turned glossy. Serve hot garnished with the chopped spring onions (scallions).

sticky rice and mango

With rice and mango being so symbolic of Thai cuisine, this is probably the most iconic of all Thai desserts. It is an unlikely marriage, but a truly luscious one, and the glutinous or sticky rice allows you to ring the changes with other fruit such as jackfruit or bananas. The sweet fragrance of mangoes marries with the savoury coconut rice in the most lip-smacking way. Thai mangoes may be hard to come by, but Indian mangoes come close in sweetness and fragrance.

SERVES 2   PREPARATION TIME: 35 MINUTES

TOOLS
Vegetable knife
Chopping board
Steamer
Deep heatproof steaming plate
   or bowl

INGREDIENTS
150g (scant 1 cup) glutinous rice
300ml (1¼ cups) coconut milk
1 tbsp white granulated sugar
½ tsp salt
2 large ripe Thai or other sweet
   mangoes

1 Put the rice in a bowl, and add just enough water to cover. Leave to soak for several hours. After the soaking period, the rice will have absorbed most of the water and be ready for steaming.

2 At this stage, add the coconut milk, sugar and salt, and stir well. Pile the rice mixture on a deep steaming plate or bowl, and steam for 30 minutes until all the moisture has been absorbed.

3 Taste a few grains and, if they are still unyielding, steam for a little longer. The rice will double in bulk when cooked in this way. When the sticky rice is ready, remove from the steamer, and leave to cool.

4 Peel the mangoes, and slice into large chunks. Serve with the sticky rice.

southeast asia
including singapore, malaysia and indonesia

The countries that make up Southeast Asia are not only geographical neighbours; they also share many cultural ties. Nowhere is this more true than in Singapore, Malaysia and Indonesia. Southeast Asian cooking is a heady mix of spicy, aromatic, soy-, chilli- and coconut-based concoctions, liberally tweaked with cross-cultural fusion elements.

southeast asia including singapore, malaysia and indonesia

Singapore, Malaysia and the Indonesian archipelago evolved from the ancient and largely forgotten Srivijaya empire, centuries before it was sacked and overtaken by the jungle, and well before Dutch and British colonialists first laid eyes on their spice-rich promise. All these three Southeast Asian regions are places of agricultural and culinary richness, and they have several dishes in common.

The cuisine is a mélange of Indian, Chinese, Arab, Dutch, British and Thai influences, with tantalizing fragrances permeating the very air. Keynote flavours include ginger, lemon grass, galangal, chillies, shallots, coriander (cilantro), coconut, tamarind and the dozen and one fresh herbs that impart their delicious perfumes to Southeast Asia's multitude of tasty curries and stir-fries.

Fish and shellfish are spiced with chillies, turmeric, ginger and coconut milk, and steamed in banana leaves. Chicken, beef and pork are cooked in heady blends of shrimp paste, shallots, galangal, kaffir lime leaves and lemon grass. Skewers of marinated chicken are grilled over charcoal; rice is drenched with coconut milk and fragrant pandan leaves. Tapioca is grated and puréed, then baked with sweet palm syrup. Delicate wafer-thin rolls of egg and coconut batter are shaped by iron plates with intricate motifs. An endless array of spicy, savoury or sweet noodles are consumed with relish. What's more, most of these dishes are still made in the traditional way, with the tools featured in this chapter.

It is not the general practice to serve desserts after Southeast Asian meals. Many of the region's sweet specialities were originally reserved for Taoist or Buddhist rituals, or to symbolize good things within the Chinese cultural pantheon. Over the years, some have become popular snacks sold throughout the year, regardless of ritual links or symbolism.

The region's mixed tapestry of culinary styles is a direct result of multicultural marriages over the centuries. In particular, the combination of spices, local produce and ethnic Chinese cuisine has evolved to give a distinctive style known as Nonya cooking. The word 'Nonya' is an amalgam of *neo*, which means 'lady' in Chinese, and *hya*, which means 'gentleman-brother'; the Malay term for the community is 'Peranakan', which means 'born of the soil', as opposed to being born in China.

Also unique to Southeast Asia is the style of street food known as 'hawker' cooking. Indian, Malay, Chinese, Arab and Eurasian dishes are trotted out daily on the streets of every town, city and village by itinerant food vendors. These people are a much-loved feature of the region, with many working from nothing more than makeshift carts, lean-tos and baskets slung on poles hoisted on sturdy shoulders. Today, with urbanization, many hawkers have been relegated to covered complexes, but the authentic flavours still abound, even if the ambience is devoid of rustic charm. The culture of food is so fundamental to Southeast Asia that its culinary heritage is kept alive and ever delicious, even if not outdoors.

OPPOSITE 1 Chinese chives **2** laksa leaves (*rau ram*) **3** galangal **4** red onion **5** kasturi, or musk, limes (*kalamansi*) **6** kai-lan, or gai-lan (Chinese broccoli or kale) **7** red chillies **8** garlic **9** lemon grass **10** pandan leaf **BELOW 1** fried tofu **2** tempeh **3** black rice **4** yellow bean paste **5** shrimp paste (*belachan*; *terasi*), **6** fish balls **7** sambal oelek **8** coconut milk **9** chilli sauce **10** fish cake **11** dried whitebait (*ikan teri*; *ikan bilis*)

street hawker tools

Despite many Southeast Asian cities being rapidly urbanized, street hawkers remain a fascinating feature, sometimes with several family members working at the same stall. Noodles, satay, fritters and pastries, porridges of black sticky rice and coconut milk, fresh fruit cocktails and intriguing parcels of banana and pandan leaves are among the typical fare these tools help to produce.

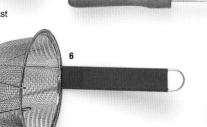

1 WOVEN PANDAN LEAF FAN
An enduring sight in Southeast Asian streets is the mobile satay man. Given that he never knows when he will have his next customer, his charcoal brazier is ever at a ready glow. This fan, fashioned from an entire dried pandan leaf, sparks the embers of the brazier to roaring life in a few seconds. Given the humid climate and hot, smoky nature of this particular type of street hawker's job, it is also used to cool the cook!

2 6 SHORT-HANDLED STRAINERS
These are used for quick blanching in small or shallow pans for delicate foods such as seafood and thinly sliced meats. Each requires a certain amount of dexterity, with a twist of the wrist, to blanch, shake, drain and turn out the food into a bowl.

3 4 NOODLE STRAINERS
Before metal and plastic became the basic materials for strainers in Southeast Asia, bamboo was the mainstay. Many street hawkers in rural areas still use the implements of old, while others prefer modern wire models. Long handles are both practical and the safest option for blanching noodles in deep pots of scalding-hot water.

5 PERFORATED LADLE
This handy tool is for scooping froth and pieces of blanched food from pots.

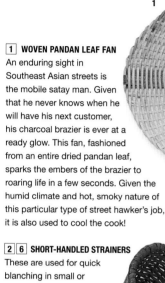

7 BAMBOO SKEWERS
Usually between 16cm (6¼in) and 20cm (8in) long, these sharp bamboo skewers are used to spear small pieces of seafood or meat for grilling. It is advisable to soak the skewers in cold water before use, to minimize scorching on the grill. In Indonesia and Malaysia, larger bamboo stakes are fashioned into gripping forks that hold a whole bird for grilling. Small slivers of bamboo are used to secure leaf containers during cooking.

penang spring rolls

Penang cooking is perhaps most famous for this spring roll, and its generic name does it little justice. It is a far cry from the greasy-spoon Chinese takeaway variety. The wrapper is made from bean curd sheets instead of wheat-flour skins. Bean curd sheets are sold at most Chinese supermarkets.

SERVES 4   PREPARATION TIME: 35 MINUTES

TOOLS
Cleaver
Chopping board
Wok and slotted spoon
Long chopsticks

INGREDIENTS
500g (1lb 2oz) pork mince
    (ground pork)
3 spring onions (scallions),
    finely chopped
1 egg, lightly beaten
1 tsp five-spice powder
1 tbsp light soy sauce
2 tbsp sesame oil
1 tbsp dark soy sauce
½ tsp freshly ground black
    pepper
2 large sheets bean curd skin
groundnut (peanut) or other
    vegetable oil for deep-frying

1 To make the filling, mix together the pork, spring onions (scallions), beaten egg, five-spice powder, soy sauce, sesame oil and black pepper.

2 Lay out a bean curd skin on a flat work surface and, with a clean damp cloth or damp kitchen paper, lightly wipe down to soften any crackly bits. Cut into rectangles measuring about 20cm x 13cm (8in x 5in). Repeat with the remaining bean curd skin.

3 Take one of the rectangles, and position with a long side facing you. Put 2 tbsp of the pork mixture in a horizontal line along the nearest end of the skin, about 6cm (2½in) in from the edge and leaving about 7cm (2½in) at either side for folding over to enclose the filling. Roll the skin over, and pat the filling in firmly. Roll once more, and tuck in the ends on both sides before completing the rolling. Repeat with the remaining rectangles of bean curd skin and filling until all the filling has been used. Allow to rest for 10 minutes.

4 Heat enough oil for deep-frying in a large wok. Deep-fry the spring rolls for 4–5 minutes until crisp and golden, turning with a pair of long chopsticks so that the rolls brown evenly all over. Remove from the wok, and briefly drain on kitchen paper. Serve hot, sliced into diagonal pieces, on a bed of lettuce and accompanied by a sharp chilli and garlic dip.

HONG SAI CHOI fried vermicelli xiamen-style

'Xiamen-style' indicates that this crisp noodle dish is made in the manner of those from the eastern province of Fujian in China. One of the key characteristics of this style of Chinese regional cooking is to combine seafood and meat or chicken in the same dish. This version comes from chef Hong Sai Choi, who is superbly well versed in Fujian-style cooking.

SERVES 2–4   PREPARATION TIME: 30 MINUTES

TOOLS
Cleaver
Chopping board
Small pot
Bamboo strainer
2 woks and ladle
Wire strainer

INGREDIENTS
100g (1 cup) beansprouts
groundnut (peanut) or other
    vegetable oil for deep-frying
100g (3½oz) rice vermicelli
150g (5½oz) skinless chicken
    breast fillet, thinly sliced

125g (4½oz) raw prawns (shrimp),
    peeled and deveined
80g (3oz) green sweet (bell) pepper,
    deseeded and sliced (about 1 cup
    sliced, or 1 small pepper)
80g (3 oz) red sweet (bell) pepper,
    deseeded and sliced (about 1 cup
    sliced, or 1 small pepper)
1 chicken stock (bouillon) cube,
    crumbled
½ tsp oyster sauce
pinch of sugar
½ tsp sesame oil

1 Blanch the beansprouts in a small pot of boiling water for 1 minute. Drain and set aside.

2 In a wok, heat enough oil for deep-frying until smoking hot. Fry the vermicelli a handful at a time until crisp, golden and puffed. Using a wire strainer, lift out the cooked vermicelli, and set aside.

3 Remove all but 2 tbsp of the oil from the wok. Stir-fry the chicken and prawns (shrimp) for 3 minutes until cooked. Remove and set aside.

4 Stir-fry the red and green peppers for 1 minute, then return the chicken and prawns to the wok with the blanched beansprouts, crumbled stock (bouillon) cube, oyster sauce, sugar and sesame oil, and stir-fry for 1 minute.

5 Briefly reheat the vermicelli in a separate wok for about 1 minute. Transfer to a serving bowl or plate, spoon the sauce over and serve immediately.

beef satay

As a culinary ambassador, satay is up there among the greats. It is also a dish that every Southeast Asian country claims as its own! As Muslims eschew pork, you won't find this meat being featured in any Malaysian satay, and the usual meats are beef, lamb and chicken. The number of skewers you end up with obviously depends on how long each satay stick is and how much meat you use. Lemon grass does double duty here, when bruised at the root end to make a feathery pastry brush.

MAKES 20–24 SKEWERS   PREPARATION TIME: 45 MINUTES

TOOLS
Cleaver
Chopping board
Mortar and pestle
Medium pot
Charcoal grill or barbecue, or
   electric grill (broiler)
Bamboo satay skewers, each
   about 20cm (8in) long

INGREDIENTS
500g (1lb 2oz) boneless beef
   sirloin, trimmed of fat
3 tbsp groundnut (peanut)
   or other vegetable oil
1 stalk lemon grass, bruised at
   the root end to make a brush
sweet chilli sauce, to serve
Satay marinade
2 tbsp ground coriander
1 tbsp ground cumin
1 tsp ground turmeric
1 tsp chilli powder
150ml (⅔ cup) coconut milk
1 tsp salt
2 tsp sugar
3 tbsp groundnut (peanut) or
   other vegetable oil

For the peanut satay sauce
2 dried red chillies, seeded
   and soaked in warm water
4 shallots, chopped
2 garlic cloves, chopped
2.5cm (1in) piece of galangal
   or fresh root ginger, chopped
1 stalk lemon grass, white part
   only, chopped
1 tsp ground coriander
½ tsp ground cumin
1 tbsp groundnut (peanut) oil
250g (1½ cups) unsalted roasted
   skinless peanuts, finely
   chopped
1 x 400ml (14fl oz) can coconut
   milk, plus extra if needed
1 tbsp dark soy sauce
1 tbsp palm sugar or soft
   brown sugar
pinch of salt
1–2 tbsp freshly squeezed lime
   or lemon juice

1 Soak the bamboo skewers in cold water for at least 30 minutes, to prevent scorching when grilling. Cut the beef into strips about 2cm (¾in) wide, and put in a bowl. Blend together all the ingredients for the marinade, and pour over the beef. Leave to marinate in the refrigerator for at least 30 minutes.

2 Meanwhile, to make the peanut satay sauce, drain the chillies, and roughly chop. Using a mortar and pestle, grind the chillies, shallots, garlic, galangal or ginger, lemon grass, coriander and cumin to a paste. Heat the oil in a heavy saucepan over a medium-high heat, and fry the spice paste for a few minutes until aromatic. Reduce the heat to medium, and add the peanuts, coconut milk, soy sauce, sugar and a pinch of salt. Stir until combined. Cook gently until the sauce boils and thickens, stirring constantly and adding a little extra coconut milk or water if the sauce becomes too thick. Remove from the heat, check the seasoning and add the lime or lemon juice to taste. Keep warm until needed.

3 When ready to grill the satay sticks, heat a charcoal barbecue or electric grill (broiler) until hot. Thread 3 or 4 strips of beef onto each skewer, pressing the meat around each skewer to firm up. If cooking over charcoal, grill for about 5 minutes on each side. Use the lemon grass stalk, dipped in a little oil, to baste the meat as you cook, to impart a delicious lemony tang. Or sit the satay sticks on a rack, and pop under a hot grill (broiler) to cook for 8 minutes, turning once and basting two or three times.

4 Serve hot alongside the peanut satay sauce and sweet chilli sauce for dipping.

grilled spatchcock poussin with spices

The spicy, smoky flavour of this chicken dish is irresistible when cooked over charcoal. If you are having a barbecue, allow a whole poussin for each guest. They cook faster and are more succulent than mature birds. This recipe requires two steps: boiling, then grilling.

SERVES 4   PREPARATION TIME: 45 MINUTES

TOOLS
Cleaver
Chopping board
Thick wooden or metal skewers
Frying pan
Mortar and pestle
Charcoal grill or barbecue,
   or electric grill (broiler)

INGREDIENTS
4 poussins or baby chickens
   (Cornish game hens)
200ml (scant 1 cup)
   coconut milk
4 kaffir lime leaves
1 tsp salt
For the spice paste
3 fresh red chillies
4 garlic cloves
½ large onion
1 stalk lemon grass, tough outer
   layer removed (use 4cm
   (1½in) of root end only)
2 slices fresh root ginger

1 To spatchcock the poussins (hens), lay each one on a work surface breast-side down, and cut along one side of the backbone with a cleaver (or use a sturdy pair of kitchen scissors if you find this easier). Rotate the poussin 180 degrees, cut along the other side of the backbone; discard the backbone, or reserve to make a stock. Open up the poussin, turn over so that it is cut-side down and flatten with a cleaver. Use 2 skewers to keep the poussin lying flat, running them diagonally through each breast and wing to the opposite thigh.

2 Pour the coconut milk into a large frying pan. Add the poussins, lime leaves and salt, and bring to the boil. Reduce the heat slightly, and simmer for 5 minutes, turning the poussins so that each is evenly cooked and coated in the coconut milk mixture.

3 Using a mortar and pestle, grind all the spices until fine, and add to pan. Simmer for a further 10 minutes until the sauce has reduced by half – it will be redolent and slightly oily by now. Remove the poussins, and reserve the sauce.

4 Grill the poussins over the hot coals of a charcoal grill or barbecue until slightly charred, basting liberally with the sauce. If you are using an electric grill (broiler), sit the poussins on a rack in the grill pan, and cook under the preheated grill for about 8 minutes on each side. To check whether the birds are done, pierce the meaty part of a thigh with the point of a sharp knife or skewer; the juices should run clear. Serve hot with bread or rice.

tools for edible baskets

Asian chefs have always been at the cutting edge when it comes to presentation skills. With ingenuity being the mother of invention, many 'plates' at banquets and other festive occasions are actually edible cradles made using the special tools featured here. Such tricks are not restricted to professional chefs either. In Southeast Asia, few home kitchens are without the pietee maker, which looks like a miniature golf putter, and housewives are adept at creating diminutive cups of pastry, or 'top hats', with these implements, to be filled with all manner of cooked ingredients.

1 PIETEE MAKER

This tool comprises a heavy knob of brass with smooth grooves, attached to an L-shaped metal bar. The knob is dipped into sizzling-hot oil, then into batter, to be popped back into the oil to deep-fry into little baskets. When done to a crisp turn, the baskets come away easily from the mould. The resulting cups are shaped exactly like little top hats, then filled with cooked bamboo shoots and other fillings; these are served as amusing appetizers or canapés, called *kueh pietee* in the local dialect. The story goes that they were little finger food items for parties, hence the patois translation of *pietee*. The term *kueh* refers to all kinds of cakes, snacks and sweetmeats. Practice is needed to make perfect cups and, if the temperature of the oil is not right, you end up with bottomless cups! One advantage is that you can make the cups well ahead of serving time; they will keep in an airtight container for up to a month. Never wash the moulds with detergents; the soapy suds may linger in the joint between the knob and the bar. Just wipe clean with kitchen paper after cooking, and store in a cool, dry place.

2 LOMPANG MOULD

Also known as a flower mould, this Indonesian tool features a flower-shaped ring attached to a thin metal rod. It is dipped in a sweet batter of rice flour, sugar and coconut milk, then into hot oil to make cakes called *kueh lompang*, or swaying flower cakes, because they are light enough to flutter in a stiff breeze.

3 4 5 BASKET MOULDS

The 'basket' referred to here is actually made of strips of yam, potato or noodles, arranged in such a way that, when deep-fried, they produce little edible bowls that are then used to contain various stir-fried ingredients. The traditional model comprises two large perforated ladles shaped to fit one inside the other. The handles are of bamboo or wood, set at a right angle to the bowls. Strips of yam or sweet potato are first dusted with cornflour or tapioca flour, then laid into the larger ladle to form a kind of nest. The smaller ladle is then used to press down firmly on this nest. The flour acts as a binding agent and, when deep-fried, these baskets hold their shape firmly. The modern version is much like a pair of wire mesh sieves held together by a hinge. Also available are perforated models without handles. These float freely in the hot oil during cooking; they are more difficult to use because there is nothing to help to keep the basket ingredients compressed while cooking in the oil.

making edible baskets

Yam is the preferred ingredient, thanks to its crisp, starchy texture and delicious flavour. Potatoes can also be used; they need to be long enough to yield strips of 10–12cm (4–5in).

1 Cut the vegetable strips as thinly as possible, to make them pliable.
2 Arrange the strips in the mould so that there are no visible gaps between the strips at the base of the mould. Dust thoroughly with cornflour to seal.
3 For an attractive brim, allow 4cm (1½cm) above the top of the mould.

prawns in a yam basket

An impressive dish for dinner parties, this spectacular basket filled with succulent stir-fried prawns (shrimp) is easier than it looks, especially when you have the right tools for the job. Gently swirling the yam basket around in the oil a little while it is deep-frying will help it to brown nicely.

SERVES 4   PREPARATION TIME: 30 MINUTES

TOOLS
Cleaver
Chopping board
Yam basket mould
Wok and ladle

INGREDIENTS
1 large yam, cut into fine strips
4 tbsp cornflour (cornstarch)
groundnut (peanut) or other
    vegetable oil for deep-frying
salad leaves, to garnish
For the filling
3 tbsp groundnut (peanut) or
    other vegetable oil
2 garlic cloves, crushed
1 small carrot, diced
1 celery stick, sliced
20 button mushrooms,
    wiped clean with damp
    kitchen paper
400g (14oz) tiger or king prawns
    (jumbo shrimp), peeled and
    deveined, with tails left intact
2 tbsp sesame oil
1 tsp freshly ground
    black pepper
1 tbsp freshly squeezed
    ginger juice
2 tbsp oyster sauce
1 tbsp cornflour (cornstarch)

1 Toss the strips of yam in the cornflour (cornstarch). Lay them in the lower ladle of the basket mould, overlapping the strips slightly. Press down firmly with the upper ladle.

2 Heat enough oil for deep-frying in a wok over a medium-high heat. When the oil is smoking hot, carefully lower the basket mould (both upper and lower parts) into the oil, and fry the yam until crisp and golden.

3 Gently lift the mould out of the oil, and prise the yam basket loose. Briefly drain on kitchen paper, then place on a serving dish that has been dressed with salad leaves.

4 To make the filling, carefully wipe out the wok with kitchen paper. Heat the oil in the cleaned wok, and stir-fry the garlic for 1 minute. Add the carrot, celery and mushrooms, and stir-fry for 2 minutes. Add the prawns (shrimp), sesame oil, black pepper, ginger juice and oyster sauce, and continue cooking for a further 5 minutes.

5 Blend the cornflour (cornstarch) with a little water to make a paste, and add to the wok. Stir until the sauce thickens slightly and turns glossy. Transfer the contents of the wok to the yam basket, and serve immediately.

kueh pietee

Crispy little cups, or 'top hats', of featherlight fried batter, these exotic 'vol-au-vents' are unique to Southeast Asia, where they are known as *kueh pietee*. Made with a special mould (see page 244) and filled with a savoury mixture of yam beans and bamboo strips, they make delightful appetizers or finger food for parties.

MAKES 40   PREPARATION TIME: 1 HOUR

TOOLS
Cleaver
Chopping board
Wok and ladle
Vegetable shredder
Sieve
Small, deep pot
Pietee maker
Small, deep cup
Long chopsticks

INGREDIENTS
For the batter
300g (2½ cups) plain
    (all-purpose) flour
1 tsp salt
3 eggs
groundnut (peanut) oil for
    deep-frying
For the filling
200g (7oz) Chinese yam bean
    or swede
400g (14oz) canned bamboo
    shoots, rinsed and drained
4 tbsp groundnut (peanut) oil
4 garlic cloves, crushed
3 tbsp preserved yellow beans
3 tbsp dark soy sauce
fresh coriander (cilantro) leaves,
    to garnish
chilli sauce, to serve

1 To make the filling, peel the yam bean or swede, and cut into fine julienne about 3cm (1¼in) long. Do the same with the bamboo shoots.

2 Heat the oil in a wok over a medium-high heat, and fry the crushed garlic for 2 minutes. Add the preserved yellow beans, and mash lightly with the wok ladle. Add the julienne vegetables, and stir-fry for 2 minutes. Pour in the soy sauce and 500ml (2 cups) water, bring to a boil over a high heat and keep boiling for a further 10 minutes. Reduce the heat to medium, and simmer for 20 minutes or until almost dry. Set aside to keep warm.

3 Meanwhile, to make the batter, put the flour in a bowl, and make a well in the centre. Add 600ml (scant 2½ cups) water, a little at a time, mixing into a batter the consistency of pouring cream. Season with the salt, and stir well.

4 Break the eggs into a separate bowl, and beat lightly. Add to the batter, stirring until well incorporated. Strain through a sieve, and leave to chill for 1 hour.

5 Heat enough oil for deep-frying in a small pot, making sure that the depth of oil is greater than the depth of the pietee maker. Pour some of the batter into a small, deep cup. When dipped, the base of the mould should not be able to touch the bottom of the pot or the cup; otherwise the delicate batter will smear.

6 When the oil is smoking hot, immerse the mould in it for at least 5 minutes to heat thoroughly. Lift out the mould using a pair of long chopsticks, and gently and carefully shake off the excess oil.

7 Dip the mould quickly and without quivering into the batter, making sure that you do not dip the mould beyond its rim, or the resulting fried cup will be 'locked' onto it.

8 Dip the coated mould into the hot oil. Within 1–2 minutes, the batter will turn light brown. When it is golden brown, lift out the mould, and gently prise the cup off using chopsticks. Set aside to drain on kitchen paper while you cook the remaining cups.

9 To serve, place about 2 tsp of the warm filling into each cup, and top with fresh coriander (cilantro). Serve with chilli sauce.

pots and pans

The wok is the favoured pan for everyday cooking in Southeast Asia. But other types of pot receive frequent use, not only in making specialities, but also for common dishes such as soups. Pressure cookers speed up cooking of key staples, and, in households of Chinese descent, the steamboat is a very popular form of communal cooking and eating.

1 PRESSURE COOKER

This is an indispensable utensil for a number of dishes that require long, slow cooking without the attendant reduction of liquids. Braised belly pork in five-spice powder, beef rendang and green mung beans in coconut milk, for example, take less than half the normal time to cook when made in a pressure cooker. It also eliminates the need for pre-soaking when cooking local staples such as dried soya beans and black sticky rice.

2 DOUBLE-BOILER

This modern version of the old Chinese utensil is used for slow simmering and stewing. The water boils in the aluminium base, conducting steam heat to the upper porcelain container. It can be used for custards and other eggy mixtures, slow-cooked herbal stews such as chicken with ginseng, and soups containing delicate ingredients.

3 ELECTRIC STEAMBOAT

Today's electric steamboat is related to the ancient Mongolian firepot used in China and Korea. The modern versions are cleaner and safer to use than the traditional charcoal-fired models, but lack their rustic appeal. Steamboats are used in several parts of Asia; typical ingredients differ according to available ingredients and favourite local dipping sauces. In Thailand, a spicy *tom yam* version is produced, while the Sichuanese steamboat is flavoured with chillies and at one time included poppy heads.

4 WIRE MESH SPOONS

Individual brass or aluminium wire mesh spoons are specially made for dunking raw foods into the steamboat. Each diner is given one in which to place preferred foods for cooking. It is a unique way of cooking to a desired consistency or doneness, and prevents portions floating around and becoming overcooked. When all the food is eaten, the resulting broth is usually very rich from all the different flavours of meat, poultry, seafood and vegetables that have been cooked in these spoons.

5 6 SIMMERING POTS

Southeast Asian households have a range of quality pots and saucepans to do jobs that the wok does not do well, such as blanching, soup and stock making, and cooking noodles and congee. Nonstick models are useful to prevent scorching.

steamboat

The last word in tabletop cooking, the steamboat is both a festive meal and a heart-warming way to entertain. The work lies solely in the preparation of raw ingredients; these can be anything you like, as long as they are sliced into bite-sized pieces. A rich stock is made from either chicken bones or stock cubes, then transferred to the moat of the steamboat. Traditionally, the stock is heated by charcoal lit under the moat; electric models are also available. Diners help themselves to whatever they fancy, and cook the food pieces to suit their individual taste.

SERVES 10–14   PREPARATION TIME: 45 MINUTES

TOOLS
Large pot
Cleaver
Chopping board
Steamboat
Wire mesh spoons

INGREDIENTS
4 litres (4 quarts; 16 cups)
   chicken stock
400g (14oz) lean pork fillet
400 g (14oz) beef fillet
400g (14oz) skinless chicken
   breast fillet

500g (1lb 2oz) tiger prawns
   (jumbo shrimp), peeled
   and deveined
20 fish balls
200g (7oz) pig's liver (optional)
200g (7oz) fresh squid
   (calamari), cleaned
400g (14oz) tofu
100g (3½oz) thin rice vermicelli
   or rice sticks, soaked until soft
1 Chinese or napa cabbage
light soy sauce, chilli sauce,
   mustard and freshly cracked
   black pepper, to serve

1 Bring the stock to a boil in a large pot. Meanwhile, cut all the ingredients into bite-sized pieces or strips, and arrange on serving plates or platters for presentation.

2 Pour the stock into the steamboat, sit the steamboat on the table and light or switch on. Take the food to the table, and set around the steamboat. Provide little dishes of light soy sauce, chilli sauce, mustard and cracked black pepper for individuals to season the cooked food to taste.

3 When the stock begins to bubble, each guest puts the food of his or her choice into a wire mesh spoon, then lays the spoon in the stock to poach the food until cooked.

4 At the end of the meal, the stock will be incredibly rich and can be kept and served as a broth, if liked.

NEIL PERRY nonya-style pork curry

Penang, where this dish called pork *gulai* originated, was once the northern Malaysian enclave for the Straits Chinese community, who were known as *babas* (for men) and *nyonyas* (for women). The term *gulai* is Penang patois for any kind of curry or sambal. This recipe comes from leading Australian chef and restaurateur Neil Perry.

SERVES 10   PREPARATION TIME: 45 MINUTES

TOOLS
Cleaver
Chopping board
Mortar and pestle
Steamer
Large pot

INGREDIENTS
5 tbsp coriander seeds
2 tsp fennel seeds
1.25kg (2¾lb) pumpkin
1.25 kg (2¾lb) boneless pork
   shoulder
10 garlic cloves
2 Spanish or sweet yellow
   onions, chopped
10cm (4in) piece of fresh
   turmeric, chopped
8 fresh long red chillies,
   deseeded and chopped

10 dried red chillies,
   soaked in warm water
100ml (scant ½ cup) groundnut
   (peanut) oil
1 stalk lemon grass
250ml (1 cup) coconut cream
2 star anise
5 cloves
5cm (2in) piece of cinnamon
   stick
salt and freshly ground
   black pepper

1 In a small dry frying pan, toast the coriander and fennel seeds separately until fragrant, then use a mortar and pestle to grind to a powder. Set aside.

2 Peel and deseed the pumpkin, cut into large chunks and steam for 20 minutes until cooked but still firm. Set aside.

3 Meanwhile, cut the pork into bite-sized chunks. Using the mortar and pestle, grind the garlic, onion, turmeric, fresh and dried chillies, and ground coriander and fennel to a paste.

4 Heat the oil in a large pot. Trim the bulb from the lemon grass, and remove and discard the tough outer layer. Bruise the lemon grass, and fry for 30 seconds before adding the spice paste. Fry over a low heat for 4 minutes.

5 Stir in the coconut cream, star anise, cloves and cinnamon. Tip in the pork, mix well and gently simmer for about 30 minutes until the meat is tender.

6 Add the steamed pumpkin for the last 5 minutes of cooking, and season with salt and black pepper. Serve hot.

coconut marinated prawns

In true Indonesian style, prawns (shrimp) are almost always cooked in their shells for better retention of flavour. If you use the largest prawns you can find, peeling them after cooking is not difficult. Also, with the spice blend being stuffed into the slit, the shell helps to keep this in place when cooking.

SERVES 4   PREPARATION TIME: 20 MINUTES

TOOLS
Vegetable knife
Chopping board
Mortar and pestle
Wok and ladle
Wire mesh ladle

INGREDIENTS
16 raw tiger or king prawns
   (jumbo shrimp)
2 tbsp freshly squeezed
   lime juice
½ tsp salt
3 tbsp groundnut (peanut) oil
lime halves or wedges, to serve
For the spice paste
4 kaffir lime leaves, chopped
2 tbsp unsweetened dessicated
   (shredded) coconut
2 fresh red chillies, halved and
   deseeded (if preferred)
3 garlic cloves, roughly chopped
3 shallots, roughly chopped
thumb-sized piece of fresh
   turmeric or ½ tsp ground

1 Snip off the feelers and legs on the prawns (shrimp). With a sharp knife, make a deep slit down the back of each prawn, being careful to slice through the shell, but not all the way through to the other side. Wash and pat with kitchen paper until very dry.

2 To make the spice paste, using a mortar and pestle, grind together the lime leaves, coconut, chillies, garlic, shallots and turmeric until very fine. Mix with the lime juice and salt. Stuff each prawn cavity with about 1 tsp of the spice paste, and pat in well. Rub any remaining spice paste all over the outside of the prawns.

3 Heat the oil in a wok over a medium heat, and shallow-fry the prawns until they turn pink and opaque; this takes only a matter of minutes. Remove and drain on kitchen paper, and serve hot with a side salad or sliced cucumber, and lime halves or wedges for squeezing over.

chicken in red sambal

Sambal in Malay simply means 'cooked spice paste'. These days, there are many proprietary brands of this spice paste, but it is not difficult to make your own, and you can adjust the heat from the chilli to suit your taste. This extremely versatile master paste can be made in a large batch and refrigerated for several weeks.

SERVES 4   PREPARATION TIME: 1 HOUR

TOOLS
Vegetable knife
Chopping board
Blender
Wok and ladle

INGREDIENTS
4 whole chicken legs (drumstick
 and thigh), trimmed and
 skinned
½–1 tsp salt
2 tbsp groundnut (peanut) or
 other vegetable oil

For the red sambal
8–10 dried red chillies, soaked
 in hot water until soft
3 large onions, about 450g (1lb)
 in total weight, chopped
6 garlic cloves, chopped
40g (1½oz) shrimp paste
200ml (scant 1 cup) groundnut
 (peanut) or other vegetable oil
1 tbsp sugar
2 tbsp tomato purée (paste)
1 tsp salt
juice of 2 limes

1 First, make the sambal. If you prefer a paste that is not too fiery, remove some of the seeds from the soaked dried chillies. Grind the chillies, onions, garlic and shrimp paste in a blender until fine.

2 Heat the oil in a wok, and fry the sambal paste over a low heat for about 15 minutes, turning over constantly until the oil separates. It may seem like a lot of oil, but this is essential to keep the paste moist once it is cooked.

3 When the paste is nearly done, add the sugar, tomato purée, salt and lime juice. Taste and adjust the seasoning if needed. Remove from the heat, and leave to cool. Once the sambal paste has cooled completely, transfer to an airtight jar, and refrigerate. This makes about 600g (1¼lb) sambal; any leftover sambal will keep for several weeks stored in an airtight jar in the refrigerator, and you can use as needed.

4 Cut each chicken leg into two pieces at the leg joint, and rub all over with the salt. Bring a small saucepan of water to the boil, and poach the chicken legs in the simmering liquid for 10 minutes until nearly done. Drain and allow to cool.

5 Just before serving, heat the oil in a wok, and fry the chicken lightly all over for 3 minutes until slightly charred.

6 Top each portion with 1 tbsp of the sambal, and serve with plain rice and sliced cucumber.

SRI OWEN beef rendang

This dish moves from boiling to frying in a continuous process, says writer and cookery teacher Sri Owen, who is the author of several highly regarded works, including *Sri Owen's Indonesian Food*, *New Wave Asian* and *The Rice Book*. 'As the water in the coconut milk is driven off, the oil remains, until eventually the meat has absorbed the oil and has become almost black, quite dry but richly succulent, while the solid residue from the oil forms a kind of dry relish.' Brisket is the cut of beef Sri recommends for this dish, but silverside or stewing steak is also suitable.

SERVES 6–8   PREPARATION TIME: 45 MINUTES

TOOLS
Cleaver
Chopping board
Mortar and pestle
Pressure cooker
Ladle

INGREDIENTS
5 shallots, finely sliced
6 fresh red chillies, roughly
    chopped, or 3 tsp chilli powder
4 garlic cloves, roughly chopped
2.5cm (1in) piece of fresh root
    ginger, roughly chopped
1.5kg (3lb 3oz) brisket, cut into
    2cm (¾in) strips or cubes
1 tsp ground turmeric
1 tsp chopped galangal or
    ½ tsp galangal or laos powder
2.3 litres (scant 10 cups/
    scant 2½ quarts) coconut milk
1 bay leaf
1 fresh turmeric leaf or
    1 stalk lemon grass
2 tsp salt

1 Using a mortar and pestle, grind the shallots, chillies or chilli powder, garlic and ginger to a fine paste.

2 Put all the ingredients in a pressure cooker, and cook for about 1 hour.

3 Release the pressure by running the cooker under a cold tap, then open the lid and stir well. The coconut milk will have rendered down to be mostly oil.

4 Return the pan to the heat, uncovered, and fry the rendang for about 15 minutes until the coconut oil has become thick and brown. Serve hot with rice.

bali chicken

Fruits such as mango, jackfruit and carambola are made liberal use of in Indonesian and especially Balinese cooking. This is a very moreish dish, with a delectable blend of flavours and perfumes from the spices and green mango.

SERVES 4   PREPARATION TIME: 45 MINUTES

TOOLS
Cleaver
Chopping board
Mortar and pestle
Wok and ladle

INGREDIENTS
4 skinless chicken breast fillets
about 1½ tsp salt, plus extra for
   sprinkling
2 green mangoes
250ml (1 cup) coconut milk
1 tsp sugar
1 tbsp freshly squeezed lime juice
fresh mint or sweet basil leaves,
   to garnish

For the spice paste
2 fresh red chillies
1 tsp whole black peppercorns
4 candlenuts or macadamia nuts or
   blanched almonds

1 Slice the chicken breasts horizontally into 3 or 4 escalopes, and rub with about ½ tsp of the salt. Peel the green mangoes, and cut into julienne. Sprinkle with a little salt, and leave to sweat for 20 minutes. Squeeze out the moisture, and set aside.

2 Using a mortar and pestle, grind the chillies, peppercorns and nuts to a rough paste. Pour the coconut milk into a wok. Add the spice paste, 1 tsp salt, sugar and lime juice, and bring to a boil. Add the chicken pieces, reduce the heat slightly and simmer for 10 minutes until cooked through. Add the julienned green mango, and cook for a further 2 minutes.

3 Serve warm, garnished with mint or sweet basil leaves.

nonya coriander duck

Deceptively simple, this dish requires assiduous watching over the wok, pan or whatever utensil you choose to cook it in, while it simmers to glazed perfection. A nonstick large wok or pot is ideal because of the long braising time involved. Traditionally, sugar cane is used as the sweetening agent. If this is not available, sugar will have to suffice, although the characteristic cane sugar fragrance will not be present.

SERVES 6–8   PREPARATION TIME: 2 HOURS

TOOLS
Vegetable knife
Chopping board
Large nonstick wok and ladle

INGREDIENTS
1 oven-ready duck
2 tbsp ground coriander
1 tsp freshly ground
    black pepper
½ tsp ground cloves
5 tbsp thick dark soy sauce
3 tbsp groundnut (peanut) or
    other vegetable oil
6–8 shallots, chopped
6 garlic cloves, coarsely ground
1 small bunch of fresh coriander
    (cilantro), chopped
2 tsp salt
4 or 5 pieces of sugar cane,
    each about 10cm (4in) long,
    lightly crushed, or 2 tbsp
    palm or demerara sugar
4 spring onions (scallions),
    sliced diagonally into 5cm
    (2in) lengths

1 Clean the duck thoroughly, making sure that the insides are free of blood and traces of offal. Wipe dry with kitchen paper, and rub all over with the ground coriander, black pepper, cloves and soy sauce. Leave to marinate for 15 minutes.

2 Heat the oil in a nonstick wok or pan (make sure that you have a lid at the ready), and fry the shallots for a few minutes until starting to turn golden. Add the garlic, and fry for a further minute until golden brown but not burnt.

3 Put the duck in the wok or pan, and fry, turning constantly, until every inch of skin has sizzled and browned. The reason for using a nonstick pan is obvious: the skin of the duck browns evenly without scorching.

4 When the duck is well sizzled, add just enough water (about 200ml/scant 1 cup) for braising – you do not want the bird to be swimming in water – and simmer for 1½ hours or more. It is important, while the duck is simmering, to keep turning the bird and spooning gravy all over. Cover the pan occasionally – for about 10 minutes each time – so that the compressed steam cooks the duck faster, and top up with a little more water if it is becoming too dry. Add the chopped coriander (cilantro), salt and sugar cane or sugar about halfway through the cooking time, and the spring onions (scallions) 15 minutes before the end. When the sauce is thick and glossy, the duck should be done.

5 Serve whole, or cut into slices, and let diners cut and come again as they wish. Serve the gravy on the side with plain rice as an accompaniment.

opor ayam

Opor ayam hails originally from Indonesia and is in reality a mild curry. The coconut milk gives it a subtle flavour and aroma, with hints of tartness from the tamarind or lime juice. As a final flourish, it is garnished with fried unsweetened shredded or desiccated coconut.

SERVES 4   PREPARATION TIME: 45 MINUTES

TOOLS
Cleaver
Chopping board
Wok and ladle
Mortar and pestle
Small frying pan

INGREDIENTS
4 whole chicken legs (drumstick
    and thigh)
500ml (2 cups) coconut milk

2 stalks lemon grass (use 5cm
    (2in) of the root end only),
    bruised
2 kaffir lime leaves
1 tsp salt
1 tsp sugar
1 tbsp tamarind concentrate or
    2 tbsp freshly squeezed lime juice
2 tbsp unsweetened shredded (flaked) or
    desiccated (shredded) coconut
1 fresh red chilli, finely sliced (optiona)

For the spice paste
2 fresh red chillies, roughly chopped
5 candlenuts or macadamia nuts
½ large onion, finely chopped
3 garlic cloves, roughly chopped
1 tbsp ground coriander
1 tsp ground fennel
2 thin slices fresh galangal
60g (2oz) shrimp paste

1 Remove the skin from the chicken if preferred, and cut each chicken leg into 4 pieces. Pour the coconut milk into a wok or large heavy pan, add the chicken and bring to the boil.

2 To make the spice paste, using a mortar and pestle, grind together all the ingredients to a smooth paste. Add the paste, lime leaves, lemon grass, salt, sugar and tamarind concentrate or lime juice to the wok or pan with the chicken, and simmer for 25 minutes.

3 In a small dry frying pan, toast the coconut over a medium heat for a few minutes until golden brown. Sprinkle over the chicken as a garnish, together with the chilli (if using), and serve hot with plain rice or flat bread.

pork ribs in black bean sauce

Black beans and black bean sauce are almost exclusive to Malaysian and Singaporean Chinese cooking, and both go particularly well with pork. The sauce, readily available in jars, sometimes comes with ginger and garlic, and is quite concentrated. Simmering the pork ribs first ensures that the meat is more succulent and absorbs seasonings better.

SERVES 4   PREPARATION TIME: 45 MINUTES, PLUS SEVERAL HOURS' MARINATING

TOOLS
Cleaver
Chopping board
Wok or large pot
Steamer
Steaming dish

INGREDIENTS
8 large meaty pork ribs
2 tbsp light soy sauce
2 tbsp sesame oil
1 tbsp black bean sauce
1 tbsp crushed fresh root ginger
3 garlic cloves, finely chopped
2 fresh red chillies, chopped

1 Cut the ribs into 6cm/2½in pieces. Bring 500ml (2 cups) water to the boil, and add the soy sauce. Simmer the ribs for 20 minutes. Drain and allow to cool; reserve the stock for another use.

2 Blend together the sesame oil, black bean sauce, ginger, garlic and chillies, and use to marinate the cooked ribs in the refrigerator for several hours.

3 Place the marinated ribs in a shallow steaming dish, and put in a steamer. Cover and steam for 15 minutes. The ribs will have absorbed much of the black bean flavour and be more tender because they have been simmered first. Serve hot with plenty of napkins for wiping sticky fingers.

Cook's note To make your own black bean sauce, simply mash some whole fermented black soya beans, and mix with a little groundnut (peanut) or other vegetable oil and the aromatics of your choice.

TYM SRISAWATT lamb cutlets in penang sauce

A former restaurateur, Tym Srisawatt is passionate about improving the standards and authenticity of Thai cuisine in the United Kingdom. Married to a Malaysian, Tym has the added advantage of being exposed to another cuisine closely related to her own, which has enriched her understanding of the region's culinary evolution. This recipe comes from her husband Tony's birthplace.

SERVES 4   PREPARATION TIME: 50 MINUTES

TOOLS
Mortar and pestle
Cleaver
Chopping board
Frying pan
Wok and ladle

INGREDIENTS
500g (1lb 2oz) lamb cutlets
  (lamb rib chops), trimmed
  of any excess fat
2 tbsp groundnut (peanut) or
  other vegetable oil
2 tbsp Penang curry paste
  (see below)
150ml (⅔ cup) coconut milk
5 kaffir lime leaves
1 tbsp fish sauce such as
  nam pla
1 tbsp palm sugar
fresh coriander (cilantro) leaves,
  chopped, to garnish
For the Penang curry paste
6–8 large dried red chillies
1 tsp coriander seeds
1 tsp cumin seeds
2 tbsp skinless raw peanuts,
  roughly chopped
1 tsp salt
1 stalk lemon grass, trimmed
  and tough outer layer
  removed, cut into thin rounds
2 tsp chopped galangal
1 tbsp chopped coriander
  (cilantro) root
5 shallots, finely chopped
5 garlic gloves, finely chopped
1 tsp shrimp paste

1 To make the Penang curry paste, put the dried chillies in a bowl, and cover with hot water. Leave to soak for about 30 minutes until soft. Drain, then halve lengthways to remove any seeds and membrane.

2 Meanwhile, in a dry frying pan over a medium heat, toast first the cumin seeds, then the coriander seeds and lastly the peanuts for 3–5 minutes each until fragrant. Using a mortar and pestle, grind the cumin and coriander seeds into a fine powder. Set aside with the peanuts.

3 Put the soaked chillies in the mortar with the salt, and pound into a smooth paste. Add the lemon grass, and keep pounding until smooth, then add the galangal and coriander root. Pound again until the paste is smooth once more. Now add the toasted peanuts, shallots, garlic and ground cumin and coriander seeds. Grind into a paste, add the shrimp paste, and pound to mix well. Set aside. (You need only 2 tbsp paste for the recipe; any leftover paste will keep in an airtight jar stored in the refrigerator for up to 1 week.)

4 To cook the dish, pat the lamb cutlets dry with kitchen paper. Heat the oil in a wok over a medium-high heat, and fry the chops on both sides for 2–3 minutes to seal in the juices. Remove to a plate, and keep warm.

5 Put 2 tbsp of the Penang curry paste in the wok with the coconut milk, lime leaves, fish sauce and sugar. Stir together until well blended, then bring to a gentle boil.

6 Return the lamp chops (and any juices) to the wok, and gently simmer for 10 minutes. Alternatively, fry the chops for 5 minutes on each side until done, and serve Western-style with the reduced sauce poured over the top. Garnish with chopped coriander (cilantro), and serve hot with plain rice.

Cook's note If you do not have the time or inclination to make your own Penang curry paste, you can find it in Thai and other Southeast Asian food stores and supermarkets. If it is not available, use any Thai red curry paste instead (see page 186).

fried pork satay

Satay is indigenous to most of Southeast Asia, and it does not always come on skewers. This classic Singapore version, *sate babi goreng*, comes from the Nonya, or Straits Chinese, heritage, and is less fiddly to make because there are no skewers to deal with – but it is no less delicious than the popular street-hawker variety. The pork is simply fried slowly until the spice paste and coconut milk become a thick redolent sauce.

SERVES 4   PREPARATION TIME: 25 MINUTES

TOOLS
Cleaver
Chopping board
Wok and ladle

INGREDIENTS
500g (1lb 2oz) boneless
   pork chop or tenderloin
   with a little fat
3 tbsp groundnut (peanut) or
   other vegetable oil
200ml (scant 1 cup) coconut milk
1 tsp sugar
1 tsp salt
5 kaffir lime leaves, shredded
1 cucumber, deseeded and cut
   into julienne, to serve
For the spice mix
2 tbsp ground coriander
1 tbsp ground cumin
1 tsp ground fenugreek
½ tsp chilli powder
1 tsp ground turmeric

1 Slice the pork into pieces about 1cm (½in) thick and 5cm (2in) square. Blend together all the spices for the spice mix with a little water – just enough to make a thick paste. Heat the oil in a wok over a low heat, and fry the spice paste for 5 minutes until the oil separates and the spices are fragrant.

2 Add the pork to the wok, and stir-fry for 5 minutes before adding the coconut milk, sugar and salt. Reduce the heat to low, and simmer, uncovered, for 20 minutes, stirring constantly to aid evaporation and the reduction process.

3 Add the lime leaves in the last 5 minutes of the cooking time, and increase the heat to reduce the sauce even more. Serve hot with bread or rice, and cucumber julienne.

serving items

Meals throughout Southeast Asia are communal, served simply on banana leaves and ordinary plates and bowls. For special occasions such as weddings and birthdays, however, presentation becomes spectacular, with glorious colourful bamboo baskets to hold bulky items. The preserved fruits and sweetmeats traditionally served at Chinese New Year and during Taoist festivals are presented in smaller decorated baskets, many exquisitely crafted to please the various deities.

1 PAINTED BASKETS

Traditional painted baskets of woven bamboo called *sia na* were used for containing gifts during weddings in earlier times. Some of these could be large enough to hold bottles of wine, syrups, and whole suckling pigs, fruits and the like. Smaller ones were used for cakes and treats, carried by members of the groom's family to the bride's home on the important day, to sweeten their thoughts and lives. Much of this craft is now dying, but with ingenuity the same designs have been cast in porcelain for the same functions. Some baskets are single-tiered; others are stacked two or three high. They make ideal serving utensils for snacks and side dishes such as prawn crackers, fried shallots, peanut wafers and other titbits.

2 LACQUERED STACKING BASKET

Throughout Southeast Asia, basketware remains a fundamental element in the home. As well as serving a utilitarian purpose, baskets are often fine objets d'art, such as this multi-tiered model meant to contain sweet treats and candies for festive occasions.

3 PORCELAIN BANANA LEAF RICE PLATE

Banana leaves were traditionally used as disposable plates throughout Southeast Asia. Rural Indonesians and Malaysians still eat from leaves and other natural containers, and even in more urbanized areas banana leaves are still very much associated with meal presentation, often used to line serving and dining plates, especially for festive and other special-occasion dishes. They bring a colourfully rustic touch to any Sotheast Asian meal, and are used in South India, too. Today, you can also find these porcelain versions in good Asian tableware outlets.

CUTLERY (NOT SHOWN)

The standard place setting for most Southeast Asian meals served with rice would be a dinner plate, fork and spoon, the cutlery usually of stainless steel or local materials such as horn or brass. To the surprise of many non-Southeast Asians, chopsticks are not a key player in this part of the region, being used only when noodles are served. The knife, as used in the West, never makes a showing at Asian tables, because it is considered a chef's tool and therefore too barbaric to used at the table. Nor does it serve any purpose in traditional meals because no Asian dish requires food to be cut up at the table – all ingredients are cut into bite-sized pieces during preparation. If soup is served during a meal, whether it is presented in individual bowls or in a large bowl placed at the centre of the table, a porcelain spoon and rest would be provided.

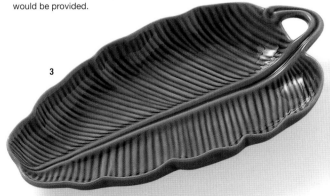

gado gado

The world and a half knows of this iconic Indonesian salad of tofu and vegetables. There are also several other versions, known by different names, found in Singapore, Malaysia and Thailand. Essentially, it is a mix of boiled and raw vegetables and firm bean curd, drenched in a mild peanut sauce. The bean curd used here is a firm variety sold in most Chinese stores and called *tau kwa* in the Chinese Fujian dialect.

SERVES 4   PREPARATION TIME: 1 HOUR

TOOLS

Vegetable knife
Chopping board
Mortar and pestle
Wok and ladle
Small pot
Large pot

INGREDIENTS

1 or 2 yard-long (snake) beans
    or 6 long French beans
½ Savoy cabbage
½ cucumber
2 pieces of firm bean curd
2 tbsp groundnut (peanut) or
    other vegetable oil
3 hard-boiled eggs, cut into
    quarters
roasted skinless peanuts,
    to garnish
handful of pea shoots or
    watercress, to garnish
    (optional)

For the peanut sauce

6 dried chillies, roughly chopped
1 tbsp shrimp paste
5 shallots, roughly chopped
1 tbsp tamarind concentrate
1 tsp sugar
1 tsp salt
2 tbsp chopped roasted
    skinless peanuts

1 To make the sauce, using a mortar and pestle, grind the chillies, shrimp paste and shallots to a fine paste. Mix 150ml (⅔ cup) water with the tamarind concentrate, and bring to the boil in a small pot. Reduce the heat slightly, and simmer for 5 minutes. Add the ground paste, sugar and salt. Simmer for a further 5 minutes, then add the chopped peanuts. Set aside to keep warm (or use cold if you prefer).

2 Next, prepare the vegetables and bean curd. Cut the beans into 5cm (2in) lengths, wash and drain. Slice the cabbage into bite-sized pieces. Peel the cucumber, remove and discard the soft core and cut the flesh into diagonal pieces about 1cm (½in) wide.

3 Cut each piece of bean curd into two, then again into slices ½cm (¼in) thick. Heat the oil in a wok, and fry the bean curd pieces until light golden brown. Remove from the wok, drain on kitchen paper and keep warm.

4 Meanwhile, bring a large pot of water to the boil, and blanch the beans and cabbage for 3 minutes. Drain.

6 Arrange the vegetables, bean curd, cucumber and hard-boiled eggs on a large serving plate or platter. Scatter with roasted peanuts and pea shoots or watercress (if using). Serve immediately with the warm or cold peanut sauce in a small bowl for dipping.

Cook's note Gado gado also works well with the satay sauce given on page 240.

nasi lemak

Nasi lemak began its culinary life many decades ago as a street-hawker dish, when a simple portion of coconut rice would be wrapped in a banana leaf and flavoured with a thick hot sambal. Today it is a veritable smorgasbord of delicious proportions and may include a curry, pickles, prawn crackers, omelette and fried fish, as well as the sambal. Together, the result is more than the sum of its parts and is typically served for breakfast. Below is a recipe for coconut rice and a few classic accompaniments. The whitebait used is not fresh, but a dried product called *ikan bilis* that is sold in most Chinese and Southeast Asian food stores. The fried tamarind-marinated mackerel opposite can be included as part of the meal; alternatively, serve a beef stew or chicken curry instead.

coconut rice

Rinse 400g (2½ cups) jasmine rice, and soak in water for 30 minutes. Rinse again, drain and put on a steamer tray. Wash 2 pandan leaves and tie into knots, then press them down into the rice. Pour in 400ml (1⅔ cups) coconut milk, and season with 1 tsp salt. Mix well. Place in a steamer, and cook for 15 minutes. To serve, mound on a banana leaf-covered plate, and top with wok-fried eggs and sambal; serve some sliced cucumber and other side dishes in baskets or in small bowls or plates.

wok-fried eggs

Put 4 eggs in a saucepan of cold water, bring to the boil and simmer for 6 minutes. Drain, and cool under cold running water, then remove the shells. In a clean wok, heat 1 tbsp groundnut (peanut) oil. Add the eggs, and roll them around the pan until a brown skin forms. Cut in half before serving, topping with the sambal if desired.

hot chilli sambal

Using a mortar and pestle, grind 1 chopped large onion, 3 chopped garlic cloves, 4 chopped fresh red chillies and 2 tsp shrimp paste to a fine paste. Heat 4 tbsp groundnut (peanut) or other vegetable oil in a wok, and fry the spice paste over a low heat until fragrant. Add 1 tbsp tomato purée (paste), 2 tbsp tamarind paste, 1 tsp salt and 1 tsp sugar, and continue cooking for a further 1 minute. When the mixture is thick and aromatic, transfer to a bowl, and set aside to cool.

fried whitebait and peanuts

Shake off any excess grit from 200g (7oz) dried whitebait or *ikan bilis*. Heat 3 tbsp groundnut (peanut) oil in a wok, and stir-fry the whitebait for 4 minutes until brown and crisp. Remove and set aside. Add 200g (7oz) skinless raw peanuts to the wok, toss to brown lightly and serve alongside, or mixed through, the fried whitebait.

fried tamarind-marinated mackerel

A faithful companion to coconut rice, these mackerel pieces are first steeped in tamarind paste, drained and fried until crisp, to give a dish known as *ikan goreng asam*. The sweet flesh of the mackerel takes on a special flavour when served with hot chilli sambal. As with any food with a tamarind coating, the fish will turn dark brown when fried – do not worry, as this is normal.

SERVES 4   PREPARATION TIME: 25 MINUTES

TOOLS
Cleaver
Chopping board
Wok and ladle
Draining rack

INGREDIENTS
1 large mackerel, about 600g
   (1lb 5oz), gutted and cleaned
2 tbsp tamarind paste
1 tbsp light soy sauce
groundnut (peanut) or other
   vegetable oil for deep-frying

1 Cut the mackerel into 4 thick steaks, discarding the head and tail fin.

2 In a bowl, blend together the tamarind paste, soy sauce and 150ml (⅔ cup) water. Add the fish, and leave to marinate for 10 minutes.

3 Heat enough oil for deep-frying in a wok. Drain the fish, and pat dry with kitchen paper. When the oil is hot, deep-fry the fish for about 4 minutes, turning once during cooking.

4 Drain on a rack, then serve alone with a little sambal (see page 254 and opposite), or as a part of a *nasi lemak* meal.

tools for cakes and snacks

In Southeast Asia, cakes and cookies are traditionally associated with symbolism and festive rites, especially during Taoist festivals. Those that originated in China are still held in reverence for their yin–yang symbolism. Others have evolved from a blend of Indonesian, Malay and Chinese cultures. Some of the most distinctive sweetmeats of Southeast Asia have transcended their festive and symbolic roles to become everyday snacks sold by street hawkers, restaurants and gourmet retailers. Such is their popularity that traditional moulds have been given high-tech treatment. Once in danger of becoming extinct, these now take pride of place in the region's culinary cultures.

1 2 LONGEVITY CAKE MOULDS
Paisley-shaped or round templates, featuring motifs symbolic of long life and prosperity, are carved from wooden blocks to make moulds.

3 MOONCAKE MOULD
Mooncakes are made of rice flour dough and filled with sweet almond or mung bean mash, pressed into the mould, gently knocked out and steamed or baked. The moulds are made of hardwood and carved with designs symbolic of the moon and its role in mythology.

4 COOKIE MOULDS
These types of mould are for small cakes known as *kueh koyah*. *Kueh koyah* are made of mung bean flour and usually feature leaf or fruit motifs. Plastic models of the moulds are also available.

5 CURRY PUFF MOULD
Curry puffs, the half-moon-shaped Anglo-Indian pastries with crimped edges, were traditionally shaped by hand, but this fold-over plastic mould makes the job easier, neater and faster.

6 ROUND CUTTER
Rings of aluminium in various sizes are used to stamp out rounds of pastry and dough.

7 BRASS CRIMPER AND ROLLER
A clever double-ended tool for decorating and shaping crumbly cookies of rice and coconut milk.

8 MELON BALLER
Shown here is a heart-shaped version of a melon baller. In Southeast Asia, melon balls are often served piled up in large fruit shells, or added to sweet drinks, and are sometimes used as a filling for sweet rice and wheat flour cakes, instead of red bean paste.

9 BOAT-SHAPED TART MOULD

Looking like a little aluminium boat, this type of mould is used for the pastry base of pineapple and fruit tarts, which are usually served during Chinese New Year.

10 GROOVED METAL TART MOULD

This oval mould contains an inset piece of wood for shaping pastry cases. It stamps each case to give a raised rim, and mashed pineapple is then piled inside for baking.

11 12 KUEH BOLU MOULDS

These moulds make little egg-based sponge cakes known as *kueh bolu*. The traditional model is brass or copper, with a lid designed to contain hot charcoal on its top, while the mould itself is heated on a clay oven. The modern version is much the same, but runs on electricity. The moulds are shaped with floral and animal motifs symbolic of luck or prosperity, or simply to look pretty for festive occasions.

13 14 LOVE LETTER MOULDS

Kueh belandah, or love letters, are traditional egg rolls, wafer-thin and crisp, that originated in China, but are now made mainly in Southeast Asia. The moulds were originally made of iron, and featured two plates etched with heraldic designs that were clasped tightly together and attached to long handles for manipulating over a charcoal brazier. The modern electric version looks like a waffle-maker. The word *belandah* refers to a genus of crabs that mate for life and are always found in pairs in coastal areas of Malaysia. The belief is that the cakes were originally made to hide secret messages between lovers – and from warring factions.

curry puffs

These Malaysian snacks look like small Cornish pasties or empanadas, and are usually filled with a curried potato and chicken or lamb mixture. They are believed to have evolved during colonial days when British expatriates and rubber plantation owners, missing their traditional pasties, asked their cooks to come up with something similar containing meat and potato. Given that most cooks in those days were indentured workers from southern India, spices were usually featured in cooking, and so it was that Malaysia came to create a nice fusion-style curried pasty. If you do not wish to make your own dough, use 400g (14oz) ready-made shortcrust pastry.

MAKES 20   PREPARATION TIME: 35 MINUTES

TOOLS
Chopping board
Cleaver
Small rolling pin
7cm (3in) biscuit (cookie) cutter
Wok and ladle
Curry puff mould
Wire mesh strainer

INGREDIENTS
For the pastry
300g (2½ cups) plain
  (all-purpose) flour, plus
  extra for dusting
pinch of salt
60g (4 tbsp/½ stick) butter
  or hard cooking margarine
For the filling
2 tbsp curry powder
1 tbsp groundnut (peanut) or
  other vegetable oil, plus extra
  for deep-frying
2 garlic cloves, crushed
300g (10oz) lamb mince
  (ground lamb)
150g (5½oz) potato, peeled
  and finely diced (about 1 cup)
1 tsp salt
1 tsp sugar

1 To make the pastry, mix together the flour and salt in a bowl. Rub in the butter with your fingertips until the mixture resembles breadcrumbs. Add 75ml (¼ cup plus 1 tbsp) water, and knead well until the dough comes away from the bowl. On a floured work surface, roll out the pastry until about 3mm (⅛in) thick, and cut out circles of the dough with the biscuit (cookie) cutter. Set aside.

2 Mix the curry powder with 2 tbsp water to make a paste. Heat the 1 tbsp oil in the wok, and gently fry the crushed garlic until just starting to turn golden; be careful not to burn, as it will taste bitter. Add the curry paste, and stir over a low heat for a few minutes without letting it burn.

3 Add the meat and potato. Keep stirring until the meat is cooked and the mixture is moist but not watery. Mix in the salt and sugar, then leave to cool.

4 Place a circle of pastry in the curry puff mould, and add 1 tbsp of the meat mixture. Close to seal the edges, so that you end up with a half-moon-shaped parcel with crimped edges. Repeat with the remaining dough circles.

5 Clean out the wok with some kitchen paper, and heat enough oil in it for deep-frying. When the oil is hot, deep-fry the curry puffs for 3–4 minutes until golden brown, turning halfway through cooking. Cook in batches if necessary, so that you do not crowd the wok. Drain the curry puffs on kitchen paper, before serving hot or warm.

CHRIS TAN spiced ni-tamago

In this recipe from Singapore-based food writer Chris Tan, soft-centred boiled eggs steeped in a flavourful marinade are served in classic ramen-bar style. You can eat them on their own or on top of ramen – or even on hot buttered toast.

SERVES 3–4   PREPARATION TIME: 30 MINUTES, PLUS 45 MINUTES' STEEPING

TOOLS
Medium pot
Large pot

INGREDIENTS
750ml (3 cups) light pork or
   chicken stock
1 garlic clove, left whole and
   unpeeled
1 tbsp crushed rock sugar
2 petals star anise
3cm (1¼in) piece of cinnamon
   stick
1 whole clove
4–5 tbsp premium shoyu
   (Japanese soy sauce)
½ tsp sesame oil
¼ tsp salt, or to taste
6 large fresh eggs, preferably
   free-range
300g (10oz) ramen noodles,
   cooked and drained
   (optional)
toasted sesame seeds,
   to garnish
fresh Chinese or ordinary
   chives, to garnish

1 Put the stock, garlic, rock sugar, star anise, cinnamon and clove in a saucepan. Bring to a steady simmer over a medium heat, and continue to simmer until reduced to just over half its original volume. Stir in the soy sauce and sesame oil. Allow to cool, then taste and adjust the seasoning with salt, more soy sauce or sugar as needed; it should be a little saltier than broth, with a concentrated meaty flavour.

2 Bring a large pot of water to the boil over a medium heat. Carefully lower the eggs into the water, and boil for exactly 6 minutes. Immediately lift out the eggs and plunge into a bowl of ice water to stop the cooking. When the eggs are cold, lightly tap all over to crack the shells, then carefully peel – they will be soft. Place in a thick plastic freezer bag, and gently pour in the cooled reduction. Press out as much air as you can, then tie a firm knot in the neck of the bag. Tie or hook the bag onto a support so that it hangs in midair: this allows the marinade to fully surround the eggs. Leave to stand for 45 minutes.

3 To finish the dish, untie the bag, and carefully lift the eggs out of the marinade; the latter can be reused immediately for another batch of eggs (but no more than that) if desired. The yolks of the eggs should be thick but still runny; steep for 1–2 hours longer if you prefer firmer yolks. Serve the eggs whole or cut in half, rolled in toasted sesame seeds. If you like, sit the eggs on a bed of cooked ramen noodles, and garnish with chives.

kueh bolu

The name of these charming festive cakes, *kueh bolu*, literally means 'round cakes', not on account of their shape, but in homage to the moon. Once reserved for Chinese New Year, *kueh bolu* are now eaten all year round, thanks to the ease with which they can be made in the modern electric moulds (see page 271). These cakes are easy to produce, but for best results it is essential that you beat the eggs with an electric whisk.

SERVES 4   PREPARATION TIME: 40 MINUTES

TOOLS
Electric whisk
Mortar and pestle
Electric kueh bolu mould
Pastry brush

INGREDIENTS
6 eggs
140g (scant ¾ cup) sugar
pinch of salt
50g (½ cup) plain
   (all-purpose) flour
4 tbsp coconut milk
2 pandan leaves

1 Crack the eggs into a large bowl. Add the sugar and salt, and beat with an electric whisk until the mixture is white and frothy. Stir in the flour and coconut milk, and blend until the batter is smooth.

2 Using a mortar and pestle, grind the pandan leaves to extract the liquid essence. Strain into the batter.

3 Heat the kueh bolu machine, and thoroughly oil each mould with a pastry brush. Pour a little batter into each mould to fill to just below the rim (top left below); the cakes will swell a little when cooked. Clamp down the lid of the machine, and cook for about 3 minutes until the cakes are golden brown.

4 Allow to cool in the mould before gently removing each cake from the machine using a pair of chopsticks (bottom left below). These little sponge cakes will keep for a few weeks in an airtight tin.

longevity cakes

The Chinese name of *ang ku kueh* translates literally to 'red turtle cakes' for two reasons. In Chinese culture, red is symbolic of prosperity, while the turtle represents longevity. Each mould is usually etched with the design of a turtle or a Chinese character for prosperity, and the cake is dyed red for good measure.

SERVES 4   PREPARATION TIME: 1 HOUR, PLUS OVERNIGHT SOAKING

TOOLS
Cleaver
Chopping board
Saucepans
Steamer
Longevity cake moulds
Banana leaves

INGREDIENTS
200g (7oz) sweet potato, diced
  (about 1½ cups)
400g (2½ cups) glutinous
  rice flour
300ml (1¼ cups) coconut milk
3 tbsp sugar
pinch of salt
½ tsp natural red food colouring
For the filling
500g (2½ cups) shelled mung
  beans, soaked overnight
500g (2 cups) granulated sugar

1 In a small pan, simmer the sweet potato in enough water to cover for 5 minutes, then drain and mash well with a fork. Mix with half of the glutinous rice flour, half of the coconut milk, and the sugar and salt.

2 Bring the remaining coconut milk to a slow simmer, and mix with the remaining glutinous rice flour. Stir well to give a thick dough.

3 Combine both doughs, and knead on a floured board for 5 minutes. Add the food colouring, and knead to incorporate thoroughly.

4 To make the filling, drain the soaked beans into a steamer tray, and cook for 15 minutes or until very soft. Mash well.

5 Put 200ml (scant 1 cup) water and the sugar in a pan, and boil until the sugar has dissolved and the liquid has become a thick syrup. Add the mashed beans, and cook over a low heat until the mixture is very dry and thick. Set aside to cool.

6 Oil the palms of your hands, and divide the dough into lemon-sized balls. Flatten a little, then make a deep dent in the centre of the dough and fill with 1 tbsp of the bean filling (opposite top left). Close up and seal.

7 Press the filled ball into a mould (opposite top centre), and apply gentle pressure so that the design of the mould is deeply etched on the surface of the cake when turned out (opposite top right).

8 Blanch the banana leaves in hot water for 1 minute to make them more pliable, and cut into squares slightly larger than the cakes. Sit a cake on each square, place in the steamer and cook for 15 minutes. Serve cold.

glossary of ingredients

appam flour A type of rice flour used to make appam, a South Indian speciality, and hoppers, which feature in Sri Lankan cuisine.

asafoetida powder This powder ground from a species of giant fennel is very pungent and should always be used sparingly. Its overpowering odour mellows during cooking to produce a flavour not unlike onion or leeks. Used primarily in Indian cooking, particularly South Indian cooking, it is also favoured by followers of Jainism, who do not eat root vegetables. Also known as *hing*.

Asian pear The fruit from a species of pear tree, *Pyrus pyrifolia*, native to China, Japan and the Korean peninsula. Also called nashi pear, Japanese pear, Korean pear and apple pear.

basmati rice A variety of long-grain rice prized for its perfumed fragrance and delicate flavour, basmati rice is grown in the Himalayan foothills of India and Pakistan.

beansprouts Sprouts germinated from mung beans are commonly used in Chinese cuisine, as well as in other parts of Asia such as Thailand and Vietnam. These are the thick, crunchy sprouts commonly sold in supermarkets, and they should always be used as fresh as possible, whether you are cooking them or serving them raw. Also called mung beansprouts.

black bean sauce Made from fermented soya beans, this sauce is widely available in jars ready-made from Chinese and Southeast Asian food stores. There is also a hot version containing chillies.

fermented black beans This intensely flavoured Chinese condiment is made by salting and fermenting dried soya beans. Also known as *douchi*, it is available in most Chinese supermarkets or food stores.

bok choy A member of the Brassica family, bok choy comes under the broad umbrella of Chinese cabbage, or *Brassica rapa*. Within this there are two subgroups: *pekinensis* and *chinensis*, and it is the latter to which bok choy belongs. Bok choy has white stems and dark green leaves, while baby bok choy has pale green steams and leaves. It is also known as pak choi. Choy sum is a member of the same group, and is smaller and more delicate, with pale green leaves and yellow flowers; it is sometimes known as flowering white cabbage or flowering Chinese cabbage. All three are interchangeable in recipes.

bonito flakes Dried flakes of smoked bonito fish, these are commonly used as a seasoning in the Japanese stock dashi. Also available as a ground powder.

candlenuts Used widely in Malaysian and Indonesian cuisine, these nuts with a very high oil content come from the flowering tree of the same name (*Aleurites moluccana*). Macadamia nuts make a good substitute if you cannot find candlenuts. They have a similar texture, but lack the candlenut's more bitter flavour.

cardamom There are two types of the spice cardamom – green cardamom and black cardamom – both from the ginger family. The whole seed pods have a papery shell and enclose small black seeds. Green cardamom pods are small and pale; black cardamom pods are larger and dark brown. Both whole pods and seeds are used in cooking. Cardamom is also ground to use as a powder.

chapati flour Used to make the bread of the same name, chapatti flour is a blend of wheat and malted barley flours. It can be found in Indian grocers and supermarkets. Also known as *atta*.

rice wine This alcoholic beverage is made by fermenting glutinous rice or millet. The Chinese rice wine Shaoxing, from the Zhejiang province, is considered particularly fine. Buy good-quality rice wine from Chinese and Japanese supermarkets, and other Asian food stores.

Chinese black vinegar This aged rice vinegar is made by fermenting malt and glutinous rice (sorghum or barley are sometimes used instead), and is somewhat similar to balsamic vinegar. Chinkiang vinegar, from the province of the same name, is considered the finest.

chilli bean paste *See* kochujang.

Chinese chives Chinese chives have flat leaves and a strong, garlic-like flavour, which has led to the alternative name of garlic chives. They are also called *gow choy* or *ku chai*. Flowering Chinese chives are the same plant with the flower in bud at the top.

Chinese salted vegetable This is the generic name for green, fleshy vegetables with a firm texture that have been pickled in salt. The greens used and even the pickling and fermenting methods may vary slightly across regions and countries, but the principle remains the same. Salted vegetable is widely used in cooking throughout China and into Indochina and the rest of Southeast Asia. It is available from Chinese and other Asian supermarkets.

crisp-fried garlic and shallots Exactly what their name implies, these crispy golden shreds of garlic and shallots, or a combination of both, can be bought ready-made in large packets from Asian food stores and supermarkets, particularly Thai or other Southeast Asian grocers. They are often used as a garnish, sprinkled over dishes to add flavour and texture.

curry leaves Leaves from the small tree *Murraya koenigii*, which is native to South and Southeast Asia. Curry leaves are used extensively as a flavouring in South Indian and Sri Lankan cooking, and have a distinctive bitter taste and a curry-like aroma. They can be used fresh, frozen or dried; like bay leaves, they are not eaten.

daikon Large white root vegetable with crisp flesh and a fairly mild flavour used in Japan and other parts of Asia such as India. Also called mooli or white radish.

dashi Japanese stock commonly made with bonito flakes and seaweed such as kombu. There are several different varieties and ingredient combinations. Dashi is also available as a concentrate or powder.

dumpling skins, or wrappers Also called *shao mai* skins or *siu mai* skins, these delicate round wrappers are made from wheat dough (with no egg). They are used for the steamed dumplings integral to Chinese dim sum. Potsticker skins, or wrappers, are slightly thicker than dumpling skins, and made to withstand pan-frying, then steaming without tearing or splitting. Wonton skins, meanwhile, are made from an egg flour dough and come in a square shape; they are about the same thickness as dumpling skins, but the egg in the dough helps them to stand up to deep-frying and using in soups.

fish sauce Extremely pungent and concentrated condiment made from fermented fish and used in cooking, particularly for curries and sauces, throughout Indochina and other parts of Southeast Asia. Fish sauce is also used in parts of China and Korea. Recipes vary slightly from country to country, with Vietnamese fish sauce having a stronger flavour than Thai fish sauce, for example. In Thailand it is called *nam pla*, while in Vietnam it is known as *nuoc mam*.

five-spice powder This spice mix is used in both Chinese and Vietnamese cooking. It is usually made up of star anise, cinnamon, cloves, fennel seeds and Sichuan pepper.

galangal From the same family as ginger, galangal has a stronger, more earthy flavour and aroma than its cousin. It is used extensively throughout Indochina and the rest of Southeast Asia, and is often found in curry pastes. It is sold fresh, frozen and dried, or ground into a powder. Fresh and frozen galangal provide the best flavour. Also known as laos root when whole, or laos powder when dried and ground.

ghee Indian term for clarified butter. Ghee is available from Indian supermarkets and other South Asian food stores.

glutinous rice As the name suggests, this short-grain rice is particularly sticky when cooked. It is grown in China, Korea, Japan, Thailand, Vietnam, Laos and Indonesia. Glutinous rice is used to make the flour of the same name.

jaggery Flavourful unrefined sugar commonly used in India that is made from the sap of palm trees or sugar cane. Sold in cakes, it is available from Indian supermarkets and other South Asian food stores. See also palm sugar.

jasmine rice A fragrant long-grain rice similar to basmati rice that is commonly used in Thai, Vietnamese and other Southeast Asian cooking, and is slightly sticky when cooked. Also called Thai fragrant rice.

kaffir lime leaves Highly fragrant leaves from the kaffir, or makrut, lime tree, *Citrus hystrix*. They are used as a flavouring in Indochinese and other Southeast Asian cooking. The leaves are a glossy dark green and are distinctively joined in a 'chain'. They can be used whole or shredded, and are available fresh, frozen or dried, depending on where you live. Fresh or frozen leaves have the best flavour.

kochujang This Korean hot chilli bean paste is made from fermented soya beans. Variations of hot chilli bean paste are also used in Chinese regional cuisine, particularly that of Sichuan. Available from Korean food stores or Asian supermarkets.

kombu Dried edible seaweed usually sold in strips or sheets, and commonly used to flavour dashi. Also called konbu.

laksa leaves Laksa leaves have a strong minty and peppery flavour and sharply pointed leaves. Also called Vietnamese mint or *rau ram*.

lotus seeds Lotus seeds are available fresh, dried or canned, depending on where you live. They are used extensively in traditional Chinese medicine, as well as in desserts. If you cannot find them, blanched almonds can be substituted. Also called lotus nuts.

Maldive fish flakes Similar to the Japanese bonito flakes, Maldive fish flakes are made by drying bonito fish under the fierce sun of the Maldive islands. It is also available in ground as a powder.

mirin Japanese rice wine similar to sake, but with a far lower alcohol content and a sweet flavour. Mirin is used as a condiment in sauces and marinades.

miso Used in Japanese cooking, miso is a thick soya bean paste made by salting and fermenting soya bean and rice or barley. White miso has a fine texture and sweet flavour; red miso is saltier.

napa cabbage Another member of the *Brassica rapa* family, napa cabbage is also called Chinese white cabbage or snow cabbage. It falls under the *pekinensis* cultivar group and is lighter in colour than bok choy (pak choi).

nori Edible seaweed available in sheets and used for rolling sushi. It is red when untoasted, but turns a dark green once subjected to heat.

palm sugar Unrefined dark sugar that is made from the sap of coconut palms and palmyrah palms. Palm sugar has a far stronger flavour than ordinary sugar, and is usually sold in round cakes or balls. It is known as *gul Melaka* in Malaysia and *gula Jawa* in Indonesia. It is available in Southeast Asian food stores and supermarkets. Also called coconut sugar or Java sugar.

palm vinegar A cloudy, mild-flavoured vinegar made from the sap of coconut palms that is especially popular in the Philippines, but also used elsewhere in Southeast Asia.

paneer A fresh curd cheese made in India that is similar in texture and flavour to feta cheese.

pandan leaf The sword-shaped leaves of the screwpine (*Pandanus* spp.) are used as food wrappers in Southeast Asia, but are also tied together into a bundle and used to add flavour and aroma to rice and curries. The leaf's essence is also used to flavour cakes. Also known as pandanus leaf, screwpine leaf, *bai toei* and *daun pandan*.

panko Crisp toasted Japanese breadcrumbs made from the white part only of bread and coarser in texture than ordinary breadcrumbs.

rice paper wrappers Thin and extremely fragile, these wrappers are used to make Vietnamese spring rolls and summer rolls. Also called spring roll wrappers, Vietnamese rice paper or *banh trang* wrappers.

rock sugar Crystallized in large chunks, rock sugar can be either clear or yellow in colour. It is not as sweet as granulated sugar and is found in Chinese supermarkets and Asian grocers. Also called yellow rock sugar, Chinese sugar and Chinese rock sugar.

sansho Also called sansho pepper. See Sichuan pepper.

Sichuan pepper The dried outer seed pods of the prickly ash tree (*Xanthoxylum* spp., particularly *X. simulans*), this tongue-tingling spice has a lemony flavour that is not as hot or pungent as black pepper. It features prominently in Sichuan cuisine, hence the name, and is also used in Japan (where it is known as *sansho*), Korea and the cuisines of Tibet and Bhutan. Sichuan pepper is often dry-roasted then crushed, before being added to food.

shichimi togarashi A classic Japanese blend of seasonings that contains dried red chilli flakes (hot red pepper flakes), ground sansho, dried mandarin zest, black hemp seeds, white sesame seeds, white poppy seeds and nori flakes. Also called Japanese seven-spice.

shiso leaves A pungent herb used in Japanese, Korean and Vietnamese cooking. It is often eaten with sashimi and is also used in salads, meat and fish dishes, as well as for pickling. Also called perilla.

shrimp paste Another pungent Asian ingredient to be used only sparingly, shrimp paste is made from salted fermented prawns (shrimp), and comes in cake form. Recipes vary slightly across regional cuisines. It is know various as *ngapi* in Burma, *belachan* in Malaysia and Singapore, *terasi* in Indonesia, *kapi* in Thailand, Cambodia and Laos, and by various names in Vietnam depending on the shellfish used.

spice sprouts These sprouts are germinated from daikon seeds and have a distinctive sharp, spicy flavour. Also called daikon sprouts.

sushi rice A short-grain variety of rice grown in Japan and specifically used for sushi.

tamarind The tart pulp obtained from the fruit pods of the tamarind tree is used in both South and Southeast Asian cooking. It is available dried in blocks, as a concentrate or paste, and as a powder. If used in block form, a smallish piece of the pulp is first soaked in hot water for about 10 minutes, then pushed through a sieve to remove seeds and fibres; the resulting liquid is added to dishes as required.

Thai basil Three main types of basil are used in Thai cooking: sweet basil, holy basil and lemon basil. Holy basil, or *bai kaprao*, has distinctive purple stems, serrated leaves and a far more peppery flavour than ordinary sweet basil. Lemon basil, or *bai maengluk*, has small, fuzzy leaves and is used in soups, salads and noodle dishes.

turmeric Like other rhizomes, turmeric can be used either fresh or dried and ground into a powder. Its most distinctive characteristic is its bright yellow colour. Fresh turmeric is available from South and Southeast Asian supermarkets and food stores.

wakame Slightly sweet edible green seaweed cultivated in Japan and Korea for centuries.

wasabi From the same family as horseradish, wasabi is used as a spice and condiment in Japanese cooking. Its roots are freshly grated or it can be bought ready-made as a paste. Wasabi should be used very sparingly; its strong flavour and heat factor can be overpowering.

water convolvulus An edible member of the morning glory family, *Ipomoea aquatica* is found in Southeast Asia and known as water convolvulus, water spinach or morning glory. It should not to be confused with other species of *Ipomoea*, also known as morning glory, which can be poisonous.

wild ginger Any of several plants from the *Asarum* genus found in Asia (mainly in China, Vietnam and Thailand). Wild ginger plants have kidney-shaped leaves and creeping roots. It is not a true ginger, but gains its name because its roots smell and taste similar to ginger. It is available from specialist grocers and Southeast Asian food stores.

list of suppliers

Depending on where you live, areas such as Chinatown or suburbs with a concentration of Asian businesses – even street markets and stalls – can be a good starting place for sourcing the utensils used throughout this book. If distance from a large city is an obstacle, there are reputable suppliers of implements and specialist ingredients to be found on-line. Below is a mixture of suppliers selling both cookware and essential Asian ingredients.

UNITED KINGDOM

The Asian Cookshop
www.theasiancookshop.co.uk

Damans Collection Ltd
36 South Road
Southall, Middlesex UB1 1RR
Tel: 020 8843 9465

Hoo Hing
A406 North Circular Road
Near Hangar Lane
Park Royal
London NW10 7TN
Tel: 020 8838 3388
www.hoohing.com
Other superstores in Mitcham,
Enfield, Leyton and Romford

Japan Centre
212–213 Piccadilly
London W1J 9HX
Tel: 020 7434 4218
www.japancentre.com

Japanese Kitchen
Tel: 01453 872 013
www.japanesekitchen.co.uk

The Japanese Knife Company
Tel: 0870 240 2248
 www.japaneseknifecompany.com

Mita Emporium
80 The Green
Southall, Middlesex UB2 4BG
Tel: 020 8571 6571

New Loon Moon
9a Gerrard Street
London W1D 5PL
Tel: 020 7734 3887

Nippon Kitchen
Tel: 020 8881 1719
www.nipponkitchen.com

Oriental Mart
6–8 Heathcote Street
Nottingham NG1 3AA
Tel: 0115 9506615 / 07789 636 744
www.orientalmart.co.uk

Quality Foods
South Road
Southall, Middlesex UB1 1SQ
Tel: 020 8917 9188

Raan Thai
Tel: 0844 414 2311
www.raanthai.co.uk

Song's Supermarket
76–78 Burlington Road
New Malden, Surrey KT3 4NU
Tel: 020 8942 8471
e-mail: css22@hotmail.com

Spices of India
Tel: 01202 873 298
www.spicesofindia.co.uk

Taj Stores
112–114 Brick Lane
London E1 6RL
Tel: 020 7377 0061
www.cuisinenet.co.uk/tajstores

Talad Thai
326 Upper Richmond Road
Putney, London SW15 6TL
Tel: 020 8789 8084

Teendeep
30 Ealing Road
Wembley, London HA0 4TL
Tel: 020 8903 8598

Tawana Supermarket
18 Chepstow Road
Notting Hill, London W2 5BD
Tel: 020 7221 6316

Thairama Ltd
16–18 London Road
Guildford, Surrey GU1 2AF
Tel: 01483 536092
e-mail: thairama_uk@hotmail.com

Wing Yip
395 Edgware Road
Cricklewood, London NW2 6LN
Tel: 020 8452 1478
Also superstores in Birmingham,
Manchester and Croydon
www.wingyip.com

General – United Kingdom

Cucina Direct
Tel: 020 8246 4311
www.cucinadirect.co.uk

Divertimenti
33–34 Marylebone High Street
London W1
Tel: 020 7935 0689
www.divertimenti.co.uk

DKB Household UK Ltd
Bridge House
Elemoor Road
Farnborough
Hampshire GU14 7UE
www.dkbhh.com

I Grunwerg Ltd
Silversteel House
29–49 Rockingham Street
Sheffield
Tel: 0114 275 6700
www.grunwerg.co.uk

Habitat
196 Tottenham Court Road
London W1
Tel: 020 7631 3880
www.habitat.net

House of Fraser
318 Oxford Street
London W1
Tel: 0207 529 4700
www.houseoffraser.co.uk

John Lewis
Oxford Street
London W1
Tel: 020 7629 7711
www.johnlewis.com

Kitchen Ideas
70 Westbourne Grove
Bayswater, London W2 5SH
Tel: 020 7229 3388

Kitchens Catering Utensils Ltd
4–5 Quiet Street
Bath, Somerset BA1 2JS
Tel: 01225 330 524

Lakeland Ltd
Alexandra Buildings
Windermere, Cumbria LA23 1BQ
Tel: 015394 88100
www.lakeland.co.uk

Selfridges
400 Oxford Street
London W1
Tel: 020 7629 1234
www.selfridges.co.uk

Typhoon Europe Ltd
Oakcroft Road
Chessington, Surrey KT9 1RH
Tel: 0208 974 4750
www.typhoonhousewares.com

AUSTRALIA

Box Hill Asian Food Centre
562 Station Street
Box Hill VIC 3128
Tel: 03 9898 7029

Ceylon Spices
511 North East Road
Gilles Plains SA 5086
Tel: 08 8261 4023
www.ceylonspices.com.au

Discount Kitchen Warehouse
Kitch N Things, 48 Mary Street
Gympie QLD 4570
Tel: 07 5482 6599
www.discountkitchenwarehouse.
com.au

Herbie's Spices
745 Darling Street
Rozelle NSW 2039
Tel: 02 9555 6035
www.herbies.com.au

Hindustan Imports
50 Greens Road
Dandenong South VIC 3175
Tel: 03 9794 6640
www.hindustan.com.au

Kim Wang Asian Supermarket
Market Plaza, 61–63 Grote Street
Adelaide SA 5000
Tel: 08 8410 1555

Kitchenware Direct
Tel: 1800 669 608
www.kitchenwaredirect.com.au

Kitchen Discounts
Tel: 1300 553 596
www.kitchendiscounts.com.au

Kongs Trading
784A Albany Highway
East Victoria Park WA 6101
Tel: 08 9362 2817
www.kongstrading.com.au
Other stores in Kewdale and
Northbridge, WA

Laguna Oriental and Indonesian
Supermarket, 772 Glenferrie Road
Hawthorn VIC 3122
Tel: 03 9818 5581

Leung Tim Choppers Co
198–200 Burwood Road
Burwood NSW 2134
Tel: 02 9744 1288

Little Saigon Market
Nicholson Street
Footscray VIC 3011
Tel: 03 9687 3505

Saini Emporium
1/910 Pittwater Road
Dee Why NSW 2099
Tel: 02 9981 1045
www.sainiemporium.com

Sanook Dee
Shop 4/5, Jacaranda Plaza
Morayfield QLD 4506
Tel: 07 5432 3370
www.sanookdee.biz

Shree Ganesh Foods
Shop 8, Balcatta Village
361 Waneroo Road
Balcatta WA 6021
Tel: 08 9349 4079
www.shreeganesh.net

Spice Mart
Shop 88, Aspley Hypermarket
59 Albany Creek Road
Aspley QLD 4034
Tel: 07 3863 4415
e-mail:info@spicemartonline.com.au

Thai Kee
399 Sussex Street
Sydney NSW 2000
Tel: 02 9281 2202

Tokyo Mart
Shop 7, Northbridge Plaza
79–113 Sailors Bay Road
Northbridge NSW 2063
Tel: 02 9958 6860

UNITED STATES

Asian Utensils
Tel: 877 469 1718
www.AsianUtensils.com

Asia Cook
Suite 30, 2850 Ocean Park Boulevard
Santa Monica, California 90405
Tel: 310 450 3270
www.asia4sale.com
Bridge Kitchenware
214 East 52nd Street
New York, New York 10022
Tel: 212 688 42200
www.bridgekitchenware.com

Broadway Panhandler
477 Broome Street
New York, New York 10013
Tel: 212 966 3434
www.broadwaypanhandler.com

Dean and Deluca
560 Broadway, New York, NY 10012
Tel: 212 226 6800
www.deandeluca.com

Global Table
109 Sullivan Street
New York, New York 10012
Tel: 212 431 5839
www.globaltable.com

Gump's
135 Post Street
San Francisco, California 94108
Tel: 800 766 7628
www.gumps.com

Indian Foods Co
Tel: 866 331 7684
www.indianfoodsco.com

India Plaza
Joyce Chen Asian Cookware
20 University Boulevard
East Silver Spring, Maryland 20901
Tel: 201 593 8905
www.indiaplaza.com

Kalustyan's
123 Lexington Avenue
New York, New York 10016
Tel: 212 685 3451
www.kalustyans.com

Katagiri
224 and 244 East 59th Street
New York, New York 10022
Tel: 212 755 3566

Pearl River Mart
277 Canal Street
New York, New York 10013
Tel: 800 878 2446
Web: www.pearlriver.com
Sunrise Mart
4 Stuyvesant Street, 2nd Floor
New York, New York 10003
Tel: 212 598 3040

Typhoon Plus, Inc.
PO Box 5068
Novato, Cailfornia 94948
Tel: 415 884 9060
www.typhoonplus.com

Williams Sonoma
150 Post Street
San Francisco, California 94108
Tel: 415 362 6904
www.williams-sonoma.com

Zabar's
2245 Broadway
New York, New York 10024
Tel: 212 496 1234
www.zabars.com

SOUTHEAST ASIA

Central Plaza
1693 Phahonyothin Road
Lardprao, Chatuchak
Bangkok 10900, Thailand
Tel: (+66) +2 937 1555
e-mail: property@centralgroup.com

Chatuchak Weekend Market
Off Phahonyothin Road
across from Morchit Bus Terminal
Bangkok, Thailand

Hocatsu (M) Sdn. Bhd.
6, Jalan SS 21/35 Damansara
Utama, 47400 Petaling Jaya
Selangor Darul Ehsan, Malaysia
Tel: (+60) +3 7725 4588
www.hocatsu.com.my

PT Hocatsu Pratama
Ruko Marina Mangga Dua Block C
7–8 Jalan Gunung Sahan Raya
No 2 Jakarta 10330, Indonesia
Tel: (+62) +21 640 4777
e-mail: sales@hocatsu-pratama.com
www.hocatsu-pratama.com

Lau Choy Seng
23/25 Temple Street
Singapore 058568
Tel: (+65) 6223 5486
www.lauchoyseng.com

Rishi Handicrafts
58 Arab Street
Singapore 199755
Tel: (+65) 6298 5927

Sia Huat
20 Pandan Road
Singapore 609272
Tel: (+65) 6268 3922
www.siahuat.com
Also Kuala Lumpur and Jakarta

Tang's Department Store
310–320 Orchard Road
Singapore 238864
Tel: (+65) 6737 5500
www.tangs.com.sg

Yue Hwa Chinese Emporium
70 Eu Tong Sen Road
Singapore
Tel: (+65) 6538 4222
www.yuehwa.com.sg
Also Hong Kong

index (id) refers to ingredient identification pictures

about the contributors

Fuchsia Dunlop A fluent Mandarin speaker, British author, food writer and consultant Fuchsia Dunlop has devoted years to researching Chinese regional cuisine. In the 1990s, she trained as a Chinese chef at the Sichuan Institute of Higher Cuisine in Chengdu, widely regarded as China's leading cooking school. The author of the acclaimed *Sichuan Cookery* and *Revolutionary Chinese Cookbook*, Fucshia has contributed to publications such as *Gourmet*, *Saveur* and *Time Out*, and makes regular appearances on radio and television.

Deh-ta Hsiung Born in Beijing, Deh-ta travelled widely in China before settling in Guangzhou and thereafter the United Kingdom. From a family of gourmets and scholars, he is considered a world authority on Chinese cuisine and is the author of many books on this and Southeast Asian cooking, including *The Complete Encyclopedia of Chinese Cooking*, *The Encyclopedia of Asian Cooking* and *Chinese Regional Cooking*. Deh-ta taught for many years at the late Kenneth Lo's Cookery School in London.

Ming Tsai Chef and restaurateur of Boston's popular award-winning Blue Ginger restaurant, which showcases innovative East–West cuisine drawing on his Chinese heritage, Ming trained in France, Japan and restaurants around the United States. He hosts and produces the public TV programme *Simply Ming*, and has been a presenter and television chef for the Food Network and on NBC's *Today*. He is the author of *Blue Ginger: East Meets West Cooking with Ming Tsai*, *Simply Ming* and *Ming's Master Recipes*.

Nina Simonds At the age of 19, Nina Simonds travelled to Taiwan, to study Chinese cuisine under the direction of Chinese master chefs. She also apprenticed in restaurant kitchens specializing in the cuisines of Jiangsu, Hunan and Canton. For the past 28 years, Nina has taught classes in cooking schools across the United States, and is the author of nine books on Chinese cuisine and culture, including the bestselling *Asian Noodles* and *A Spoonful of Ginger*. She has appeared on numerous television programmes and as a guest on the *Today* and *Martha Stewart* shows.

Emi Kazuko Leading Japanese food writer and journalist Emi Kazuko is based in London. She has written a number of authoritative and accessible books on Japanese cuisine, including the award-winning *Japanese Food and Cooking*, the bestselling *Easy Sushi*, *Masterclass in Japanese Cooking* and *New Sushi*. She has taken part in programmes such as Radio 4's *Woman's Hour* and for the BBC's World Service, and also works as a food development consultant for a major UK supermarket.

Shirley Booth Award-winning writer and film-maker, and leading authority on Japanese food, Shirley lived in Japan for a number of years. There, she studied Zen temple cooking, and she has taught Zen vegetarian cookery to both Japanese and foreigners in Japan and in Britain. She has made several films on Japanese food, and wrote the award-winning book *Food of Japan*. In 2006 she was the first UK recipient of the Japanese Ministry of Agriculture Award, for her work promoting Japanese food overseas.

Roy Yamaguchi Tokyo-born restaurateur and television chef Roy Yamaguchi graduated from the Culinary Institute of America in New York. He opened his first Roy's restaurant in 1988, after moving to Hawaii from Los Angeles. There are now Roy's in more than 30 locations in Hawaii and across the continental United States, as well as in Guam and Japan, all serving Roy's trademark eclectic mix of Hawaiian fusion cuisine. Host of the cooking show *Hawaii Cooks*, he has also published several cookbooks.

Peter Gordon Head chef and co-owner of The Providores and Tapa Room restaurant in London, Peter Gordon is considered one of the pioneers of Antipodean-style fusion cuisine in Europe. He is the author of several cookbooks, including *Sugar Club Cookbook*, *A World in My Kitchen*, *Salads: The New Main Course* and *Vegetables: The New Food Heroes*. Peter has appeared on various television programmes in the United Kingdom and United States, as well as in his native New Zealand.

Elizabeth Andoh American-born Elizabeth Andoh's path took an unexpected twist when her adviser at the University of Michigan suggested she apply for a postgraduate fellowship in Japan. Thus she found herself on the island of Shikoku in 1967. She studied at the Yanagihara Kinsaryu School of Traditional Japanese Cuisine in Tokyo, where she now lives with her husband, whom she met on Shikoku. She teaches at her school, A Taste of Culture, and has been *Gourmet* magazine's Japan correspondent for more than 30 years. She is the author of the award-winning cookbook *Washoku: Recipes from the Japanese Home Kitchen*, among others.

Doc Cheng's The history of Doc Cheng's begins in Penang in 1882, where Cheng Soon Wen, the indulged scion of wealthy parents, was born. After his father died, Soon Wen was packed off to Oxford and became a prominent member of the Royal College of Surgeons. He spent all his spare time sampling the culinary delights of Soho, Chelsea and the Brompton Road, earning a reputation as a sybarite and connoisseur of fine wines and good food. He eventually returned home to Singapore, and set up his practice on Beach Road, a few doors away from the famous Raffles Hotel. Doc Cheng, as he became known, spent more time in the hotel's bar than in his clinic. He became something of a legend, dispensing his own peculiar brand of medicine to all and sundry while imbibing at his favourite haunt. This restaurant is a tribute to the good doctor and raconteur.

Das Sreedharan London restaurateur Das Sreedharan grew up in a small village near Cochin, Kerala, in South India. Within a year of his opening the first Rasa in 1994, it had become the most famous vegetarian restaurant in London. Its reputation for excellent Keralan cuisine continues, and there are now seven more Rasa restaurants. Das has appeared on television's *The Naked Chef* and other programmes, as well as on radio and in magazines. He has also written several cookery books.

Roopa Gulati Born in England, Roopa Gulati first began to explore her taste for culinary adventure in India, her home for 18 years. A Cordon Bleu–trained chef, she blended Western and Asian styles of cooking while working as a consultant chef with India's Taj group of hotels, and cooking on a daily show broadcast live on Star TV. Roopa returned to the United Kingdom in 2001, where she is Deputy Channel editor for Good Food Channel. She is a regular broadcaster on the BBC's Radio 4 and a restaurant critic for *Time Out* magazine and guides. Her features have been published in many magazines and newspapers, including BBC *Good Food*, *Gourmet* and the *Telegraph*, and she is the author of *Curry Lovers*.

Vivek Singh After graduating from catering college, Vivek Singh joined the Oberoi Hotels group, quickly moving up the ranks to become Indian chef of its flagship Oberoi Rajvilas, in Jaipur – at the age of 26. Since 2001, as executive chef of London's Cinnamon Club, he has been revolutionizing the way people think about Indian cooking, brilliantly fusing Indian flavours and spicing with classic Western culinary styles. He is the author of *The Cinnamon Club Cookbook*, *The Cinnamon Club Seafood Cookbook* and *Curry: Classic and Contemporary*.

Cyrus Todiwala Cyrus trained as a chef with the famous Taj Group in India. He left India for Europe in 1991, where he developed his hallmark style of blending traditional Indian culinary techniques and flavours with more unexpected ingredients. Proprietor and Executive Chef of the Café Spice Namasté restaurant group, Cyrus is renowned for his innovative and fresh approach to Indian cuisine. He was awarded an MBE in 2000, in recognition of his contribution to the UK restaurant and catering industries.

Atul Kochhar At his London restaurant, Benares, Michelin-starred chef Atul Kochhar serves modern British Indian cuisine that combines the best local and seasonal ingredients with his deft mastery of Indian spicing and flavours. He has two other restaurants: Vatika, in Hampshire, and Ananda, Dublin. Author of *Fish, Indian Style* and *Simple Indian: The Fresh Tastes of India's New Cuisine*, he has been a finalist on the BBC's *Great British Menu*.

Mehernosh Mody Executive chef at London's highly regarded La Porte des Indes restaurant since it first opened in 1986, Mumbai-born Mehernosh combines traditional influences from his roots with his own progressive approach. He also draws inspiration from the French cuisine of Pondicherry and other former French outposts in South India.

Yogesh Arora Yogesh Arora worked at restaurants in Singapore and New Delhi, before joining Singapore's Raffles Hotel in July 1996. Raffles has a global reputation for fielding some of the finest restaurants in the world, and its Tiffin Room is renowned for producing excellent Indian cuisine, largely due to Yogesh's culinary genius.

Camellia Panjabi Camellia, together with her sister Namita, is a director of the Masala World group of restaurants. Chutney Mary, located in London's Chelsea, opened in 1990. Under Camellia's steerage, it has won numerous awards. The group also includes Veeraswamy, the UK's oldest Indian restaurant; the group's newest award-winning restaurant Amaya; and several Masala Zone restaurants dotted around London.

Chef Chang Rungsan Mulijan, affectionately known as Chef Chang (Chang means 'elephant' in Thai), attended the famous Saowapha cooking school in Bangkok, while working evenings at the massive Wangkeo restaurant with its three kitchens – Thai, Chinese and Japanese. In 1985 he joined the Blue Elephant Brussels, in Belgium, bringing with him culinary influences from the Thai royal court. Since then, he has become the driving force behind the burgeoning group of Blue Elephant restaurants around the world. He is also culinary major domo at the Blue Elephant Cookery Institute in Bangkok, which draws students from all over the world.

David Thompson Renowned chef, restaurateur and cookery writer David Thompson began his career on the world culinary stage with his Sydney restaurant Darley Street Thai, voted one of the top ten best Thai restaurants in the world. Today, he continues to set exemplary standards for authentic Royal Thai cuisine at his London restaurant Nahm, the first Thai restaurant to be awarded a Michelin star. He is author of the authoritative *Thai Food*.

Daranee Cobham Chef Daranee Cobham spent 15 years learning her craft at various cookery schools in Bangkok and with several Thai restaurants in England, before decamping to Monaco to open her own Royal Thai restaurant on Rue de Milo six years ago. She brings her impressive skills to bear on a distinctive menu of mainly Royal Thai dishes – skills she learned from some of the best-known experts in Royal Thai cuisine.

Marlena Spieler American food writer, author and broadcaster Marlena Spieler has written or contributed to more than 50 cookbooks and is the European food correspondent for the *San Francisco Chronicle*, contributing its 'Roving Feast' column. Her books and column have been short-listed for three James Beard Foundation awards and two Guild of Food Writers awards for Broadcaster of the Year (on British radio and television), and she has won two Association of Food Journalist awards.

Corinne Trang The 'Julia Child of Asian cuisine', according to the *Washington Post*, New York-based Corinne Trang is an award-winning cookbook author and contributor, food and travel writer, and expert on Asian cuisines and cultures. She also works as a food and beverage consultant and recipe developer. Her books include *Authentic Vietnamese Cooking*, *The Asian Grill* and her most recent cookbook, *Noodles Every Day*.

Tom Kime British-born chef, author and food writer Tom Kime has worked in several highly regarded restaurants, including London's River Café and the award-winning Darley Street Thai, in Sydney, Australia. At the latter, under the tutelage of David Thompson, Tom learned the refined traditions of Royal Thai cuisine. He has written four books, *Exploring Taste and Flavour*, *Street Food*, *Asian Bites* and *Tom's Table*, and regularly contributes to magazines such as *Olive* and BBC *Good Food*, as well as making television appearances.

Alan Davidson The late British diplomat and historian Alan Davidson was best known for his works on food and gastronomy, and was the author of the encyclopedic *Oxford Companion to Food*. His *Mediterranean Seafood*, published in 1972, has since become an iconic reference work. It was followed by *Seafood of South East Asia* (1979) and *North Atlantic Seafood* (1979). He was a noted expert on Lao cuisine, which he introduced to the West through his two books *Traditional Recipes of Laos* and *Fish and Fish Dishes of Laos*. Davidson was also founder and organizer of the Oxford Symposium on Food and Cookery.

Somkid Bhanubandh Somkid has run the Thai restaurants Sreeracha and Thai Marina in Eastbourne, in the south of England, since the 1980s. She learned from past masters in Royal Thai cuisine whose banquets have been served to visiting royalty and heads of state. Her Eastbourne establishment is noted for a unique menu that marries the best of Royal Thai cuisine with elegant European and fusion presentation, winning her a legion of fans.

Hong Sai Choi This talented chef whose ancestors hail from the Fujian province of Eastern China first worked at the Furama Hotel in Singapore. The in-house restaurant went on to become a beacon of exquisite Chinese cuisine under Hong's steerage. He is an expert in the preparation of choice viands such as abalone, scallops and bird's nest – dishes regarded as the epitome of Chinese fine dining. Sai Choi currently works at the Huang Ting Restaurant, Beijing, part of Hong Kong's Peninsula Hotel Group and regarded as a bastion of fine Chinese cuisine.

Neil Perry Regarded as Australia's number-one exponent of Asian cuisines, Neil Perry is co-owner and executive chef of a number of critically acclaimed restaurants in Australia. In Sydney, his current stable consists of three restaurants: his flagship fine-diner Rockpool, the modern Chinese restaurant Spice Temple, and upmarket steakhouse Rockpool Bar & Grill. Spice Temple represents a foray by Perry into more traditional Asian cuisine, specifically regional Chinese food given a sophisticated polish. The original incarnation of Rockpool Bar and Grill in Melbourne has been awarded two coveted 'chef's hats' in Australia's highly regarded *Sydney Morning Herald/The Age Good Food Guide*.

Sri Owen Born in Sumatra, Indonesia, Sri Owen moved to the United Kingdom in 1964. She began cooking for her teacher husband's friends, one of whom was a literary agent, and this led to the publication of her first book in 1976. Since then she has become an internationally renowned author, lecturer and cook whose admired and authoritative books include *Sri Owen's Indonesian Food*, *The Rice Book*, *Indonesian Regional Food and Cookery* and *Healthy Thai Cooking*. One of the grande dames of the British foodie scene, Sri is on the committee of the UK Guild of Food Writers and the Oxford Symposium on Food and Cookery.

Tym Srisawatt Tym studied Thai cooking at the famed Wandee Culinary Institute in Bangkok. After coming to London, she opened Mantanah Thai restaurant in Norwood, South London, with her husband, Tony Yeoh. A small, unpretentious place, within a few years it had won a clutch of awards, especially for Tym's vegetarian dishes. When Mantanah was sold, Tym became a consultant chef to Eastbourne's Thai Marina. She devotes much of her energy to the UK Thai Restaurant Association's efforts to upgrade and authenticate Thai cuisine in Britain.

Christopher Tan Writer, food consultant and photographer Chris Tan has contributed articles, photographs and recipes to magazines such as *Saveur*, *Appetite* and *The Peak*, and is also a food columnist for Singapore's *Straits Times*. He gives talks on cuisine and culture at venues that have included the National Museum of Singapore and the Culinary Institute of America, and has authored, co-authored and styled food for many cookbooks, including *Slurp: Soups to Lap up and Love*, *Inside the Southeast Asian Kitchen* and *Wartime Kitchen*.

acknowledgments

AUTHOR'S ACKNOWLEDGMENTS

As a believer in karma, I would like to mention the propitious telephone call from literary agent Teresa Chris, who asked if I knew anyone who could write a book on Asian cooking tools. I said I could do it myself and so it came to pass that I met up with Jacqui Small, to whom I give my most heartfelt thanks in offering me the commission for the original edition of this book (published in 2003), as well as for her inimitable style, vision and commitment to this new incarnation in revised and expanded form.

I would be very remiss in not thanking all those people who were involved in bringing the original edition into book form. Most of all I would like to thank my then-editor Jenni Muir for her inexhaustible patience, unstinting help in sourcing guest chefs, and remarkable skill in making sense of my often convoluted copy. Thanks also go to the art director of the first edition, Valerie Fong, for her invaluable, brilliant artistic and cultural input, unflagging energy and logistical help throughout the hectic weeks of photography.

I am also indebted to Tym and Tony Yeoh for their invaluable assistance in sourcing rare Indochinese tools and information on Thai culinary heritage that brought the first edition to fruition. To all my family who turned their kitchens inside out for family-owned tools. To photographers Michael Paul and Nat Rea for inspiring work in capturing the true essence of the food and tools.

Importantly, I would also like to express my heartfelt thanks and appreciation to the people who are responsible for putting their professional stamp on this new, very much 'rejuvenated' edition of the book. Indeed, in some ways, this feels like a new book entirely, with more than double the number of recipes, new tips and techniques, and its greater emphasis on the varied and delicious food that makes up the many Asian cuisines – and much more besides. So thanks must go to the project editor on the new edition, Siobhán O'Connor, who has helped me to shepherd this book through its gestation into new and improved form. I am grateful for her passion, enthusiasm, creative input and culinary knowledge – not to mention her skills with the written word and her commitment to authenticity and accessibility – as well as her assiduous attention to improving and expanding what was already there and her help in tracking down new guest chefs to expand the culinary repertoire within these pages. A big thanks, too, must go to the art director Maggie Town, whose designer's vision and creative skills are responsible not only for the new look of the book, but also for the beautiful photographs of new recipes. Thanks also to food stylist Sunil Vijayakar, without whose deft hand and culinary eye the food would never have looked so tempting, and photographer Sian Irvine, who captured it all so wonderfully on camera.

Finally, thanks to my friends and fellow chefs, and the Blue Elephant Group in the UK for their guest contributions, to the chefs of the Raffles, Furama and Shangri-La hotels in Singapore and to all the chefs from the global front. Special thanks to Typhoon Europe Ltd, and Yoshikin (UK) for the loan of their items.

PUBLISHER'S ACKNOWLEDGMENTS

Thanks to Emi Kazuko and Roopa Gulati for help with photography, sourcing equipment and advice on culinary matters in their specialist fields for the first edition of this book, and special thanks for the recipes they have contributed to this second edition. Betty Fong's help in preparing the first edition was also greatly appreciated.

We would like to thank the following for contributing recipes to this book (in order of appearance): Fuchsia Dunlop, Deh-ta Hsiung, Ming Tsai, Nina Simonds, Emi Kazuko, Shirley Booth, Roy Yamaguchi, Peter Gordon, Elizabeth Andoh, Doc Cheng's Restaurant, Das Sreedharan, Roopa Gulati, Vivek Singh, Cyrus Todiwala, Atul Kochhar, Mehernosh Mody, Yogesh Arora, Camellia Panjabi, Chef Chang, David Thompson, Daranee Cobham, Marlena Spieler, Corinne Trang, Tom Kime, Alan Davidson, Somkid Bhanubandh, Hong Sai Choi, Neil Perry, Sri Owen, Tym Srisawatt and Chris Tan. All guest recipes are used with permission.